The nonfiction *New York Times* bestseller as suspense-charged as any political thriller, *Breakthrough* captures an unwavering "quest for truth in the age of media obfuscation" (Gavin McInnes, Fox News *Red Eye*)

"Splendid. . . . Fast-paced. . . . O'Keefe's tale will have your stomach churning and your blood boiling. . . . His raw, genuine, and tightly focused rage is the beating heart of *Breakthrough*, a call to action and a playbook for aspiring citizen journalists."

—*Watchdog Wire*

"Gripping. . . . In *Breakthrough*—which serves simultaneously as a memoir, a manifesto, a tell-all, and an activist handbook—O'Keefe describes being thrust under the national microscope. The reader watches a young man grow up, wise up, and toughen up."

—*Yahoo News*

"A how-to guide for modern activists . . . [and] armchair patriots who think *someone else* is better qualified to engage in direct action."

—J. Christian Adams, publisher, PJ Media

"O'Keefe is courageous." —Glenn Beck

"A latter-day Mike Wallace." —Dennis Miller

"A grand slam home run."

—Rush Limbaugh, on the NPR investigation

"Go watch this video. It's enlightening, it's enraging."

—Governor Chris Christie, on the NJEA video

BREAKTHROUGH

OUR GUERRILLA WAR
to EXPOSE FRAUD and SAVE
DEMOCRACY

JAMES O'KEEFE

THRESHOLD EDITIONS

New York London Toronto Sydney New Delhi

Threshold Editions
A Division of Simon & Schuster, Inc.
1230 Avenue of the Americas
New York, NY 10020

First Threshold Editions paperback edition June 2014

THRESHOLD EDITIONS and colophon are trademarks of Simon & Schuster, Inc.

For information about special discounts for bulk purchases, please contact Simon & Schuster Special Sales at 1-866-506-1949 or business@simonandschuster.com.

The Simon & Schuster Speakers Bureau can bring authors to your live event. For more information or to book an event, contact the Simon & Schuster Speakers Bureau at 1-866-248-3049 or visit our website at www.simonspeakers.com.

Designed by Aline C. Pace

Manufactured in the United States of America

10 9 8 7 6 5 4 3 2

Library of Congress Cataloging-in-Publication Data

O'Keefe, James, 1984–
    Breakthrough : our guerrilla war to expose fraud and save democracy / James O'Keefe.
— First Threshold Editions hardcover edition.
    pages cm
    Summary: "Controversial ambush journalist James O'Keefe shows the reader what happens when a young citizen journalist challenges some of America's most powerful and protected organizations"— Provided by publisher.
    1. Citizen journalism—United States. 2. Journalism—Political aspects—United States. 3. Project Veritas. 4. O'Keefe, James, 1984– I. Title.
    PN4784.C615O44 2013
    071'.3—dc23
                                                                                        2013003391

ISBN 978-1-4767-0617-7
ISBN 978-1-4767-0618-4 (pbk)
ISBN 978-1-4767-0619-1 (ebook)

Dedicated to the idealist sitting in a classroom or an office whose conscience tells him to take a stand against the status quo and whose courage allows him to ignore the world around him, which tells him to sit down, shut up, and comply

———————

"Journalism as Guerrilla Theater. The reporter as life actor . . . we begin to see things in a different focus."
—Abbie Hoffman, *Mother Jones Magazine*, 1979

CONTENTS

PROLOGUE

Through the Plexiglas

On the morning of January 25, 2010, I woke curled up in a fetal position, on a green mattress stained with seminal fluid, to the sound of my fellow prisoners chanting the Qu'ran.

With me were my pals Stan Dai, Joe Basel, and Bob Flanagan. We had spent the night in the St. Bernard Parish jail, just outside New Orleans. I was not sure that any of us had even slept, but no matter. I was on my way to have my mug shot taken—the one that would appear on the front page of the Sunday *New York Times*.

Welcome, friends, to the world of citizen journalism.

We had been arrested the morning before. The feds had shuffled us from cage to cage in the Hale Boggs Federal Building downtown, shackled us hand and foot, chained our hands to a heavy leather waist belt, and bused us out to St. Bernard's. There they dressed us in orange jumpsuits, Tim McVeigh–style, and assigned us our scummy mattresses. In the morning, they shackled us, moved us again from cage to cage, bused us back to Boggs, and stuck us in another cage deep within the building's bowels.

I will reveal the details of our offense in due time, but it was so soft we had no idea we had committed a crime or what that crime could be. We saw ourselves as journalists holding the federal government accountable, but our public servants did not see it that way, and the way they saw it was the way it was. They fully controlled both the process and the message.

As to the message, we suspected that forces within the U.S. Department of Justice were purposely leaking confidential material to keep the media stoked. But the message was not our immediate problem. It was the process, one that now had us standing shoulder to shoulder in a four-by-five-foot cage. Fluorescent lights flickered eerily overhead. Vile words and images covered the cement wall behind us. A weary, middle-aged public defender introduced himself through the Plexiglas. He would tell us only that we had done something very bad. "It is important you understand what I'm about to tell you," he said as robotically as Ben Stein calling out "Ferris Bueller."

"You are being charged with a felony that carries ten years of a prison sentence. Please be advised that if you do get your own attorney, he should have federal experience. This is a very serious crime."

Throughout this inquisition, my attorney, Mike Madigan, could not reach me. He was leaving voice mails on an iPhone that had long since been confiscated. In fact, I would hear his message—"If there is a federal marshal listening to this voice mail I urge you to allow my client to call me"—only six months later when I finally retrieved the phone, now marked "property of the FBI."

"There is a misunderstanding," Dai interjected. The attorney wasn't listening. Through the Plexiglas, he saw us as he must have seen hundreds of others before us, dressed in telltale orange, dopey from lack of sleep, dazed, confused, guilty. It stunned me how quickly under these circumstances we saw ourselves much as he did.

We had all but lost confidence that logic and reason prevailed on the other side of the Plexiglas. We began to doubt the innate American expectation that the truth would find its way and justice would be done. Ten years in prison? What the hell? This was the very first time we had heard we were even being charged, and they were apparently throwing the book at us—but what book and why?

All this rushed through my mind without any fixed meaning. Then the idea descended on me like a tongue of fire. Yes, of course! They were screwing us over not in spite of the fact we were journalists but *because* we were. Three years later, the "they"—our prosecutors in the New Orleans U.S. Attorney's office—would be forced out of office in disgrace, but that item barely dented the news. Our arrest the media would never forget.

BOOK ONE

BOOK ONE

THE HOLLOW MEN

Nineteen eighty-four was not just the year I was born.

On the night of January 17, 2012, Kristen Coolidge*, home from college, talked and joked with her three younger siblings around the kitchen island while their mom, Mary*, prepared dinner nearby. The Coolidges lived in Newmarket, New Hampshire, on a quiet street lined with homes as old and picturesque as their one-hundred-year-old colonial.

Kristen heard the sounds first. Startled, she looked up and listened intently. They were footsteps—urgent, masculine footsteps—several sets of feet. She tracked them around the side of the house. Unaware, Mary labored away at the stove until a sharp rap on the seldom-used back door made her jump. She saw the outlines of three grown men dressed in winter gear and instinctively made her way to the door.

---

* Names changed to protect the innocent.

"Don't open it, Mom," whispered twenty-year-old Tim. Mary hesitated. Sensing her hesitance, the man in front flashed a badge. Mary proceeded to the door and opened it just a crack. "Can I help you?"

The lead officer—gruff, officious, his head shaved down to a military trim—wedged his foot in the opening and barged his way through. The two younger men followed, surveying the room. The Coolidges stood frozen. "We're looking for Adam Coolidge," said the lead officer, Mark Myrdeck, a retired police lieutenant now working for the New Hampshire attorney general, Michael Delaney. "We're told he lives here."

I learned about the raid as it happened. Nineteen-year-old Jenna Coolidge had the wherewithal to send me a Facebook message from her cell phone. "Hi James, three men just knocked on the door looking for Adam . . . asking about where he lives."

"What did Adam do?" asked Mary, deeply worried about her twenty-three-year-old son. Myrdeck could not give a direct answer. "We don't know if he has broken any laws. We just need to talk to him." He knew better than this. He brought with him a subpoena for Adam to appear before a criminal grand jury. He placed a dossier on the kitchen counter and left it open just enough so that the Coolidges could see photos of Adam and me.

To make sense of his visit, Myrdeck said something about how Adam disrupted a lot of families that had lost a loved one, making them feel uncomfortable. "My son is just trying to do good for the country," Mary protested, but the men were not listening.

The one person Adam had really made uncomfortable was New Hampshire governor John Lynch. Just six months earlier, a preening Lynch proudly vetoed New Hampshire state bill 129, which would have required voters to show a photo ID. In all his limited wisdom, the governor chastised a heartless legislature for passing a highly "restrictive" voter ID bill "despite any evidence that current law is insufficient protection against voter fraud."

A week earlier, Adam Coolidge and a few others had shown just how pathetically insufficient those protections were. These guys were the Green Berets of citizen journalism, the proud ground troops of Project Veritas, the nonprofit I had launched to revive investigative journalism. They had calmly walked into a half-dozen voting stations during America's most closely watched primary and were handed ballots for seven of the eight dead people whose names they volunteered.

Here we were just one week into our election fraud investigation, and we had already tripped the fascist trigger in the government-media complex. Too many people had too much at stake in a look-the-other-way electoral process to let us attack it with impunity. The harassment of the Coolidges was payback time. Six months later we would essentially be cleared of wrongdoing for our investigative reporting on voter fraud, however reluctantly, by the attorney general of the United States. But the Stasi wannabes of New Hampshire had yet to get that memo.

"She was physically shaking," Kristen said of her mom. "It was not as if they came in during the daytime or came in through the front door. They did to my mom what they hoped to do." T. S. Eliot had it nailed. "This is the way the world ends," he wrote in "The Hollow Men" nearly ninety years ago. "Not with a bang but a whimper." The crimes would be small ones, the persecution petty, the outcry limited to an old colonial in Newmarket, New Hampshire.

I wish I could have been there to help. I wish I could have gone to New Hampshire to oversee the video sting, but I could do neither. I had to direct the operation from the restored carriage house on my family's property in New Jersey. I could not leave the state without permission from, yes, my probation officer. This fellow was assigned to track me for a misdemeanor I did not even commit. That's how special I must have seemed to someone.

I was twenty-seven years old, five years into my self-created career as a citizen journalist, and I had already been arrested, imprisoned, nearly killed during my coerced "community service," commended along with Hannah Giles by the U.S. House of Representatives for exposing ACORN, publicly accused of everything from racism to rape, lauded by the governor of New Jersey for exposing a corrupt union, pursued recklessly on an interstate by a teacher I caught on tape, denounced by Keith Olbermann as the "worst person in the world," applauded for causing major resignations at National Public Radio, sued multiple times, slandered by half the working journalists in America, and finally inspired to expose voter fraud in the heat of a presidential election, which my late mentor Andrew Breitbart described over the phone to me as "the most consequential thing you ever did."

In the course of these short few years, I have received an education that few will receive in a lifetime. Some of what I learned came from books, most usefully Saul Alinsky's *Rules for Radicals,* Tom Wolfe's *Mau-Mauing the Flak Catchers,* and everything by G. K. Chesterton. Some I learned from the people who mentored me, chief among them my father, my grandfather, and the uniquely gifted Andrew Breitbart.

Much of what I learned, I learned through the cold, hard knocks of experience. To learn, I have had to sort my way through legal and media swamps into which no one has ventured before. For those who may want to follow, I have edited what I have learned into a set of guidelines, the *Veritas rules.* The rules are shaped by my larger vision, simply put, to make the world a more virtuous place.

By showing what is true and what is not, journalists can help forge a more ethical and transparent society, one in which people do what is right because they want to, not because they feel compelled to by the government. "A society with no other scale but the legal one is not quite worthy of man," Soviet dissident Aleksandr Solzhenitsyn said at his justly famous Harvard address. He was talking about us. In solving human problems, we have become increasingly bureaucratic, technocratic, legalistic. The society we have today does not oppress like Solzhenitsyn's did. It depresses.

It demoralizes. It discourages the impulse that motivated Revolutionary War general John Stark to "live free or die."

Years ago, New Hampshire adopted those stirring words as the state motto. Today New Hampshire officials intimidate families like the Coolidges over the exercise of their basic freedoms. Solzhenitsyn saw the change coming. "Whenever the tissue of life is woven of legalistic relations," he said, "there is an atmosphere of moral mediocrity, paralyzing man's noblest impulses." My colleagues and I had to fight through that paralysis in this, the critical year of the Lord, 2012. There was a lot at stake, and there were only ten months left before the presidential election.

THE CARRIAGE HOUSE

Veritas Rule #2:
You must do what you can with what you have.

As far back as I can remember, my father and grandfather would build things out of nothing. In 1987, when I was just two, my father, James O'Keefe Jr., bought a ratty, century-old house with a carriage house adjoining the property on Fairview Avenue in Westwood, New Jersey. So he would not have to apply for a zoning variance—and that process was getting more burdensome by the year—he decided to restore the carriage house on-site and not to build anew. He needed help, and the only person he knew more skilled than he at restoring old buildings was his father, James O'Keefe Sr.

Just about everyone in Westwood told them, "You can't save that building. It simply can't be done." But my dad and grandfather had the sort of vision nobody else had. The philosophy of these two wise men was never to waste, always to create. They figured if you worked smart and hard and honored the building codes, there was nothing you couldn't do.

This time, though, the two had their work cut out for them. For starters, the building leaned more severely than that famous tower in Pisa, and no matter what they did with this relic, they weren't about to make a tourist attraction out of it. Although no contractor was willing to take on the job, my father saw an opportunity where the market didn't see one. He and my grandfather borrowed a tow truck, fixed a massive belt from the truck to and around the side that leaned, righted the building, and busily reinforced the tilting side. They repeated this process all around the barn until it was squared away.

Then the fun began. My grandfather was a classic child of the Great Depression who grew up learning to make do with less. His rule was to buy new building material only when he absolutely had to. He was the original recycler and a master improviser. For the carriage house project, he devised a system to jack up the whole building an inch at a time until eventually it was five feet above the ground. That way he and his son could dig new footings and cast a new floor, then lower the building back down on top of it. In the process, they preserved the historic aspects of the building.

The engineering done, father and son took out their craftsmen's tools and went to work on the thousand little things needed to bring the carriage house back to life. The result was a showcase that would be honored by the Bergen County Historical Society in 1990 and celebrated in the local papers.

As I got older I was more or less forced to join in the fun. When I was ten, we started renovating and restoring another century-old home. I worked on that house with Dad every weekend. While other kids were off swimming and playing, I was scraping paint, carrying bricks, and holding lumber as it was being cut. I got dust in my lungs and plumber's glue in my nose. I remember one day spending all day scraping old wallpaper with a tiny scraping device until my fingers bled, and I began crying at my lack of progress. When I asked for a better tool, my grandfather encouraged me to keep on. "You do what you have to do," he said, "even it means using your fingernails."

On this project, I learned as important a lesson as any I learned as a child: real resources come from within, and those that come from without are often within easy reach. To change the world or simply improve your condition, you need only to muster them. "Tactics," Saul Alinsky wrote, "means doing what you can with what you have."

I learned to think and to work watching these two gifted men. I was not blessed with their carpentry skills, but their resourcefulness and self-reliance have informed everything I do. Like them, I would attempt to build an organization out of little more than thrift and creativity and, in my case, overextended credit cards. "My grandfather spent his life making things out of nothing," I would tell the *New York Times Magazine*. "I'm that way, too. A lot of people sit around discussing what to do. They draw up proposals, look for funding, and nothing happens. I grab my camera and go do it."

My father is still working but without the same enthusiasm. As he sees it, the town and the state have unwittingly slowed progress. "They have begun to use property as a vehicle for revenue in the building departments," he told me recently. "It's overly burdensome to the homeowner." Many of my grandfather's innovations, including handmade windows, have been regulated out of the codebook, and so it rarely pays for the two to improvise anymore. "It's a changed world, and we wouldn't make the effort today we did before," said my father.

During much of my time on federal probation I worked out of the carriage house that these men restored. For a short time, it served as the Project Veritas office. I would experience some great highs there and the occasional low, like the time a young woman attempted to infiltrate our operation and sabotage our 2012 vote fraud campaign. Bizarrely, the action she started in the carriage house would involve the attorney general of New Hampshire and ultimately the attorney general of the United States. It is amazing what you can still create out of nothing—good and bad.

THE BOOK OF RULES

Veritas Rule #3:
*Use their own flawed construct to put them into a position where
either way they can't win.*

A glee club board meeting was an unlikely setting to get my first real lesson in the soft tyranny of academic life, but there was no denying what I had just been told. Rutgers University dean Joan Carbone, who wore an LGBT pin on her lapel, leaned over and said to me quietly:

"James, I've been reading your *Centurion*. Now, let me just say a respectable journal of political opinion needs to be erudite, educational, persuasive. It needs to be about ideas. It ought not be adversarial, not polemic, not in people's faces."

As the paper's editor in chief, I was taken aback. Others had been saying much the same thing. My friend Bryan Karch, who came up with the name *Centurion,* quit because he felt the paper was not being "educational." The choir conductor felt much the same way. He told me the paper as currently conceived would ruin my "job opportunities."

I almost buckled to Carbone's request, but the duplicity of it all began to weigh on me. Here was a dean at a public institution discouraging a student from exposing facts and reporting them, not for his own good, but for hers. Dean Carbone had no use for journalists who did what journalists were supposed to do—hold those in power accountable. Before we came on the scene, the university was accountable to almost no one, certainly not to the editors of the official student newspaper, the *Daily Targum*. Much like the national media cocktailing with government officials at White House correspondents' dinners, the *Targum* editors were chummy with the administration. The reasons, I suspect, were the same in New Brunswick, New Jersey, as in Washington, D.C.—ambition, shared politics, and a pinch of fear.

Without intending to, Carbone gave me an education in the ways of the world. In 2012, my pals and I would take on electoral corruption in one state after another and in the federal government as well, but in 2004, I was cutting my muckraker's teeth on a state university and its staff. It was good training. The patterns of corruption and hypocrisy I observed at Rutgers I would see again and again on the campaign trail.

The campus environment brought out the contrarian in me. I resented the campus ethos, I suppose, the way my father did the local zoning board. It was just so damn totalitarian. Just about everyone on the faculty and most of the students seemed to think alike, and the weight of that groupthink rested heavily on those of us who thought otherwise.

During my freshman year I expressed my dissent in an opinion column for the *Daily Targum*. My thoughts, however, got lost in a sea of orthodoxy and complacency. I wanted to make a difference, and I wasn't doing it there. I also wanted to create a social fabric in the midst of all this soullessness. I wanted to get people to care.

I got the idea for starting an alternative paper at an unlikely place: Harvard University. I was there with the Men's Glee Club, and I spotted someone reading a journal from Tufts University called *Primary Source*. I liked the idea of it. So in my sophomore year, I and a few like-minded souls—Matt Klimek, Joe Nedick, and Justine Mertz—launched the *Centurion*.

We found an easy mark in the *Daily Targum*, which had grown too comfortable with the administration to challenge it in any way beyond the trivial. In early 2004, for instance, the *Targum* had joined with the administration in celebrating the life of a certain Rutgers alumnus, "the exceptional scholar, athlete, political activist and performer" Paul Robeson. Robeson was the first Rutgers graduate to get his mug on a postage stamp. The university unveiled the stamp at the Kirkpatrick Chapel, and the *Targum* people were giddy at the thought of it.

"Orthodoxy means not thinking—not needing to think," wrote George Orwell in *1984*. "Orthodoxy is unconsciousness." To honor Robeson in 2004, years after the Soviet archives had been opened and examined, one had to be totally unconscious.

Yes, he was a scholar and athlete, and I am sure he had his virtues. As to "political activist," however, that was just a nice way of saying "Stalinist." Hell, in 1952, during the heart of the Korean War, Robeson was awarded, and proudly accepted, the perversely named "Stalin Peace Prize." In 1953, shortly after Stalin's death, he penned a tribute to this genocidal monster titled "You My Beloved Comrade." Please!

We put Paul Robeson's face on the front cover of the *Centurion* with the quote "Glory to Stalin." On the contemporary campus, this was like taking a crowbar to political correctness. It pained the campus muckety-mucks that we knew about Robeson. It pained them even more when we shared what we knew. We made the authorities defend the indefensible, and the only thing they and their student minions could do in response was to shut us down—or at least try to. They set copies of the *Centurion* on fire, stuffed them in garbage cans, and generally made them disappear. And I was the one who got lectured by the dean to be "respectful." Think about that.

The closer we hit to home, the more irritated the administration grew. In the December 2004 issue of the *Centurion*, we tallied the donations the faculty had given to that year's presidential candidates. The results won't shock anyone who has spent time on any major American campus. A total of 104 faculty members donated to John Kerry. One donated to George W. Bush. The bottom line: $52,000 for Kerry and $500 for Bush. This was about the level of ideological diversity you'd find in Robeson's beloved Soviet Union.

To add a little mischief to our reporting, we decided to honor those professors whose office doors were most thoroughly decorated with political propaganda. The competition was intense. I remember liking the contribution of one professor, an apparent dyslexia sufferer, who posted, "Buck Fush." Having selected our winners, we went to the offices of those so honored, presented their "Centurion Award" on a lovely plaque, and recorded their responses on video. Ivory tower or not, these professors responded with an impressive range of obscenities. Those who were most impressive we presented with a framed "cursing like a drunken sailor" award.

It was about this time, 2004 to be precise, that I discovered Saul Alinsky. Yes, the same Saul Alinsky who inspired Hillary Clinton and Barack Obama, but well before Alinsky became a household name. An adjunct named David Knowlton, that rare teacher with real-world experience, taught a course called "Business and Government." Knowlton, in fact, was a former student of Alinsky and attempted to teach our class to see past ideology to *tactics*.

A pipe-smoking lobbyist, Knowlton caught my attention with stories about how community organizers would undermine power structures by making their adversaries live up to their own rules. I remember one story in particular about a bar owner in Chicago who tried to discourage African-Americans from frequenting his bar by requiring multiple IDs from them but not from whites. The local NAACP branch wanted the bar shut down, but Knowlton wrote "TACTICS" on the chalkboard and asked us to think analytically about how to solve this crisis.

Then he went on to describe the actual solution. The organizer found fifty African-Americans with multiple IDs and sent them into the bar during happy hour. He ordered them each a drink and asked them to sip it very slowly; when white people arrived at the door, they were to stare at them like they didn't belong. After just a night or two, the owner saw his business slipping away and asked the black patrons what he could do to appease them. They told him to just stop asking blacks for multiple IDs. This was an inexpensive solution to the problem that required no legislation and no outside intervention, and it provided a lesson I heard often in class: "You must operate with the world as it is, not with the way you wish it to be." I was instantly captivated.

I started by noting Alinsky's tenth rule: *"The major premise for tactics is the development of operations that will maintain a constant pressure upon the opposition. It is this that will cause the opposition to react to your advantage."* To keep the pressure on the administration, we launched a series of what we called "campaigns"—demand-oriented, videotaped sessions that backed the administration into no-win predicaments.

In one campaign, we went around planting American flags in the classrooms, forcing campus authorities to either accept them or reject them. If they accepted them, good, we won. If they rejected them, we won again by exposing their rejection and creating the headline "Rutgers Officials Reject American Flags in Classrooms." Our first media stir came when NJ 101.5, the state's largest radio station, reported on the Rutgers vice president's denial of our request. The president, Richard McCormack, responded to the adverse publicity as weak-kneed officials often do. He appointed an "independent commission." Just by making a demand and recording the reaction, we had caused the president to respond and gotten media coverage in the process. We had *created* news that spoke to the nature of the university. This was how it all began. Little did I imagine that a few years later we would be forcing the president of the United States to respond to the news we created.

In another campaign, we moved to have the university erect a statue to an alumnus who surely deserved to be honored, the esteemed libertarian economist Milton Friedman. Friedman won the Nobel Prize for his work. As we reminded the university, the Nobel beats the Stalin Peace Prize any day. We then went around campus asking wealthy professors to "give back to the community"—they like that phrase when applied to others—and pay for the erection of a Friedman statue. Some actually signed the petition to give money!

In our most notable campaign, we appropriated Alinsky's fourth rule: *"Make the enemy live up to their own book of rules."* The rules in this case involved the university "policy against verbal assault, defamation, and harassment," which, in real English, translates into "speech code." As the rulebook reminded us, "Intolerance and bigotry are antithetical to the values of the university, and unacceptable within the Rutgers community." Among the unacceptable forms of bigotry, of course, were those involving "sexual orientation." A campus protest along these lines would prove to be our inspiration.

Some background: One of the great Rutgers traditions is the "grease truck." There were several around campus, and they competed by offering the biggest, greasiest, most caloric sandwiches on the planet. The names of the sandwiches—Fat Mom, Fat Dad, Fat Bitch—spoke to the nature of the competition. In 2005, at the suggestion of a couple of campus lesbians, Ayman Elnaggar, owner of the RU Hungry?, offered an instant classic called "The Fat Dyke." The university, however, was not amused and forced Elnaggar, who did not even know what the offending word meant, to put duct tape over the sandwich name. Censorship, anyone? The orthodoxy on these subjects was soul deadening. Only through the magic of video and the tactics I was learning, we decided, could we show just how deadening it was.

"Ancestry" was another of the sensitivities protected by the campus speech codes. Given my ancestry, I felt I had as much right to be offended as anyone else on the Rutgers campus. For the record, I am as Irish as the O'Keefe name implies. I am six feet, two inches tall, and I have blondish hair. My great-great-great—I lost count—grand something or another reportedly died in the Irish potato famine, so I know what suffering is about. I could no longer endure an ongoing campus defamation of my ancestors. I had to respond.

As Tom Wolfe has reminded us, "Mau-mauing was the ticket. The confrontation route was the only road," and any aggrieved ethnic group could do it. So on St. Patrick's Day, 2005, I put Wolfe's tactics to the test. Three of my pals and I arranged a sit-down with Rutgers dining hall administrator Carolyn Knight-Cole. After some introductions, my friend Greg went to work.

> **GREG:** Well, we're with the Irish Heritage Society. I am the personal adviser to James, Natalie, and Kian. Basically, they have had some unpleasant and uncomfortable experiences in the dining halls.

Note the word *uncomfortable*. Greg was using the language of the university. Strange as this may seem, making fellow students or instructors "uncomfortable" has been grounds for expulsion on any number of campuses. The Foundation for Individual Rights in Education has thoroughly documented these cases.

Alinsky's real contribution to provocateurs like us was the insight that people are rarely swayed by intellectual argument. Argument may be used to steady them on the first step, but after that it is a matter of escalating experience. Greg turned it over to me, and I escalated, as Knight-Cole dutifully took notes about our discomfort.

> **JAMES:** We wanted to bring a matter to your concern. We noticed that the dining halls here at Rutgers serve Lucky Charms, and we think that this promotes negative stereotypes of Irish-Americans. And we don't

think that's acceptable in an academic setting, especially one of higher learning. We brought a box for you to look at here, and there is what appears to be an Irish-American on the front cover.

KNIGHT-COLE: Okay.

JAMES: And he is portrayed as a little, green-cladded gnome, a huckster, and we think that undermines the importance and severity of St. Patrick's Day, especially during the month of March. So basically what we are trying to—

KNIGHT-COLE: Can you tell me that again. You feel that he is portrayed as . . . ?

JAMES: I think he is portrayed as a green-cladded gnome, and as you can see, we're not short and green. We have our differences of height, and we think this is stereotypical of all Irish-Americans.

I carried on for a while longer about "our history" and "what happened to us." Kian Berry was struggling to keep himself from laughing. Greg was pure deadpan. He had actually printed out the university's "policy against defamation and harassment."

GREG: If I might interject quickly, the university's policy against verbal assault, defamation, and harassment starts off by saying that intolerance and bigotry are antithetical to the values of the university and are unacceptable.

Greg then read those rules in their mind-numbing meaninglessness as though they mattered and concluded with the clincher: "Basically these students and others who could not be here today are made to feel very uncomfortable whenever they go to the dining hall."

Greg honored a fundamental Veritas rule: *Put them into a position where they can't win either way.* We put the bureaucrats in a bind. Either they showed themselves insensitive to the feelings of a "marginalized" ethnic minority or they went along with the absurd proposition that Lucky Charms could not be served in the dining hall. It was pure lose-lose, based entirely upon the university's own flawed construct.

The administrators took the lesser of the losses. They told us they would remove Lucky Charms. Good gosh, we thought, if we had time enough and allies enough we could bring the university to a standstill. We could start by asking for a ban on Froot Loops to keep the LGBT community from feeling uncomfortable and go on from there until we subverted the whole silly tyranny of the place.

We recorded the Lucky Charms encounter and posted it on YouTube to great effect. This was my first real excursion into video journalism, and instantly I knew what I had to do. Strategic video had the potential to help people, young people especially, see the moral mediocrity that Solzhenitsyn warned about and rise above it. Law school, to which so many idealistic students gravitate, was not the way to change the world. Journalism was—a hidden camera, a sensational video, a great scoop, someone caught on tape saying something true, something they would never say on a podium. I would later try law school myself, but it would only confirm what I learned at Rutgers: no brief can compete with a video.

MR. O'KEEFE GOES TO WASHINGTON: PART I

Veritas Rule #4:
Find someone who can act and take action.

On a May morning in 2007, I found myself on my knees vomiting in a bathroom stall of the Leadership Institute. I could not believe what was happening to me. The turn of events had so shocked and unnerved me that my body rebelled. I was retching and, in my moments of near composure between heaves, trying to talk on the phone with a supportive friend. This citizen journalism thing was a little harder than I thought, especially if done on behalf of someone else.

This misadventure began some months earlier. Starting in 2006, soon after graduating from Rutgers, I had gone to work at the Leadership Institute, or LI, as we call it, in Arlington, Virginia. The institute's mission was to train young conservative activists. My adventures at Rutgers had caught their attention. For me, working for LI was something of a dream job. I traveled the country recruiting young provocateurs. I helped them start their own publications and, on occasion, instructed them in how to make videos about their own campus follies.

During this time I met Lila Rose. Lila was a human whirlwind, a force of nature. The third of eight children, she was homeschooled through twelfth grade by her evangelical parents in California's Silicon Valley. At the age of fifteen, she founded a pro-life organization called Live Action. When we first got together she was a diminutive but dynamic freshman at the University of California, Los Angeles—poised, beautiful, outspoken, fearless, godly. It was Lila who opened my eyes to the casual criminality of the abortion industry. The fusion of my tactics and her wisdom would make us a dynamic duo.

Lila was about as bold as an eighteen-year-old could possibly be. Better still, she had an appreciation of my nonlinear thinking. In October 2006, just a few months after our Rutgers flag-planting campaign, I asked Lila if she would be willing to do the same thing on her campus. The best way to train someone I knew—something LI did not quite understand—was to teach in the field, hands-on, not just in the classroom.

Lila agreed without hesitation. "How about tomorrow?" I said. Lila was game. The next day we met up with UCLA's dean of students, Robert J. Naples, and had a perfectly wonderful conversation. In this innocent era, the dean did not even worry about being taped. He should have. The best training exercise for Lila was being there in the moment, improvising on the spot.

JO: We just want to put the American flags in classrooms.

LR: We're very concerned about diversity.

"Diversity!" I liked that. Right out of the chute, Lila was showing her grasp of the mau-mauing art. The dean was not quite sure why the American flag was a problem, but he was determined to think one up.

DEAN: It's a statement of political expression. Now what if someone wanted to put the Uganda flag . . .

JO: There is a difference; this isn't Uganda.

DEAN: I think the Supreme Court has not suggested that there is a difference. Why don't you just put the flag on your back or carry it around with you?

LR: Could we put the American flag in your office, Dean?

DEAN: (voice cracking) Sure, I don't have a problem with that.

Ah, the catalytic moment when the flak catcher agrees to go against his own political grain! Of course he had a problem with it, but he knew he had an even greater problem if he resisted. What he did not expect is that we would put the flag up right there and then. He started backtracking quickly.

DEAN: I think it's a waste of your money to put it in here. You can give me a flag. I may take it down though. I think you should put them up where they should go.

LR: Okay.

JO: Okay, do you want it then?

DEAN: No.

We were just warming up. Lila's heart was really in the life movement, and she would soon convert to Catholicism. As she told me with no small regret, the Arthur Ashe Student Health and Wellness Center on the UCLA campus was actually encouraging students to have abortions. With the flag sting successfully behind us, I proposed to Lila an even bolder project: her posing as a pregnant student at the health center. Lila had qualms about doing anything under false pretenses, but this was a cause that demanded action.

I played along as her boyfriend. As expected, a UCLA official gave us all types of highly politicized advice about the mere "collection of cells" this faux-pregnant freshman was nurturing within her. Ben Wetmore, my creative mentor at LI, and I spent some mischievous time dreaming up ways to market a "greatest hits" CD of the awful things Lila and I had been told. In time, Lila would put out a publication called the *Advocate,* whose back cover actually promoted the CD.

Psyched by the UCLA sting, Lila and I raised our sights. We didn't even know it at the time, but Texas activist Mark Crutcher had already orchestrated phone stings with abortion providers around the country. He recruited a young actress to pose as a pregnant thirteen-year-old girl with a boyfriend in his twenties. In more than 90 percent of the clinics she called, clinic staff proved eager to help her skirt the law to get an abortion.

We had independently decided to do a similar sting, but on video, and we were naïve enough to go after the mother of all abortion providers, Planned Parenthood. Lila would pose as a fifteen-year-old, which wasn't hard given her size and youthful looks, and I as her twenty-three-year-old boyfriend. We would soon enough see if the Planned Parenthood staffers in Los Angeles were willing to aid and abet both statutory rape and illegal abortion.

It did not take us long to find out. When Lila consulted with a staffer at the first clinic we visited, the woman obliged Lila at every turn.

LILA: He's twenty-three, and . . . um . . . I am fifteen. Do I have to report that?

STAFFER: It depends on how old you are. Let me double-check that.

When the helpful Planned Parenthood staff member returned a few minutes later, she seemed to have her strategy worked out.

STAFFER: If you're fifteen, we have to report that. If not, if you're older than that, we don't need to.

LILA: But if I just say that I'm *not* fifteen, then it's different?

STAFFER: That's correct.

LILA: So if I say—

STAFFER: You could say "sixteen."

LILA: Okay, so I say "sixteen." Okay, so I could just write, I could just write that I'm sixteen.

STAFFER: Figure out a birthday that works, and I don't know anything.

If the worker had reported that Lila was fifteen, the boyfriend would have faced charges for statutory rape. The worker acknowledged as much. Instead, the fifteen-year-old would agree to let the child in her womb be killed—an illegal act in itself—the clinic would destroy the evidence, the boyfriend would skate, and Planned Parenthood would improve its cash flow. I don't care what Planned Parenthood's politics are, but if their supporters cannot see the wrong in what they are doing, they aren't looking.

It was time to absorb another Alinsky rule into the Veritas rulebook: *"Whenever possible go outside the experience of an opponent. Here you want to cause confusion, fear, and retreat."* I shot some background footage outside the clinic with me as Mustang-driving, cigarette-smoking, whiskey-drinking boyfriend, edited the footage into a funky MTV style, and posted the video on YouTube.

Planned Parenthood had no experience with this kind of culture jamming. Its execs could have let the video float around the Internet and cause minimal damage, but they overreacted. Their attorneys, in overkill mode, sent a letter to Lila at her home threatening not just a lawsuit, but criminal action for taping the Planned Parenthood employees in California. We had forced the opposition to react to our advantage. This billion-dollar corporation was trying to take down an eighteen-year-old girl for exposing its own lawbreaking. It was poetry in motion.

I was back at LI by now, and Lila's parents called me looking for reassurance. "Don't worry," I reassured them as I struggled to come up with a justification on how Lila would be safe. We had provoked Planned Parenthood just as I hoped we would, but I was treading new water here. A bit distracted wondering what hell a billion-dollar corporation could unleash, I showed the letter to my office mate and shared our story. We were doing what LI wanted me to do, namely change the world. I even forwarded a copy of the letter to a reporter I knew at CNS News, the Christian News Service.

As it turns out, my office mate took the Planned Parenthood cease-and-desist letter and went straight to his boss with it. "Why?" I asked him. He turned his back to me and walked down the hallway. "Company man," I muttered under my breath. Next thing I know, I was called before an LI board and put on probation. Stunned, I headed back to New Jersey to help my father and grandfather on a building project. I did have a plumbing merit badge after all, and if worse came to worst, I suppose I had a career to fall back on, but it was not the career I wanted. I was shaken.

Duly chastised, I returned to LI a week later. In the meantime, the Planned Parenthood letter I had sent to CNS was magically working its way through the media stream, finally landing on the desk of Bill O'Reilly's producer. An outspoken abortion foe, O'Reilly asked

Lila on the show to discuss the video sting and the Planned Parenthood reaction. She agreed, and she and her pro bono attorney, David French from the Alliance Defense Fund, held forth in fine style on *The O'Reilly Factor.*

O'Reilly played audio excerpts from our video, and they had the desired effect. It was hard for even the most ardent abortion rights advocate to defend a clinic worker saying, "Figure out a birthday that works, and I don't know anything." The story went seriously viral. Sean Hannity would run with it as well. I should add that O'Reilly gave me credit on air. When I heard Lila mention my name on national TV, I admit it was something of a rush. Even the company man who ratted me out said, "Wow, you're famous." I'd get over that kind of praise quickly.

But I would never get over the sensation of breaking through. And this was just the first step of our own personal DEFCON—our "alert posture," as the air force might say. The media exposure worked. After Lila appeared on *The O'Reilly Factor,* Planned Parenthood backed down from pursuing criminal or civil action. A strategy had emerged, and I could not have predicted it.

When I returned to work the next morning, I learned that the LI people were not nearly as jazzed as I was. I got called into another meeting with a couple of execs, Director of Publications Jeff Fulcher and Vice President Steven Sutton. "What you do is important," they told me, "but you can't do it here." Perplexed, I asked, "But if you get rid of people who do what I do, how are you going to raise money?" I never did get a good answer to that one. They fired me on the spot. I was shocked, but it soon got worse. A colleague forwarded me a fundraising letter LI was sending out in which they were bragging about my direct-action campaigns during the course of the year with two different students. This is what made me sick. This is what sent me to the stalls, looking for answers between heaves. Getting fired I could take. This duplicity I could not. I was devastated.

The message was crystal clear: the Beltway—right, left, and center—is an unprincipled swamp. Its denizens spend most of their time raising money to keep the lights on. The creative fires do not burn here. Those who light them are quickly sent home. Others lose heart working long hours for bad pay under indifferent management. Meanwhile, the cynical and soulless all too often find their way to promotions and permanent positions in the oligarchy. At least there was Lila, and she never wavered. "Stay strong," she told me at my worst moment. "You can't resist what you are born to do."

The guy we called "Juicer," the office hulk so named for his presumed steroid use, handed me a box, told me to fill it up quickly, ushered me out of the office, and shut the LI doors behind me. I was through with D.C., and D.C. was through with me. For all the heartache, I would need one more slap in the face before I learned to stay away from Washington.

In the way of a postscript, the LI's founder and head honcho, Morton Blackwell, reached out to me after the ACORN bust in 2009. He wanted to use what Hannah Giles and I had accomplished as a way to promote the Leadership Institute. "You're a national hero, and I'm just the president of LI," he told me, and then suggested a variety of ways we could work together, as "my example would be an inspiration for many." I wrote a lengthy, soul-cleansing email in response and then, wisely, chose not to send it. Blackwell would not have liked what I had to say.

Without a doubt, dozens of young idealists, if given the most basic tools and some sound management, could reshape Washington and the world beyond it. Unfortunately, most of them end up having their dreams crushed, or worse, going to law school, and in the fall of 2007, that is exactly where this disillusioned fool was headed.

BUSHWHACKING

Veritas Rule #5:
The law will always surround you. Learn it.

Angels have appeared periodically throughout my life, and in the fall of 2007, one showed up in the guise of a scruffy young Southern Californian surfer dude. He would help save me from a fate not exactly worse than death, but close—law school—and I still don't know his name.

Cut loose by the Leadership Institute, I enrolled in Western Law School in Fullerton, California, the heart of Orange County and all that Orange County entails. From day one, I knew I did not belong there. I don't think in straight lines, and law school is about as linear as it gets. The more I studied a case, the more difficult it became for me to identify the relevant issues. "There is something wrong with you," my torts professor said without much in the way of sugarcoating. She didn't specify what.

Another prof got more specific. She accused me of "bushwhacking," meaning my mind was attracted primarily to cases with big, gaping holes in them. Five years later, I would spot gaping holes in the voting laws of various states and bushwhack them. I am still not sure I know why bushwhacking is bad.

While my profs were carrying on about their off-the-shelf course work, I was daydreaming about what innovative new videos I could make to change the world. I had at least one good idea on file. In the summer of 2007, working with Lila and her UCLA-based publication, the *Advocate*, I had made some calls to Planned Parenthood facilities in a few states with one-party consent laws and taped them. Using the Alinsky playbook, I had hoped to show how taxpayer-funded abortionists thoroughly failed to honor their own rules on the subject of race.

What I learned through Lila was that the abortion industry targets African-Americans, in part, I suspect, because they are so vulnerable. Thanks to the clever marketing strategies of Planned Parenthood and their competitors, a pregnant black woman is three times more likely to abort her child than is a pregnant white woman. But profit alone is not what moves the abortion industry.

Planned Parenthood founder Margaret Sanger was a stone-cold eugenicist. One of her two stated motives in launching the birth-control movement was "to prevent the sexual and racial chaos into which the world has drifted." As she saw it, this supposed racial chaos was due to the fact "that the least intelligent and the thoroughly degenerate classes in every community are the most prolific." Unlike the Nazis, who simply wanted "fit" women to outbreed the "unfit," Sanger did not want the "unfit" to breed at all.

After making the calls, however, I had run out of both time and money to do anything with the audio we gathered. But as my itch to start making videos grew, and my interest in law school shriveled, I decided to get back in the game. It was not easy. I had no equipment and no cash. I made the happy acquaintance, though, of the aforementioned surfer. In that he had to do something to pay for his board wax, he manned a high-end iMac at a Cal State lab. I offered to pay him to use the equipment, but he wouldn't take money. When the opportunity presented itself, he just let me use the iMac free for a few hours. That was all it took, and it began a trend. Instead of reading case law, I started sneaking across the street to make videos.

In late February 2008, the *Advocate* began releasing the videos and their accompanying transcripts. The most damning was one with Autumn Kersey, vice president of marketing for Planned Parenthood of Idaho.

JO: I want to specify that abortion to help a minority group, would that be possible?

PP: Absolutely.

JO: Like the black community for example?

PP: Certainly.

JO: The abortion—I can give money specifically for a black baby, that would be the purpose.

PP: Absolutely. If you wanted to designate that your gift be used to help an African-American woman in need, then we would certainly make sure that the gift was earmarked for that purpose.

JO: Great, because I really faced trouble with affirmative action, and I don't want my kids to be disadvantaged against black kids. I just had a baby; I want to put it in his name.

PP: Yes, absolutely.

JO: And we don't, you know we just think, the less black kids out there the better.

PP: (Laughs) Understandable, understandable.

JO: Right. I want to protect my son, so he can get into college.

PP: All right. Excuse my hesitation, this is the first time I've had a donor call and make this kind of request, so I'm excited, and want to make sure I don't leave anything out.

When the video aired in February 2008, the Idaho Planned Parenthood made a few halfhearted apologies and then denounced Lila as "a known anti-choice extremist." We had seen this before. "They do not change their ways," Lila told the *Idaho Statesman*. "They attack the whistle-blower."

The furor around the call caused Kersey major embarrassment, and other calls like it caused national Planned Parenthood at least a temporary dent in its reputation. The media were talking about our efforts. The USA Radio Network was on to us. Kirby Wilbur was playing our clips on the air. A Fox News affiliate was following up. The *Drudge Report* had even linked to the Planned Parenthood videos in red. *We were making news.* Emails were flowing in from all over. My adrenaline started rushing again. I was back in the game. We had created our own art, our own undeniable truth, *veritas.* I didn't care whether I was mentioned on air or not. I cared that our action, in classic Alinsky style, generated reaction. We forced the media to pile on, and we were breaking through.

We were indeed! In late April black pastors ramped up the public shaming by holding a protest in the District of Columbia charging Planned Parenthood with "genocide." This protest got decent coverage, including national Fox News. Fox played the following audio exchange between me and a worker in an Ohio Planned Parenthood clinic:

JO: When I underwrite an abortion, does that apply to minorities, too?

PP: If you specifically want to underwrite it for a minority person, you can target it that way. You can specify that that's how you want it spent.

JO: Okay, yeah, because there's definitely way too may black people in Ohio. So, I'm just trying to do my part.

PP: Hmm. Okay, whatever.

We were changing the world. Citizen journalism, I knew, was my calling, but I had a hard time convincing anyone else that there was a calling to be had. The news cycle moved on. The buzz quickly subsided. Planned Parenthood brushed us off and kept on doing what they do.

For several months, the videos showing Planned Parenthood in all its racist glory were the most watched "Planned Parenthood" videos on YouTube. But curiously, on the very night of Barack Obama's acceptance speech at the Democratic National Convention, YouTube took these four short videos down without warning or explanation. If you tried to access the videos, all that you would see in their place was a statement claiming a "terms of use violation" due to "inappropriate content."

The timing was suspicious. YouTube flags offending videos promptly, not seven months after posting, and there was nothing offensive about our videos. Let me speculate here. Google bought YouTube in 2006. In the 2008 election, Google employees gave more than $800,000 to the Obama campaign, the third most among all corporations. (Goldman Sachs was first, something for the Occupy Wall Street crowd to chew on.) Google CEO Eric Schmidt openly stumped for Obama and donated $25,000 to his inaugural. I can't imagine he pulled the plug on the videos, but I can imagine that someone down the food chain felt empowered in this Obama-friendly environment to do just that. Planned Parenthood, after all, supports President Obama even more ardently than does Google or Goldman Sachs.

Still, the internal buzz never completely subsided. Nothing in law school could ever match that emotional surge. The tactics I was exploring worked. They just needed to be scaled. One young woman saw their potential much as I did. In September, she wrote an online article about Google's shutdown of our videos. It was titled "The Truth Is Too Scandalous for YouTube" and her name was Hannah Giles.

CHINCHILLA JOURNALISM

Veritas Rule #6:
Always use props.

There I was on this very early morning in late July, driving fast and north on rural 301 on Maryland's eastern shore, the Delmarva fog hovering over the tall pines and grassy pastures that flanked the road. Stan Dai and Hannah Giles were as alert as birds, while Queenie Bui, the "second prostitute," slept soundly in the backseat.

"Damn," I said. Stan and Hannah looked at me quizzically. "Damn, damn, damn." I watched through the rearview mirror as a Maryland trooper heading south pulled a U-turn, humped over the grassy median, and sped toward us. I pulled my sister's car, a 2001 Mercury Grand Marquis with 220,000 miles and a missing hubcap, onto the shoulder.

"Oh dear Lord," I prayed under my breath, "please don't let me get arrested. Please don't let me get arrested." I shot glances at the mirror and chewed on my nails as the officer approached. What Stan and Hannah did not know is that I had a warrant out for my arrest in New Jersey.

I hadn't paid my parking tickets for the last two years. I was afraid the trooper would arrest me and impound the car.

My critics would later insist that right-wing billionaires had to be funding what would prove to be a remarkably successful sting on a notoriously corrupt organization, but they were profoundly wrong. I was so broke that summer I had to hit up Stan for the gas and take a longer route over the Chesapeake Bay to avoid paying tolls on I-95 through Baltimore.

That morning, the future hung by the narrowest of threads. If we did not get this clunker up to Philadelphia and Baltimore that day, President Obama would not have signed a bill to defund ACORN two months later, passed by both houses of Congress, and this voter registration/housing/whatever outfit would not have disbanded within six months.

"You were going eighty-eight in a fifty-five zone," drawled the trooper in a practiced monotone. "It'll feel a lot worse if you hit a deer at this speed." So saying, he handed me a ticket, walked briskly back to his squad car, and sped off. The mission was still a go.

It had all started about a month earlier, on June 15, 2009, to be exact. On that fateful day, I received a Facebook message from Hannah Giles, the young woman who wrote about how YouTube pulled down our videos some months back. "How are things?" Hannah asked. "Working on anything exciting at the moment?"

I told her about my then project about the rights of Guantanamo Bay prisoners. "I have more footage I'm releasing soon," I wrote. "'Adopt-a-detainee,' where I get signatures from Boston hippies to adopt Gitmo detainees into 'loving homes.' We call ourselves the 'love-thy-prisoner campaign.'"

In her response, Hannah told me what she was up to and then added, "p.s. have you ever done undercover stuff with ACORN housing???" I was intrigued. I had a deep suspicion about this outfit ever since I saw a news clip from Baltimore, where ACORN workers busted into foreclosed homes, seized them, and squatted there without the media or police saying boo. Color me naïve, but I always thought breaking down other people's doors was against the law.

ACORN stands for Association of Community Organizations for Reform Now. At its peak, just before Hannah and I got into the game, ACORN had more than 500,000 members spread over more than 1,200 neighborhood chapters in 100 or so cities. Everyone was wary of these guys. They had received multimillions in tax dollars and invested them in their many and sundry shell games.

The ACORN operation grew out of the welfare rights movement of the 1960s. The fact that the organization *professed* to "help poor people," especially poor people of color, was enough to secure the media's good graces. Yet during the forty years of its existence, ACORN failed in its mission in every conceivable way. At the end of the day it had become so indifferent to that mission that when the brother of its founder embezzled as much as $5 million from its coffers, ACORN refused to press charges for fear of exposure.

In the 1990s ACORN metastasized into the housing business, bigtime. Its housing MO was to bully bankers into giving home loans to people who could not afford them. Its henchmen succeeded well enough at this racket to help bring the economy to its knees in 2008. The media chose not to make the connection. Even if they had, in 2009 ACORN had the clout to survive just about any allegation thrown its way.

On the eve of the 2008 election, for instance, the *New York Times* spiked Stephanie Strom's potentially game-changing story on ties between ACORN and the Obama campaign. Strom knew, as Matthew Vadum reports in his book *Subversion,* that whistle-blower Anita Mon-Crief was giving the Obama campaign fits. She had testified in a Pennsylvania court in 2008 that Team Obama had given ACORN a list of Obama donors who "maxed out." In other words, they had given all they legally could to the Obama campaign but could still donate to ACORN. ACORN, in turn, could then use these donations to get out the vote for Obama, a violation of any number of election laws and of ACORN's nonprofit charter. Strom had written several articles based on MonCrief's information. MonCrief had proved to be a reliable source, too reliable perhaps.

"I have just been asked by my bosses to stand down," Strom told MonCrief in a recorded phone message at the time. "They want me to hold off on coming to Washington. Sorry, I take my orders from higher up sometimes." When the charge that the *Times* spiked the Strom story surfaced months later, public editor Clark Hoyt moved into damage control mode. Although conceding that the story had been killed, Hoyt dismissed as "nonsense" the charge that it had died an unethical death.

Protesting too much, Hoyt claimed that even if MonCrief's charges had borne out, they were not "momentous enough to change an election." No one who knew the *Times'* history believed its editors would have killed a comparable story about a Republican. In fact, the *Times* ran a flimsy story in mid-2008 campaign about an alleged affair between John Mc-Cain and a lobbyist ten years earlier. This front page got the paper sued.

This was the nature of the Goliath we were up against, a powerful national organization with a hold on both the White House and the media. Only a madman would have predicted that a couple of twenty-somethings working off a credit card and internship money could expose ACORN's dark heart and force it to disband; journalism can still work when it is tried.

"What's your idea with the ACORN?" I wrote Hannah back. "I'm always looking for new video ideas and have surveillance equipment and activists." At the time, I did not even know ACORN's history with vote fraud. Hannah was thinking ahead.

"So what if two girls dressed for 'business' walk in and ask to apply for housing," she asked, "and make the nature of their business clear and ensure that they can make the payments, but they need the house to make money safely etc., essentially using the house for prostitution but putting it nicely." Hannah added, "Think it might work?"

"I love it!" I responded. Now came the moment of truth. Finding someone to pull off a sting is a whole lot harder than finding someone to talk about it. There are not many Lila Roses in the world. "Would you be willing to play the role of one of the prostitutes?" Hannah was indeed, and that brings me to an experience-driven Veritas rule: *"You will get a wave of creative adrenaline from time to time. Go with the flow."* We did just that. In our Facebook exchanges, Hannah and I started plotting the adventure.

I offered the idea of a pimp to go along with the prostitute in the fictitious scenario. "It might be good to have a pimp come along wearing a fur coat, gold chains, and the undercover camera (I have one in a satin tie)," I wrote. "When you placate them it has to be extremely over-the-top to prevent people from saying 'what does that prove?'" This recommendation evoked still another new Veritas rule: *"Always use props."* In the course of this story, you will see just how useful props can be.

I elaborated to Hannah: "My strategy has always been good content. As explosive as possible." This, in fact, became the essential Veritas rule (#1): *Content is king. Without strong content, nothing else matters.* Content is what provoked Planned Parenthood into suing. Content would drive ACORN into its fatal tailspin.

We continued to talk tactics on Facebook for weeks. My friend Ben Wetmore, an inspired idea guy who helped Lila and me with the Planned Parenthood sting, joined the conversation. The plan was coming into shape. We wanted to provoke ACORN staff into one of those catalytic—"the less black people the better"—moments, the kind that reveals the soul or, as the case would have it, the soullessness of an organization. We never imagined the nationwide impact this would have.

The plan went operational late that July. Hannah, I should add, is a national treasure. Only twenty at the time, she had the poise of a woman twice her age. Smart, athletic, attractive, she was not afraid to get creative. "I asked my sister if she would send the fox fur and she said no," Hannah wrote about a prop we both thought would be useful. "I guess it doesn't make much sense for a pimp to have a fur during the summer even though it would be good for film."

Ah, the problem of the pimp fur. I walked over to my bed, clasped my hands behind my head, and thought for a moment. At twenty-five, I was still living at home. There are many ways to rationalize getting fired, leaving law school, and living at home, but they all smell of indecision at best, failure at worst. Yet there was something about Hannah's energy and eagerness that downright inspired me. I got up off the bed, then walked down the hallway and up a spiral staircase to ask my grandmother, who lived with us, whether she had a fur coat I could borrow. Why not disgrace my unemployed self a little further?

"Now, why exactly do you need this, Jamie?"

"There is just something that I need to do, and I need um . . . ah . . . a fur coat to do it."

"Is there something about you that I don't know?"

"No. I mean, I'll show you when I'm done, but if you have something, anything that could work, that would be great."

I didn't really expect much, but my grandmother found a thirty-year-old chinchilla shawl and placed it on my bed that afternoon. I should warn any aspiring pimps in the audience: chinchilla sheds like a bitch. I wasn't sure I would have anything left of it by the time I was finished. I borrowed my grandfather's wide-brimmed derby and my little sister's famous Mercury Marquis with the missing hubcap and drove down to Hannah's D.C. apartment. There I met up with Hannah, Stan Dai, one of my co-conspirators, and an Asian-American woman Stan knew named Queenie Bui. We practiced for hours inside Hannah's apartment and recorded our rehearsals on video.

"You don't want to start out completely absurd," said Stan. "Start out relatively subtle." When Stan talked we listened. He had a military intelligence background and, more importantly, a gift for mau-mauing.

JO: I need to buy a home.

SD: Good. This will force them to start talking about foreclosure.

HG: I need a house to perform our work.

SD: That's great, then you might want to say you've got twenty to thirty people coming in and out.

JO: We need to have a place that is safe and where we can have a lot of people.

HG: We don't want any police officers coming around.

JO: We provide services to the inner-city community to make people happy.

So began our exercise in role-playing. We explored euphemisms for prostitutes, story lines, names for ourselves, and scenarios. As with any good caper, we needed to understand both the lay of the land and the psychology of our target. I had even done some reconnaissance work, going into the D.C. office before the sting, taking an application, and casing the joint as a robber might case a bank.

In the practice session, we began to further develop the scenario. I transitioned to a situation in which I was still a pimp, but I wanted to run for political office down the road. And as far as pimps go, I was a relatively good pimp. Hannah was going to ask for a place of her own to escape a second, more abusive pimp. "And the girls can give me the prostitution money," Hannah suggested, "and I can give it to James to run his campaign." We high-fived each other. We liked that angle: money laundering into a pimp/boyfriend's political campaign.

Just when we settled into that idea, Stan offered a refinement. "Try to maneuver them into asking questions," he said. "I think the tagline should be 'ACORN wants to register illegal immigrants who are prostitutes.'" This got us brainstorming some more. Somehow the name El Salvador came up during the course of discussing illegal immigrants, and it just sounded right. This was the way to brainstorm a video—organically, step by step, fueled with creative adrenaline.

Queenie was skeptical about being involved in the project at all, especially as a prostitute. Although I understood her reluctance, to this day I struggle with people in "the conservative movement" who resist all action for fear of ruining their careers. Their timidity makes Hannah's courage stand out even more. She had to contact me, fly around the country in costume, and operate at her own risk. People to this day just don't realize the guts this took. Before we launched the project, the "conservative" honchos we told about the idea thought it was stupid. "It will keep you from ever working in Washington," they told us, and from their perspective, little could be worse. Until that movement identifies and encourages more people like Hannah, it is going nowhere.

That afternoon we walked around D.C. to get in character. We walked past the Lincoln Memorial, the Washington Monument, the Capitol Building, and down the cobblestone streets of Georgetown. It was not easy for me. I am not a natural prankster. Still, once we got our groove on, you would be amazed by how many people asked to have their picture taken with us. My regalia now included a cane that I bought at Dollar General and a pair of oversized sunglasses. Hannah was wearing a halter top and a skimpy wraparound sarong that would look almost modest on Miami Beach, where it belongs, but altogether scandalous on Capitol Hill.

Different people looked at us in different ways. In Georgetown, even the nerdiest-looking white guys, bow ties and all, would fix on Hannah's butt and not give me a passing glance. In the Adams Morgan neighborhood, black guys would shoot me sly grins and say, "Big pimpin'!"

"My parents back everything fully," Hannah would later email me after seeing the raw footage, "but dad isn't too happy about some of that stuff." I couldn't say I blamed him, so we took out the more scandalous B-roll. Stan and I also practiced with our camera and audio equipment, following one practical Veritas rule: *Make sure your battery is charged and your memory chip clear.*

That night we slept to the degree anyone could sleep. At 5 a.m. on July 24, we got up to don our battle gear and charge our equipment for a 9:30 a.m. meeting. I remember standing outside leaning against the car in such a way that Hannah would not notice the missing hubcap.

I imagine that Philippe Petit, the Frenchman who in 1974 violated just about every rule of God and New York City by slinging a wire between the Twin Towers of the World Trade Center and walking across it, had a similar urge. He had his own dream, his own little posse, and his own sense of destiny. We both hoped to make the world a better place, he by entertaining it, me by exposing it. The difference, I suppose, was that the outcome would be a little more brutal if he fell off the wire than if Hannah, say, fell off her platform shoes.

It was on the way north out of D.C. on 301 that I got busted. This was the one time in my life I would be relieved to get a speeding ticket. The ticket would cost me 325 more dollars that I did not have, an early exercise in deficit spending. When we got to the Philly office, which was definitely not in one of the city's nicer neighborhoods, I parked in a Dunkin' Donuts lot to avoid putting money in the meter.

Hannah was fully tricked out in sarong, stiletto heels, pimp fur with hoop earrings, and eccentric leather shirt. I was dressed more conservatively, as befits a pimp who aspires to Congress. Stan and Queenie Bui hung around outside, posing as your average Asian tourists shooting video of everything they see in America, and Hannah and I went in. Although this office heard us out, our meeting did not generate much in the way of video interest.

From Philadelphia, we drove down to Baltimore, where we were greeted by an ACORN housing employee named Shira. When we explained our circumstances, she told us we would want to talk to tax specialist Tanja Thompson. "She is really good," Shira assured us. She had confidence that the alchemist Thompson could help us turn our criminal enterprise into a "legal business." Jon Stewart would later capture the highlights of our exchange on a very funny *Daily Show* bit titled "The Audacity of Hos." As he observed, "Clearly, this is not the first time they're hearing this."

JO: Is it against the law in Maryland? Prostitution?

Shira: Anything that the government's not getting our money from is always against the law. Let me get somebody here from taxes so they can talk to you. . . . Tanja, she wants to know how you can make it legal.

Tanja: Let me make sure there's a code for it, okay?

JO: A code for prostitution?

Tanja: We might have to name this something else . . . [looking through tax forms] performance arts. Let's see. Independent artist. You could be that. . . . Your business is a performing artist, which you are. Okay, so you're not lying. . . . So stop saying "prostitution."

JO: Got it.

Hannah volunteered that she made $8,000 a month. Thompson showed off her math skills by doing the calculations in her head—let's see, 12 times 8,000—and concluded that Hannah would make $9,600 a year. We chose not to correct her. Yes, there is something sad and tragic about this whole dumb show. If these people had not been wrecking the economy and trying to steal elections at taxpayer expense, I am sure I would have felt more sorry for them. I kind of did anyhow.

Flaunting her expertise, Thompson walked us through the various exemptions Hannah could claim. "You have to have a certain clothing. You have to have a certain grooming." Thompson imagined that Hannah could write off as much as $8,000 of her $9,000 or so annual salary. She said all this without a trace of irony or unease.

It was time to ratchet the absurdity up a level and add another variable to the moral calculus. "What might complicate our taxes," I said, "is that we have a couple girls overseas coming over." By the time Hannah and I finished elaborating, the "couple girls" turned into thirteen underage prostitutes-in-training from El Salvador. Stewart got exactly what we were doing. As he said with deep irony, "I'm sure ACORN has a line they won't cross."

JO: There's going to be thirteen El Salvadoran girls coming into this house. And they're very young. And we don't want to put them on the books.

Stewart pleaded, "Please tell me thirteen underage Salvadoran sex slaves *is* the line." It wasn't. Tanja scrupled over ways to shield their income before arriving at a perfectly logical, if utterly appalling, solution. Tanja suggested that since our young contractors were under sixteen, it was not necessary to file 1099s for them. Her ultimate solution she enthused over as happily as if she had just discovered a new planet.

Tanja: On the other part of the return you can use them as a dependent. You can use them as a dependent, because they live in your house.

"Are you [beeping] kidding me?" said a comically exasperated Stewart. "Did you hear what they just said?" Always looking out for her customers, Tanja cautioned us, "If they are underage and they are making money, you shouldn't let anyone know anyway." Shira added a further caution: "Be careful. Train them [girls] to keep their mouths shut."

In November 2007, then-candidate Obama bragged about his ties to ACORN, saying, "I've been fighting alongside ACORN on issues you care about my entire career." He was not the only politician to do so. Those bragging days were about to come to an end.

But they almost did not. After leaving the ACORN office, Hannah and I hustled back to my old jalopy, footage in hand. She rubbed my derby for luck and I threw her a misguided high-five as I slouched in the front seat, conjuring an anticlimactic getaway scene in traffic-clogged Baltimore. We had scored a major hit, but we still didn't even realize how major it would be.

Much too pleased with ourselves, Stan, Hannah, my friend Maureen Wagner, and I headed down to Solomons Island, an hour south of D.C., where I was keeping my sailboat, a Catalina 27. "What?" I can hear the folks at *TPM* shouting. "He is supposed to be broke, and he has a yacht." Well, not exactly a yacht—you can pick up a used boat like this for a few K—but a wonderful diversion. The money my peers might spend on tattoos, piercings, and cocaine, I spend on my boat. It was part of the reason I was always broke. As Kenneth Grahame has said, "Believe me, my young friend, there is nothing—absolutely nothing—half so much worth doing as simply messing about in boats." Boat people will understand.

In any case, it was a beautiful night. The cabin was well stocked, since friends traditionally brought a bottle as a gift when coming on board. We sailed out of Mill Creek into the Patuxent River. Lightning was flashing in the vague distance. Luminescent jellyfish added a magical glow to the water. The Dollar General tiki lamps—what's a nighttime sail without them?—cast an exotic spell over the boat. We were pleased with the world and ourselves and celebrating our crazy, brazen sting, the audio of which was contained in my iPhone. I was staring mindlessly at the starry sky when a freak wave hit us portside, sending the bourbon bottles flying, one of which landed squarely on my iPhone. "It was the crack heard around the world," Maureen remembers.

The glass face was shattered and dangling from the phone. I quickly pulled the sails down, turned on the motor—an old eight-horsepower Johnson outboard, which I had to clamp on to keep from falling off—and headed back to the harbor, my heart in my mouth. Up to this point, for no good reason, I had not yet transferred the audio files onto my computer. Once docked, we headed for Maureen's Honda, huddled over the phone as I tried to power it back up, and shouted with joy as that tenacious, brave apple popped back up on screen. Yes, there is a God, and he loved us!

In the way of postscript, I could not afford to replace the phone and so kept using it, dangling glass and all. It took full immersion in a hot tub a couple of months later to end that heroic puppy's life, its mission memorably complete.

MR. O'KEEFE GOES TO WASHINGTON: PART II

Veritas Rule #7:
Resist the temptation to work or live in the Beltway.
Restrict visits to twenty-four hours.

Hannah and I had little clue what to do with the footage we had shot thus far, but our intuition told us it might be a good idea to take it directly to lawmakers on Capitol Hill. I was in full "Mr. Smith" mode, bright-eyed and bushy-tailed, going to Washington to showcase fraud and abuse at a taxpayer-funded institution. Seemed reasonable enough—at least until we got there. The meeting we walked into would become the subject of lore.

Monitoring the news, we had seen a minority report on ACORN published July 20, 2009, by ranking Republican congressman Darrell Issa of the House Committee on Oversight and Government Reform. Said the report, "ACORN has committed investment fraud, deprived the public of its right to honest services and engaged in a racketeering enterprise affecting interstate commerce." This report was circulating throughout the media late that summer and inspired Hannah and me to arrange a meeting with Issa's staff. We had just seen the congressman give an exclusive TV interview on the report. The timing seemed serendipitous, or so we thought.

On July 30, 2009, we walked into Issa's D.C. office and met with Daniel Epstein, Republican counsel to the Judiciary Committee and a staff member for Issa. We brought a stereo in with us and an audio CD with our "greatest ACORN hits." Epstein, a young researcher, had little to say but smiled when his colleague John Cuaderes, deputy staff director for the House Oversight Committee, boasted that he and Epstein had done most of the research on the report that attracted us in the first place.

"We've heard you had some interesting material for us," said the fortyish Cuaderes. He had an Oklahoma drawl, a confident air, and the polished look of a Washington insider. My Leadership Institute experience taught me to be wary of such people, but I was a bit overeager and held nothing back.

"Yes, in fact we do have something unbelievable," I told him. "We have tapes of ACORN employees encouraging underage prostitution." The two staffers gasped, literally. You could hear the air rush out as their mouths dropped open.

"What did you say? What?" said Cuaderes. "We've heard about embezzlement, vote fraud, but nothing involving prostitution." Insiders though they may have been, these two staffers were still capable of being shocked.

I knelt to put the CD into the stereo, and I could see my hands shaking. I was nervous, yes, but I was also a little uneasy. The videos had yet to air on TV, and no one outside our circle had heard this audio. As I handed them each a set of headphones, I asked, "Can we have your assurance that if we let you listen to this you keep this confidential?" Maybe it was the look on their faces when I asked, but the whole scene didn't sit quite right. I felt as though this were turning into some kind of illicit exchange, like they were corner drug dealers and we were looking for a score.

Cuaderes seemed uneasy as well. I made a motion suggesting I ought not play the audio, and he only reluctantly overruled me. Epstein, meanwhile, sat quietly in the corner writing on a notepad. I knelt back on the floor fiddling with the stereo to get it ready to play, while Hannah stressed that we planned to release the videos as citizen journalists, nothing else. "It's important to James and me that we remain independent when we release this," she told them.

Cuaderes had other ideas. He wanted to sell us on partnering a release with Republicans. "Oh, you definitely want to release through us," he drawled. "We have the ability to get this into the media. We've done the research, as you know because you've read our report."

Hannah and I looked at each other for reassurance and nodded our solidarity. We were not backing down. We were doubling down. I got up from the stereo and sat on the edge of my chair.

"If our investigation is to retain its credibility," I said, "we really have to release this independently. We're coming to you because we thought you could use our findings. But we need to break it ourselves."

Cuaderes didn't like that answer. His face changed as though a dark cloud had just passed across it. "Are there any additional copies of the tape?" he said. "Yeah," I answered. "In my car."

For a moment, no one said anything. Even Epstein's pen went silent. I was trying to keep my cool, but nothing seemed quite right. It wasn't. This was the Beltway, after all. They play by a different set of rules than in the rest of America. Knowing now that he would not get an exclusive, Cuaderes said something you and I would never think to say. "Well, it sounds like you have evidence of these people engaging in criminal behavior," he said smugly. "And if you refuse to cooperate with us, then you yourselves are covering up a crime, and we cannot be an accessory to that." Not having intimidated us enough, he added, "You could be arrested and your car impounded."

Something definitely went out of me that moment. My heart dropped. My mouth quivered. My eyes lost their brightness and my proverbial tail its bushiness. This guy was colder than ice. A thousand things rushed through my mind as I tried to regain my composure and stay strong, if nothing else because Hannah was in the room. I didn't know whether they were going to call their own "juicer" or the police or what, but they just stood there, staring at us, and we were in shock. My voice shaking, I said, "Hey, we're just trying to participate in the democratic process. If that's how you feel, then I guess we're done here."

"We're going to have to ask you to leave," Cuaderes said. Again, complete silence. No one knew quite what to say. Hannah and I looked at each other and affirmed that we were on the same wavelength. We stood up as Smith made sure to escort us quickly out of the office. As we walked through the congressional hallways, I saw all these young guys hustling about with bow ties and brass-buttoned blazers, Democrats and Republicans both. They all looked alike. "This place sucks," I told Hannah.

I left the building drained, wiping the sweat off my neck after I passed through security and into the thick, swamplike D.C. air. I breathed deeply, and it almost hurt going down.

I refused to get upset this time. It was not my first rodeo, and I communicated as much to Hannah. I do not know the Bible as well as I should and do not often quote scripture, but somehow I found myself quoting Matthew 10:14: "If anyone will not welcome you or listen to your words, leave that home or town and shake the dust off your feet."

We'd have to go the non-D.C. route. We went back to Hannah's apartment and brainstormed a bit more. I had sent a few emails out to various media types who assisted with the Planned Parenthood story. Then, Greg Scott from the Alliance Defense Fund called me back and said the following: "This definitely sounds like something for Andrew Breitbart."

MEETING BREITBART

Veritas Rule #8:
Expect the media to invert Gandhi: First they fight you, then they laugh at you, then they ignore you, then you win.

I was on a Chinatown bus out of Philadelphia when the call came in. Yes, it had come to that. I was that broke. I was riding a discount bus to D.C., where my girlfriend would pick me up. But we had the goods. The day after our Baltimore sting, Hannah and I had stung the Washington ACORN office. The results were pretty much the same. Ditto for New York on August 4. In the interim I had a chance to produce the Baltimore piece and show it around as I angled for a way to make the videos public. Frankly, I did not quite know how to jump-start our PR strategy. Breitbart did.

"Hey, James, it's Andrew," he said in his surprisingly soft Southern California voice. Breitbart presumed that there was only one Andrew worth knowing, and he may have been right. All roads lead to Rome? Not in my world. From my Alinsky-trained professor in New Jersey to a Christian Defense Fund in Arizona, all roads lead to Breitbart.

You see, everyone would go on to ask me how I met up with Andrew.

It wasn't exactly direct. The previous summer I emailed David Knowlton, the Rutgers adjunct who had introduced me to Alinsky. He hooked me up with the president of Jamestown Associates, who hooked me up with their guy in D.C., who hooked me up with Mike Flynn, who referred me to his wife, Maura, a documentary producer who had shown some interest in an earlier video I had produced on bailouts. It was Maura who made the ultimate connection for me—I told her what I was doing and she told me what others already had: "Sounds like something for Breitbart." It was becoming something of a theme.

"So Maura told me you are up to something exciting," said Andrew. "What do you got?"

A bus bound for D.C. is not a great place to brag about videos involving child prostitution. So I whispered, "ACORN employees encouraging a pimp to employ child prostitutes and evade taxes."

"You're shitting me," said Andrew. "You are shitting me."

"No, we really have it. It's all on video."

I went on to describe everything in detail, whispering and covering my phone with my free hand. With one half of his brain, Breitbart was sifting my story through his uncanny BS screen. With the other half he was already strategizing on what to do with the videos. When I suggested taking them to local media, as we had done with past stories—in this case, the *Baltimore Sun*—Andrew laughed incredulously. "James," he said, "these media—the *Sun* especially—are *part* of the Democratic establishment."

"Andrew, I know they're biased. I've experienced—"

"Biased?" He laughed. "James, you don't understand."

"You don't understand," I soon learned, was a common Andrewism, born out of indignation, always righteously delivered, not to be taken personally. This was a man consumed by his passion. His enthusiasm to help me see what he saw—the unplumbed depths of media corruption—poured out of him spontaneously and sincerely.

"James," he insisted, "the *Baltimore Sun is* the Democratic Party. There is no distinction." At that moment I realized who Andrew Breitbart was, and what he was about. "The media is everything, James, everything." Andrew wanted me to publish with him. He knew how the media worked, and he did not hesitate to tell me.

"I can blow this up in a way nobody else can," he said. He then added mischievously, "Though to be honest, part of me doesn't even believe you." Andrew had an appreciation for the comic absurdity of every premise. I improvised: "Well, Andrew, I have a girlfriend living just north of L.A. I plan to visit her at her parents' next week. I can stop by your house."

I heard that little voice saying, "All roads lead to truth. All roads lead to Breitbart. Go there."

Andrew was thinking ahead. He had already begun to put his newest blog, BigGovernment.com, into the preliminary planning stages and sensed that the video could kick it off big. Still, I don't think he actually expected me to show up. I was just one of a hundred sources sent his way. I would later see him give other sources a phone call and offer them a meeting, but they would rarely provide the goods. Still, he kept listening. What made Andrew successful was that he lent these sources his ear, knowing that one day one of them would make it worth his while.

A few days later, with my ticket cost dropped onto a credit card already groaning with debt, I flew out to Los Angeles, rented a car, and met Breitbart at his modest Brentwood home. He greeted me in a long black shirt and gray sweats. His hair was short then, his feet were bare, and his toenails were painted pink. He caught me looking at his feet. "It's not what you think." He smiled. "It's my kids." I didn't doubt him. There were four of them, all under ten, all with their faces painted; lovely, animated, precocious kids dancing around the house like elves. I met his wife, Suzie, as well. Friends inevitably described her as "long-suffering" for affectionately putting up with a husband who never quite grew up himself.

Andrew got me a Fresca and we went down to his basement bunker. He must have had a hundred windows open on his iMac, and they all seemed to be in play. At the same time that he was monitoring the screen he was talking to me and checking his BlackBerry. I had to grab his attention in the passing moment when his focus fell on me. As soon as it did, he pulled up a picture of the actor Matthew Modine on Google images. "You look like this guy—the guy from *Vision Quest*," he said playfully.

Soon after I arrived, Breitbart's best friend and business partner, Larry Solov, joined us. If Breitbart did not exactly look Hollywood, Solov did—square-jawed, handsome, self-aware. At first I thought Solov was an actor friend of Breitbart. I took his presence as a good sign. They were sizing me up, appraising my soul. "Tell Larry about ACORN," Andrew asked. "I'm not an expert," I told them, but I explained the outfit as best I could, including the fact that the president of the United States used to be an attorney for the group.

Andrew had heard enough. "Let's see what you got." I opened my Acer laptop, which still housed my law school briefs, dusted off the screen, and showed the Baltimore video. I could see their mouths open wider and wider, and I knew I had them. Before it was even finished, Andrew was working on strategy and, to my exasperation, simultaneously checking his BlackBerry.

"You know they are going to say it was one rogue employee." I knew that drill already from my work with Lila. The media will work to kill new stories that don't fit their agenda. YouTube pulled the Planned Parenthood videos. CNN challenged our editing.

Breitbart was on a different page than just about anyone in the conservative media. He didn't waste energy shouting "bias." What he understood, and what I was learning, is that conservatives may have their own media, but they don't create the news. They simply aggregate and/or comment on the news that the major media produce.

Meanwhile, the majors zealously guard the power to set the agenda. Protecting their right flank are the anti-journalists. These are the salaried staff of the numerous, well-funded attack dog blogs and online journals—*Huffington Post, Daily Kos, Media Matters, TPM, Politico, Mediaite*—whose mission is to kill stories in the womb that do not fit their ideological agenda and ridicule those they cannot kill.

For me to add new information into the ether was to invite attack. One particularly unsavory strategy of the anti-journalists is to research the background of real journalists, citizen journalists included, to find some moment in time when they offended the gods of race, sex, class, and/or orientation. Let me jump ahead here. Just four days after the first ACORN video hit, the *Daily Kos* ran a piece appropriately titled "The Acorn Pimp: The bully behind the costume. (I found his blog.)"

The author, "goodidealist," dove deep into the Internet and found a diary/blog I posted as an eighteen-year-old at Rutgers. Much of the material goodidealist lifted would have offended only the readers of the *Daily Kos,* as it was vaguely incorrect from a race-obsessed perspective. Where the author found gold, or thought he had, was in my description of an incident from my freshman year.

I had been assigned to a largely black floor in the dorm, yes, the "Paul Robeson" floor. After a month without a roommate, I was assigned one, "an absolute nightmare," as I described him at the time. I continued, "Then, to my horror, he actually said to the all-black RAs that I called everyone on the floor 'niggers'—a complete lie." This fellow understood that the best way to get rid of an unwanted roommate was to accuse him of *racecrime,* knowing that in the Orwellian world of American academia even a false accusation was proof of guilt. More Orwellian still, merely telling the story of being falsely accused would contribute to my being labeled a "white supremacist."

"Maybe it was all a lie, like [O'Keefe] says," wrote the alleged good idealist, "but either way now you can judge him for who he is, in his own words. And you have a more complete picture of the prick in the Pimp costume." Either way? To the *Daily Kos,* on the subject of race, an accusation is as good as a conviction. The author never stopped to ask himself why I would post this story publicly if it were false. Still, it was an arrow to my chest. A year later George Stephanopoulos would talk about the story before seven million people on *Good Morning America.* Trust me—I understand why citizens shy away from entering the arena. Race-baiting is a powerful deterrent.

Of all the anti-journalist organs, *Media Matters,* more formally *Media Matters for America,* is the squirreliest and least scrupulous. According to the *New York Times, Media Matters* has a $10 million annual budget, most of it provided by friendly plutocrats, none richer than international man of mystery George Soros. Every day its staff of nearly one hundred little McCarthyites pores over every word said by every major commentator of a different political stripe; they are looking for something that can be used against him or her. They specialize in race-baiting. They took credit, for instance, for getting Don Imus thrown off the air for his insensitive comments about the Rutgers women's basketball team.

"Whether Media Matters has affected the course of the 2008 election—by intimidating some reporters or commentators, or forcing a change in the tone of others—is difficult to judge," wrote the *Times'* Jacques Steinberg. What was not difficult to judge was their eagerness to intimidate. Imus has never been the same since his exile. I am sure they have assigned me my own case officer.

This is what passes for journalism today, and no one could manage it better than Andrew. From the first day, he and I were on the same wavelength. I was the content producer. He was the aggregator. I was the match. He was the gasoline. Together we had the potential to ignite the major-media tinderbox, and they and their minions hated us for it.

Andrew took me out to lunch that day in his Range Rover. He had his satellite radio set where I set mine—First Wave, the alternative music from the era that defined what alternative meant. I remember listening to Depeche Mode's "People Are People" and thinking that the lyrics were entirely fitting: "I can't understand / What makes a man / Hate another man." That hatred is something I have been wrestling with since my *Centurion* days at Rutgers. Andrew dealt with it better than I do. Hell, he courted hatred. It seemed to give him life.

He took me to a homely little Mexican restaurant in Brentwood. He was chomping on his burritos and sharing disconnected bits of data—where O.J. lived, how they trashed Drudge for busting Clinton, when he worked at a pizzeria—between bites. He wanted me to believe in him. He wanted me to believe in myself as well.

On the way back to the house, we stopped at an ATM. All Andrew had to do was deposit a check, but he had the hardest time doing the simplest thing. Just as he was about to stick the envelope in, an idea popped into his head, and he did a monologue on that theme. Then he turned back to the check, but before he could finish depositing it, he began to lecture me, "James, when it comes to Hollywood . . ." It took us twenty minutes to do the deed. That was Andrew, God love him. We would have our fallings-out, but we never fell far.

The plan we decided on was to launch the videos serially, beginning with the Baltimore video. "We deprive them of information," Andrew told me, "that way ACORN can't get the government-media complex to kill the messenger before the whole message gets out." In the meantime, Hannah joined me in California, where we did several more stings, in Los Angeles, San Bernardino, and San Diego. It was obvious that ACORN had not put out an alert. We were getting more or less the same results everywhere we went.

Under any circumstances, the days leading up to the video's release on September 10, a Thursday, would have been hectic. Add Andrew to the mix and they became absolutely manic. The schedule called for a rollout of the Baltimore video through BigGovernment.com—a site whose launch Andrew accelerated to accommodate the release—an airing of the story on Fox News, and a showing of the complete video on the then–highly popular *Glenn Beck Show,* also on Fox.

On the morning of September 4, I had to bring the sole hard-drive copy of the video over to the building in Rockefeller Center where Beck's show was produced. Lacking a car of my own, I had my father drive me into the city, but the traffic was worse than usual and close to gridlock in Manhattan. Realizing I was about to be late for my scheduled appointment, I jumped out of the car and ran as if in a dream through the streets of midtown Manhattan, silver hard drive in hand, cords dangling, dodging cars and pedestrians both, my heart pounding, looking skyward now and then as the rain clouds gathered, and wondering if I'd live to be twenty-six.

Fortunately, I found my way. I rushed into the building's lobby, huffed and puffed my way through security, ran to the elevator, pushed the "up" button about thirty-five times, and ascended to Beck's spacious suite at the top of the building. There, breathless, I met Beck's producer and handed him the tape.

"Want to meet Glenn?"

The producer ushered me back to Beck's lush corner office. He was shaving when I walked in. He looked up and said, "So this is the kid?" He smiled. Beck was forty-five at the time. He was taller than I imagined him to be and not as pudgy as he appeared on TV. He was at the peak of his game then, with unheard-of ratings for the 5 p.m. slot on Fox News, and he was feeling it.

"Mr. Beck, honored to meet you. You've got to see this video." At the time, Beck and Breitbart were allies. That would not last. They were both such oversized personalities they were bound to clash. When they did, it usually involved me, went public, and got ugly. I tried my best to stay out of it, although I wound up being on the receiving end of some of the vitriol.

I got a sense of how big this story could be when Fox sent Eric

Shawn and a crew to interview me in New Jersey prior to the closely guarded September 10 release. On September 9, I started getting really wired when Beck appeared on *Fox & Friends* and teased the videos as an "exclusive" that would shake up Washington and send people to jail. During the rollout, I was scheduled to go into the city and stay with Andrew in a Midtown hotel. He was orchestrating our media. He was a maestro. My already weird life was about to get much, much weirder.

Fox News started running a news story about the Baltimore video at around 7:30 on the morning of September 10, 2009. Andrew had already posted the story on BigGovernment. Beck played the video in full that evening on his show, the whole of which he dedicated to ACORN.

The media requests flooded in, and I started to respond without Andrew's permission. One request came from the splashy tabloid the *New York Post*. They wanted a photo. I had a picture from our walkabout in Washington with me in full pimp regalia and Hannah in high ho style. I cropped out Stan Dai and Maureen Wagner, who flanked us in the original, and emailed it to the *Post*. That photo made the front page two days in a row, one day under the banner headline NUT CASE. This exposure validated the Veritas rule *Always use props*. I assure you, we would not have made the front page without them.

ACORN responded just as Andrew said they would. As ABC News reported on September 11, Alton Bennett, the president of ACORN housing, and Mike Shea, the executive director, were allegedly "appalled and angry" by the performance of their employees and insisted "this is not how we behave." They claimed that all ACORN employees "undergo rigorous training" and are expected to "comply with high standards for ethical behavior and compliance with the law." Right!

That was apology enough. Then, in what appeared to be a prepared statement, the ACORN execs went on the offensive, claiming that the video was "slanted to misinform the public." Here they shifted from misleading to flat-out lying:

The people who made this tape went to at least five other ACORN Housing offices where they were turned away or where ACORN Housing employees responded by calling the police. That is not mentioned on the tape—it is part of a long-term plan to smear ACORN Housing for political reasons and provide entertainment in the process.

Andrew may have predicted this, but even he underestimated ACORN's chutzpah. On the same day that these execs were assuring their funders that the Baltimore employees were the unhappy exception, Andrew was rolling out the other videos, starting with Washington, to prove that they were the norm.

In Washington, we had met with two women named "Boone"— Lavernia, an ACORN mortgage consultant, and Sherona, an ACORN employee. On the positive side, they were as helpful as they could be. On the negative side, they gleefully counseled us on how to create a "paper trail" to conceal my profession as pimp for Hannah and ten young girls from El Salvador. If my sideline as a pimp became known, Lavernia cautioned me, "You will not have a career. You will be smeared and tarnished for the rest of your life to come." Both women clearly understood that what we planned to do was seriously less than legal.

Unfazed by the law, the two Boones gave us detailed advice on how to run our illegal business in a legalistic manner. "The money got to go in the bank," Lavernia insisted. She recommended that, for tax purposes, Hannah establish a sole proprietorship and call herself a "consultant" or "marketer." They both acknowledged the risks that we ran. "When the police ask you, you don't know where the money is coming from," Sherona counseled me. "We're looking out for you." Lavernia warned us about nosy neighbors who might just call the police, "Whatever you do, you got to be low-key." The two women could not have been nicer. Lavernia gave us her business card, and Sherona invited us to call with any questions.

I must give credit here to Hannah, who not only looked good, but also came across so credibly and wonderfully dumb. My favorite line: Lavernia advises us, "You're not saying what she does. She provides a service." Hannah responds, "That is what America is based on, goods and services." I laugh every time I hear it.

Before they saw the D.C. video, *Salon*'s Joe Conason and the *Washington Post*'s Keith Richburg took part in a CNN round table on the subject of the ACORN sting. A third panelist, a black conservative, was piped in. The Baltimore video and its aftershocks had forced the anti-journalists into a predictable but unsustainable response. Unaware of what was to follow, they took their cues from the ACORN brass.

Richburg, the saner of the two, questioned whether the ACORN executives were telling the truth, but he worked under the presumption that they were. "And it sounds to me like that's just entrapment," he said of our sting. "You know, let's go around various offices until we can finally trick somebody into . . ."

Here Conason, a third-generation lefty as smooth as a game show host, jumped in. "It's not journalism unless they report everything that happened," he argued. "It's propaganda." Conason knows something about propaganda. He has made a slimeball career of it. He called our work "dishonest" for not reporting on the imagined ACORN employees who kicked us out or called the police. He then volunteered that Maryland was a "two-party" state, as everyone knew from the Linda Tripp affair, and that we "could be liable to civil or criminal action."

A CNN producer had somehow gotten hold of my cell number and was calling all that morning, at least seventy times and in such rapid sequence I could not make an outgoing call. The producer wanted to interview me. Andrew said no. As he explained, CNN wanted to interview me not to expose ACORN but to somehow destroy my credibility. This was a warning I could not ignore, pure inverse Gandhi: *First they attack you.* After posting the Washington video, Andrew had me fire off an op-ed to BigGovernment. He believed in preemptive strikes and eagerly ghostwrote this one:

> *So far CNN has only reported on the breaking story on blatant ACORN CORRUPTION from angles that attempt to extricate the government-funded "community organizing" enterprise from the extreme crime we caught on videotape. First CNN pushed the false ACORN line that "[t]his film crew tried to pull this sham at other offices and failed."*
>
> *To set that record straight please check the Washington, D.C., tape we dropped today at BigGovernment.com, which is also being aired on your cable news competitor with curiously higher ratings. Now that ACORN lied to you, Jonathan Klein, what are you going to do. . . .*
>
> *. . . When you air the raw ACORN footage that is now viral on the Internet, and being played on FOX NEWS and countless talk radio shows, then and only then—when America can see, hear, and smell the stench we have exposed—will I subject myself to a CNN hit job.*

Ah, the glory in that question to Klein, *What are you going to do?* It was pure media warfare. This was what I was born for. Klein, the CNN president, would be let go a year later. On his departure, the *New York Times* noted that "CNN's ratings have languished, while Fox's and MS-NBC's have improved, leading some media critics to publicly wonder how he managed to keep his job." We wondered, too.

The op-ed, by the way, went wildly viral. Rush Limbaugh read it in its entirety that afternoon. That blew me away. Friends were texting me nonstop. Andrew might have gotten used to this stuff, but my head was spinning. I stabilized it long enough to find my way back to the Fox studios to tape a segment for that evening's *Hannity* show. I rallied as best I could. Hannah, whom they beamed in from Washington, looked like a movie star. I looked like an extra from *Zombieland*.

The interview went well for all that. Hannity kept us on for ten minutes and showed clips from Baltimore. It had to freak out ACORN supporters when I cited one of their heroes. "So this is just the application of community organizer Saul Alinsky against the community organizers," I told Hannity, who had by now seen the D.C. Acorn video as well. He asked us if there would be more. "Maybe," I said, "maybe not." NAACP head Ben Jealous caught the irony of it all. "We're being out-Alinskyed by the anti-Alinskys," he tweeted in frustration.

The taping over, I headed down to the New Jersey shore for a clambake to celebrate my grandfather's eightieth birthday. When *Hannity* came back on that evening, we all gathered around the TV, popcorn at the ready. My friends were ecstatic at the way the show turned out. My grandmother, the one who lent me the chinchilla, sensed the undercurrents. "Jamie," she said, "take a deep breath. Focus on what you're doing. You'll do great."

ON TOP OF THE WORLD

Veritas Rule #9:
*Think of the worst thing they can say
and prepare your response.*

Wednesday, September 16, found me sitting in the well of a corner window forty stories above the street, shifting my gaze from the vintage radios scattered around the room to the Chrysler Building outside the window. This was the city I grew up in and around, but now I was looking at it through a different lens. I had come so far so fast. It was like climbing Mount Everest on a day's training.

We were in Glenn Beck's Mercury Radio Arts office in this Sixth Avenue building. Glenn and Andrew Breitbart did not bother looking out the windows. They were less interested in the view of midtown Manhattan than in the media landscape that lay before us. This was heady company. No one knew more about contemporary media than these guys. I listened more than I talked. Their conversation involved, among other things, two American presidents.

"You want to know why Obama was in New York yesterday," said

Andrew. "He was asking Clinton for advice on how to deal with this story. Just wanted to put that out there."

"What's your source?" asked Beck.

"Of all people this guy Bernie Kerik has been reaching out to me," said Andrew. A former New York City police commissioner, Kerik would plead guilty to various federal fraud charges a month later. He was a fascinating guy. He knew a lot and was prepared to talk before he went down.

"What he's saying?"

"When I told Kerik my theory about the Clinton meeting, he affirmed very forcefully."

Andrew then laid out his theoretical framework for the Obama visit as only Andrew could. As he explained, radical energy czar Van Jones's forced resignation just ten days earlier had shaken the White House. "This ACORN story can be ten times more impactful," said Andrew, who also noted that "Obama knows his guys don't know how to deal with damage control. Clinton does."

"This is what bothers me," said Beck. "They are just doing things awfully fast, like removing the census ties. That doesn't feel right to me."

"Especially since the majors aren't even covering the story," replied Andrew. They were ignoring us, an ironic testimony to the fact that the attacks and ridicule were not working.

"But wait until you see the impact of tonight's show," said Beck. "We have to go after the head. You've established ACORN's corrupt. We now have to follow that corruption to the top."

"Obama's realizing everybody around him is an ACORN guy."

"They all have ties."

As the guys made clear, we had stumbled onto something bigger than we knew. The president was not worried about ACORN's work in providing housing and tax services to the poor or our role in exposing this. He was worried about ACORN's pivotal role in getting him reelected. In the election fraud business, ACORN was General Motors, right down to the government subsidies.

ACORN and its voter registration arm, Project Vote, would typically hire hundreds, if not thousands, of marginal workers during an election cycle and give them incentives to register as many voters as possible. They would then overwhelm election officials with all these registrations, many of which were fabricated, and throw the system into chaos. Matthew Vadum, senior editor at the Capital Research Center, estimated that as many as four hundred thousand ACORN registrations were thrown out in 2008 alone. How many made it through no one knew. Before we put ACORN out of business, ACORN workers had been or were in the process of being *convicted* of election fraud in Arkansas, Colorado, Florida, Michigan, Minnesota, and Missouri—thirteen vote thieves in Missouri alone.

The media were desperately afraid, as was the president himself, that we or someone else would track the vote fraud scandal to the top. "I've been fighting alongside ACORN on issues you care about my entire career," Obama told ACORN leaders on the campaign trail in November 2007. "Even before I was an elected official, when I ran Project Vote voter registration drive in Illinois, ACORN was smack dab in the middle of it, and we appreciate your work." Even in the short bios on his book covers, Obama boasted of registering 150,000 new voters. I wonder how many of those were legit.

Two days before the meeting with Beck, September 14, we had released our Brooklyn video. The video showed our visit to the Bronx ACORN office and our finding it padlocked. From there, Hannah and I shuttled down to Brooklyn and hit video gold again. One ACORN staffer instructed us to bury our brothel profits in a tin and plant flowers around it to throw the IRS off the trail. "You can't say what you are doing for a living," her coworker memorably told us. "Honest is not going to get you the house."

In another era, or with a different target, every major newsroom in America would have unleashed its own Woodward and Bernstein to follow up on our work and track this corruption to its source, but that's not the way the media roll if you're investigating and exposing big government. On September 29, in an insightful commentary, PJTV contributor Bill Whittle explained the way they did work:

> *You may think that Andrew Breitbart, Glenn Beck, Fox News, and BigGovernment-dot-com were fighting against an enemy, and the enemy was ACORN, but I do not think that's the case at all.*
>
> *I think the enemy they were fighting against are the media. By not covering the story, not at all . . . Breitbart showed that the media is no longer merely biased. They're no longer even ignoring the news. The mainstream media is now in the news suppression business.*

That's not to say I wasn't getting asked for interviews, but again, these producers weren't out to congratulate me. They were out to target me. Except for Hannity, I turned them all down. "Why park in front of my parents' house?" I asked a New York CBS crew. "Why don't you park in front of the ACORN people's houses and ambush them?" Everything was completely reversed from the way journalism ought to work. It was agonizing.

Andrew had cautioned me not even to go on *Fox & Friends*. I should have listened. I certainly ought not have shown up, as requested, in the full pimp regalia I wore in the title sequences that we shot in Washington. "You're not a pimp," Steve Doocy jokingly advised the audience that same Monday morning; "you're just playing one on our show."

A bit overconfident perhaps from the *New York Post* cover, I replied, "I'm one of the whitest guys ever. I just wear ridiculous stuff and put people in ridiculous situations." For a race-baiter, this was a pony under the Christmas tree.

"That is how he assures us he is not a pimp—he is one of the Whitest Guys Ever," John Wellington Ennis fumed in the *Public Record*, "therefore on the opposite end of the spectrum from the Blackest Guys Ever, who normally tend to this kind of thing." Not one for subtlety, Ennis headlined his article THE LYNCHING OF ACORN. The racist meme—whatever a "meme" is—had entered the communication flow. My comment even set off the generally supportive Jon Stewart. "Are you fucking kidding me!?" he screamed after playing it on air. On the positive side, the comment only reinforced the fact we were inexperienced and independent.

Andrew did not see it that way. He was furious at me for my "whitest guy" comment. He was furious at me for going on *Fox & Friends*. He intuited the media response from a continent away and was convinced that I had ruined the release plan. It did not make him any happier when I failed to correct Doocy's suggestion that I dressed like a pimp in the visits to the ACORN offices. I should have.

The anti-journalists seized on every contradiction. "I think journalism is dead," I told Doocy. It may have been, but its ghosts were haunting me big-time. I wasn't eating. I couldn't even swallow food. I wasn't sleeping. I was down to 145 pounds. At six foot two, when I looked in the mirror, I saw my shadow staring back at me.

Fox had provided us a generic suite on the forty-third floor of a Eurotrashy hotel in Midtown. Now Hannah, Andrew, and I were together all the time. Although completely sleep deprived, I had to produce the San Bernardino video for a September 15 release. While I scrambled to put this thing together, I had to screen out Andrew, who, in full-blown ADHD mode, paced the floor, talking and texting—now Fox News, now Newt Gingrich, now me, now who knows who—then getting so lost in his thoughts about undoing my "white guy" screwup, he tripped over the wire to my laptop and erased all the work I had done on that video.

When finally I did finish and went to upload the video, the hotel's Internet connection failed. So now I was wandering the street in a daze, laptop in hand, looking for a hotel lobby with an Internet connection. Andrew walked by my side, texting and calling while walking, trailing a miniature posse along with him, including a reporter from London, this guy named Dan Gluck from New York's Museum of Sex, and a photographer from the *New York Post* who kept asking me to stand still so he could take a picture. They were waxing euphoric over the week's fresh, new, sexy scandal.

We found a basement in a nearby hotel where we started to upload the video to YouTube. We had to get it online by 5 p.m., when Glenn Beck came on the air. While the video was uploading, a hotel manager came in and said, "Hey, you guys can't be down here using our Internet." "We're uploading a story with national implications that will affect the president," Andrew shot back. This was New York. The hotel manager wouldn't have cared if Andrew *were* the president. Our posse then ducked the manager and scrambled up to the lobby, where the signal was better in any case. When it was finally uploaded, I shot an email to the BigGovernment producer that said, "GO!!!"

I wore a suit to Beck's studio, and his comment was "So you're wearing a suit now, huh? Where's your costume?" I would hear this line a thousand times, usually accompanied by laughter. On the upside, Beck again devoted an hour to our work, this time around the new San Bernardino tape. On the downside, he sounded edgy, frustrated.

"Is this a joke to you?" Beck asked on TV. "Do you realize what you're dealing with?" He was referring here to my *Fox & Friends* appearance. A joke to me? I turned an even whiter shade of pale. I was shocked he asked that. We had been spending our own money, flying around the country, and putting our asses on the line. Why was Beck saying these things? "No, it's not a joke. There are very serious crimes being committed," I said, trying to retain my cool.

After the show, Andrew told me Beck was just trying to bring me back to earth. I felt awful. I had pulled all-nighters three nights in a row producing the videos. I was light-years beyond exhaustion, and now the media rush was wearing off. Still, there was no rest for the weary. The whole posse shuffled over to Fox News, where Hannah and Andrew were to tape the *Hannity* show.

Once there, I helped the producer sync the audio and video for the San Diego tape and then collapsed on the couch in the greenroom. At some point, I overheard Hannity say, "What's wrong with James?" Then he walked over to me and said in a fatherly way, "You're twenty-five years old." I could not quite figure out what he meant by that as I was on the verge of passing out. I asked if Fox could put me up with some place to sleep. No one could quite manage it. So I wandered out on my own, stumbled down to the street, found a News Corporation driver to take me back to New Jersey, and slept for twenty-six hours straight.

THE EMPIRE STRIKES BACK

Veritas Rule #10:
Your manner matters more than your costume.

"You could mold this into anything you want," Tresa Kaelke told Hannah and me about our prostitution business. "You can mold it to the level of decency or indecency."

Tresa, the sole employee at the San Bernardino ACORN office, made for great theater. This hard-boiled California blowhard could have stepped right out of a Quentin Tarantino film. Fortunately, she was white. We could hold off the race-baiters for another day or two.

No ACORN employee we met was more obliging. Kaelke maintained she had once run her own "service," which at its peak allegedly earned her fifteen thousand dollars a week. Her idol was Hollywood madam Heidi Fleiss. "I have some experience in how not to get caught," she boasted of her own career in the brothel biz. Given her background, we felt free to be explicit about our plans.

HG: The guy I am supposed to be working for here just got a shipment of twelve El Salvadoran girls and they are between the ages of twelve and fifteen. . . . I would like to take them away from him and use them for myself.

JO: This is very lucrative.

I explained that I intended to use the income to fund my future political campaigns. Trying to be helpful, Kaelke cited by name several of her own political contacts, from the local assemblywoman to U.S. senator Barbara Boxer. "We lobby these people for legislation," she explained. She cautioned me, though, that if I wanted a political career like those of her pals I would have to be discreet about our business.

TK: If you're just taking money from underage prostitutes —oh my God!—that just doesn't sound good.

At this point, Hannah upped the deviation ante:

HG: [Clients] pay thousands of dollars more if they are violent with these fourteen-year-old girls. They are okay with guys hitting them if they get a little more money for it. If they are fine with that, there is nothing I can do.

TK: Again, it is how you want it to be run. Don't forget, you could mold this into anything you want. You can mold it to the level of decency or indecency.

Like just about every ACORN employee we met, Kaelke took our request seriously, treated us respectfully, and refused to be judgmental. She sent us to a friendly couple across the street, and the fellow advised us how to set up a 501(c)3 school for the girls to disguise their activity. Kaelke promised no one would leak our secret. "A soon as you leave I am going over to talk to the both of them and threaten them with their lives," she reassured us, "because I can kill people."

Kaelke was admittedly something of a bullshitter. This I began to sense when she confided that she had killed a husband who had been abusing her. "You killed him emotionally?" I asked. "No, I shot him," Kaelke replied proudly. "I just picked up the gun and said fuck you." This does not appear to be true. One of her exes did swear out a restraining order on her, but he and the others appear to live on.

ACORN responded as Andrew knew they would. California head organizer Amy Schur called the video "a gross misrepresentation of what actually happened" and demanded that "the complete and unedited video" be posted—she was unaware, presumably, that we had posted it before she asked.

Fortunately, ACORN and its media whores could not undo the raw power of those videos. At the same time they were trashing us as liars and racists, House Republican minority leader John Boehner was introducing the "Defund ACORN Act." In a Democratic-controlled House, the bill passed by a resounding 345–75 vote, with 172 Democrats voting in favor. The Democratic-controlled Senate followed by voting 83–7 to do the same thing. This legislation passed before the *New York Times* even assigned a reporter to the story.

In a *Washington Examiner* article titled THE STUNNING TOTAL DEFEAT OF ACORN, Byron York wrote, "it is not an exaggeration to say that none of this would have happened now without the *BigGovernment* undercover videos." That was us. Wow! Even better perhaps, Jon Stewart concluded his *Daily Show* segment, "The Audacity of Hos," with the question that every editor in America should have been asking: "Where are the real reporters on this story? I am a fake journalist and I'm embarrassed these guys scooped me."

All too predictably, the real reporters were busy plotting their ACORN defense. After a brief page-two item on Saturday, September 12, the *Wash-*

ington Post retaliated with back-to-back articles on September 17 and 18. Not only did we scoop the *Post,* but we also scooped them on a story they would just as soon have suppressed. They took their wrath out on us. The first of the articles, ACORN TO REVIEW EMPLOYEES' CONDUCT AFTER HIDDEN CAMERA VIDEOS, by Darryl Fears, went after Hannah.

Fears strategically informed his readers that Hannah's father, Doug Giles, served as minister of the "ultraconservative" Clash Church in Florida, where he allegedly once said that "liberals 'spit on the Word of God.'" Fears included this reference to reinforce the claim of ACORN chief organizer Bertha Lewis that "the videos were part of a relentless conservative attack." The goal of these conservatives, Lewis told Fears, was "to destroy the largest community organization of black, Latino, poor, and working-class people in the country."

On September 18, Carol Leonning joined Fears for a second whack at the Veritas piñata in an article titled DUO IN ACORN VIDEOS SAY EFFORT WAS INDEPENDENT. This time, after still another knock on Doug Giles, the reporters went after me. They ignored their own observation that I was inspired to target ACORN by "a video of ACORN workers breaking padlocks off foreclosed homes and barging in" and pulled the inevitable race card out of an already stacked deck.

According to Fears and Leonning, I "targeted ACORN for the same reasons that the political right does." What could that reason be? What else? I hoped to derail ACORN's "massive voter registration drives that turn out poor African Americans and Latinos against Republicans." If you've never been subject to this kind of ritual defamation, let me warn you, it hurts. You could have lived your life up to that moment as innocently as the Easter Bunny, but the second these guys sense there is even the possibility they can invent a racial issue, they will take a great big healthy bite out of your reputation and savor every swallow.

Trusting the *Washington Post,* the Associated Press corrupted this race-baiting gibberish even further: "James O'Keefe, one of the two filmmakers, said he went after ACORN because it registers minorities likely to vote against Republicans." I talked to one of these reporters on the phone, wanting badly to explore his motivations and throw them back in his face. Andrew was a master at this. I was still learning.

On September 21, 2009, Leonning sent me an email that revealed just how petty and perverse was the *Post*'s thinking. In her research, she apparently came across a notation on my blog in which I thanked the Leadership Institute for buying a four-thousand-dollar HDTV monitor to edit my videos. She then mustered up the nerve to ask, "Why did you not mention this as part of the financial support you received?" In fact, I never did *receive* the monitor. It was LI property. It never left their facility. Even if I had received it, why would that have mattered in the ACORN investigation? Why was our funding the issue? The *Post* was trying to find anything—anything—in order to blur the manifestly damning truth caught on camera.

"Before I answer any more questions," I responded in my email back to Leonning, "I want you to print a retraction. It appears to me that you, Carol, and your colleague Darryl Fears are alone responsible for introducing race to the discussion." Fearing litigation, I suspect, both the *Post* and the Associated Press each felt compelled to issue corrections, which, of course, almost no one read. Wrote the *Post*:

> This article about the community organizing group ACORN incorrectly said that a conservative journalist targeted the organization for hidden-camera videos partly because its voter-registration drives bring Latinos and African Americans to the polls. Although ACORN registers people mostly from those groups, the maker of the videos, James E. O'Keefe, did not specifically mention them.

As Andrew helped me see, these reporters refused to see our motives for what they were—a desire to expose actual malfeasance. Instead they projected their anxieties onto us. Big government was the soup they swam in. Race-baiting was one way to defend it. Dave Weigel of *Slate* would confide to me a few years later that many of these journalists saw everything through a lens of "racial justice," and "justice" was for them a utilitarian concept.

The *New York Times* suppresses more stuff, more consequentially, than any other media outlet in the world. Like the *Post*, the *Times* tried not to notice the ACORN furor. The paper ran its first staff-written article on the subject on September 15, five days after the airing of the initial video and three days after the *Post* had run its front-page story. It was not as if the *Times* had spent the interval doing in-depth research. Reporter Scott Shane did not even contact me until September 17, two days later.

The headline—CONSERVATIVES DRAW BLOOD FROM ACORN—alerted sensitive readers that this article would focus on those blood-sucking "conservatives." But why "conservative"? We did no political editorializing. The *Post* had no way of discerning my politics from our work product. The abuses we highlighted the *Post* editors would consider abuses as well. Even the Planned Parenthood stings focused on behavior that they might themselves condemn—eugenics, statutory rape, illegal abortions. What we were doing was pure Alinsky—forcing the establishment to honor its own rules.

Regardless, as reporter Scott Shane saw it, ours was just another right-wing effort "to dig up dirt" on individuals and "trumpet" that dirt on talk radio. Later in the article, he unearthed a liberal advocate who obligingly described our tactics as "McCarthyite." I sense some small differences between two guerrilla journalists working on their own dime and a powerful, subpoena-wielding U.S. senator, but perhaps I misread my history.

Shane also repeated uncritically the nonsense from Bertha Lewis, who claimed, as Shane phrased it, that we "had spent months visiting numerous Acorn offices, including those in San Diego, Los Angeles, Miami and Philadelphia, before getting the responses [we] were looking for." No, Scott, we exposed major mischief in Baltimore on day one, in Washington on day two, and Brooklyn on day three, and we didn't do half bad in San Bernardino, either. Curiously, Shane failed to mention our Brooklyn sting, the fourth we attempted, the video of which was released the day before. Most newspapers would have led with the local angle, but not the "Grey Lady." She suppressed it.

When Shane weighed in again three days later, his article—A Political Gadfly Lampoons the Left via YouTube—managed to both politicize and trivialize the downfall of America's most fearsome grassroots organization. To show his disdain, Shane worked in a Lucky Charms reference in the very first sentence. Only after three paragraphs on Lucky Charms and four more paragraphs on this and that did he inform the reader that "a succession of Acorn workers advised the pair on how to smuggle Salvadoran girls into the country, falsify a loan application to buy a house for use as a brothel and even claim the under-age prostitutes as dependents for tax purposes," not, as Seinfeld might say, that there is anything wrong with that.

Then too, Shane could not quite figure out how I dressed for the interviews. That should not have been hard to do. In the Baltimore video, when we had Stan Dai do the exterior shooting, the viewer can clearly see me walk in and out of the office dressed in white pants and a dress shirt. I am, after all, a future congressman.

In the initial story, however, Shane described me as "dressed so outlandishly that [I] might have been playing in a risqué high school play." This was corrected in later versions, but ACORN supporters lobbied hard for exculpation based on this one minor editorial mistake. Better late than never, the paper's public editor, Clark Hoyt, set things straight a year after the flare-up.

For starters, Hoyt conceded that the *Times* was "slow" in covering the sting and the "resulting uproar" that followed. He then admitted that the *Times* erred in describing my attire but dismissed the notion that the whole story would "fall apart over the issue of what O'Keefe wore." Said Hoyt forcefully, "If O'Keefe did not dress as a pimp, he clearly presented himself as one: a fellow trying to set up a woman— sometimes along with under-age girls—in a house where they would work as prostitutes."

Hoyt then added what should have been the clincher: the video's *"most damning words match the transcripts and the audio, and do not seem out of context."* Finally! A Pulitzer Prize–winning ombudsman reveals that nothing relevant was taken out of context. Redemption! It is too bad the rest of the media chose to ignore this.

PIMP PROTOCOL

Veritas Rule #11:
If you do your job right, expect to break new legal ground.

Mike Madigan isn't just any lawyer. He is a "superlawyer," one who served as federal prosecutor in more than one hundred jury trials and then spent the next thirty years as a hard-core criminal defense attorney. Going back, Mike was Senator Howard Baker's counsel on the Senate Watergate Committee. So what was he doing representing me, a law school dropout?

Well, it had nothing to do with libel law. Although I have been called a liar in a thousand different ways, I have not once been sued for libel or defamation. I have, however, sued others successfully for libeling me. Of course, you would not know that from reading the *New York Times*.

No, our brand of journalism has opened up new frontiers of law in everything but libel: civil defense law, criminal defense law, constitutional law, election law, municipal law, workplace law, entertainment law, you name it. We have actually succeeded in creating new areas of the law. One case that we provoked involved ACORN, the U.S. Department of Housing and Urban Development, the Justice

Department, and President Obama and got major coverage in the *New York Times*. Cited deep in the *Times* article and every other was a reference to a "pimp and a prostitute seeking financial advice." I must say I was proud to see how much legal chaos I was causing, although I was not pleased to see so many lawyers enriched.

I particularly disliked enriching them myself. I have spent so much time on the phone talking to lawyers I've learned how to manage them, direct them, and, most important, conserve their time. One of the dozen or so lawyers who represented me described the attraction to the chaos we were causing: "It's a lawyer picnic, James, and everyone gets some pie but the client." I had never thought my year in law school would come in handy, but it most certainly has.

Madigan was a trip. In the highly publicized "Africa Sting" trial, he got a client off who had been stung by a legion of FBI agents equipped with recording devices. The *Times,* in fact, cited him for potentially "spelling the end of undercover stings in [federal] prosecutions." Now he was representing the stinger who would go on to sting the Justice Department. Hollywood screenwriters struggle to make up stuff like this.

Before meeting Madigan, I expected your basic Beltway, stuck-up, elitist politico, but that was not Madigan at all. A sawed-off Irishman with red stubble of a beard, he walks like Yoda, swears like a longshoreman, and is as mercurial as the actor James Caan, whom he vaguely resembles. Although he could surely afford better, he drives a nineties-era two-seater, carries a dirty red duffel bag into court—"jury relates to it"—and talks like he never once left Brooklyn. He also has a gift for strangely placed F-bombs. Our first conversation went something like this:

MADIGAN: Hey, huh, James, is that you? Yeah, I uh . . . got your flight confirmation number to get to D.C. Got a pen?

ME: Okay, ready.

MADIGAN: K . . . E . . . 2 . . . I. Damn, I can't figure out whether this is a fucking *O* or a zero. . . .

That was pure Madigan. Breitbart, who was Irish by birth, Mike Flynn, one of Breitbart's editors, Madigan, and I referred to our little cabal as the "Irish mafia." I was probably more idealistic than his average client, but you don't have to be an idealist to distrust the feds as both he and I did. That comes with experience.

Madigan and I would spend hours debriefing in Washington. In one of these conversations I told him how humbled I was to be sitting in this glass conference room in D.C. when my legal abilities were so lacking. He answered, "While you can't do what I do, nobody can do what you do." That gave me a new perspective. So did his bill.

In March 2012, while my colleagues at Project Veritas were moving from state to state trying to save the republic from vote fraud, I was in Washington being deposed. What follows are some highlights from the deposition in that suit. They show better than I can ever tell you the amoral clownishness of the foes we were fighting.

Questioning me was one Eugene G. Iredale, Esquire. Stricken from the court transcript was a whole lot of lawyerly bickering between Iredale and Madigan, two old-school septuagenarian street fighters. I struggled to keep from laughing when they went at each other's throats.

Q: Sir, could I ask your full name.
A: James Edward O'Keefe III.

Q: And Mr. O'Keefe III, do you mind if I dispense with "the Third"?
A: You can call me James if you'd like.

Q: Let's go with Mr. O'Keefe.

A: All right.

Q: Have you ever had your deposition taken?

A: No.

Q: You understand that a deposition is a proceeding under oath?

A: Yes.

Q: And you will agree to do that?

A: Yes.

So far so good. It went downhill quickly. Iredale questioned me about the fact that I was paid by Andrew Breitbart to broadcast the videos. That a journalist would actually be paid for his work product seemed to offend this high-priced, San Diego–based attorney, but in the scheme of things that was just a minor absurdity. We moved on.

Q: Well, the investigative videos involved your tape-recording people, right?

A: Yes.

Q: Without telling them you were videotaping them, right?

A: Yes.

Q: Right? And you knew all the time in California at least that that was against the law of the state of California, correct?

A: I don't believe I violated any laws at the time. I don't believe I violated any laws now.

Q: Well, let's see. You know a lady named Lila Rose, do you not?

A: I do.

Q: And through Lila Rose you became familiar with certain California laws concerning nonconsensual taping, correct?

A: That's correct.

Q: And you understood that Lila Rose was the subject of a lawsuit because, in connection with one of your projects, she had engaged in nonconsensual taping of conversations with people.

A: There was never a lawsuit under my understanding. What lawsuit are you referring to?

Q: Well, what was your understanding?

A: My understanding was that we had gone into Planned Parenthood locations, but I don't believe there was an expectation of privacy, and I don't believe I violated any laws whatsoever. I didn't believe that then. I don't believe that now.

Remember, the father of Lila's imaginary unborn baby had committed statutory rape. As a health organization, Planned Parenthood is a mandatory responder in child abuse cases. If the clinic was not going to take this responsibility seriously, we thought that journalists should. I then had to ask myself how much privacy was a mandatory responder entitled to when aiding and abetting a rapist. I know that Planned Parenthood founder Margaret Sanger called for "drastic and Spartan" measures to stop an "ever-increasing army of under-sized, stunted, and dehumanized slaves" from overrunning America, but I felt no obligation to help her.

As I learned early on, the nation's progressives have been controlling the media narrative for a century. If they wanted to make a "social justice" champion out of Margaret Sanger, they could do so. If they wanted to paint ACORN as a civil rights group in the tradition of Martin Luther King, they could do that, too. What our videos were doing was ripping a hole through that narrative and allowing the people inside to expose that narrative for the fraud it was. To stop us, the government-media complex and its allies within the government have tried to criminalize the one effective medium at our disposal, the video sting.

> **Q: What you did in San Diego was essentially the same modus operandi as you used in all the other offices, correct?**
>
> A: Modus operandi. Would you clarify that?
>
> **Q: In other words, you pretended to be a pimp.**
>
> A: That's correct.
>
> **Q: And Hannah Giles pretended to be a prostitute?**
>
> A: Yes.
>
> **Q: You engaged ACORN employees in conversation?**
>
> A: Yes.

Having asserted this, Iredale posed a string of questions to establish that Andrew was somehow responsible for what we did, all the better to sue his widow and children. He was particularly eager to ferret out my funding sources:

> **Q: [Breitbart] was trying to get the money that he didn't have at his fingertips and he was trying to find a benefactor of some kind who might donate some money?**
>
> A: My understanding is that, from what I could tell, he was trying to find a way to get that money because it wasn't on his fingertips, as you suggested.
>
> **Q: Did he say what he intended to do to get the funding?**
>
> A: He did not share that with me.

Iredale was desperately hoping to trace the money trail back to Rupert Murdoch or the Koch Brothers or some other right-wing plutocrat. You can imagine his chagrin when he realized that I had funded those ACORN videos off my own woefully overextended credit cards. After some more haggling about financial and technical details, Iredale zoomed in for the kill.

Q: Now, you're not a pimp.
A: No.

Q: Have never been a pimp?
A: No.

Q: And in order to study for your role, as you performed it in San Diego, what did you do in order to try to appear to be a pimp?
A: I didn't really have to do much—much more than script out in my head some of the things I would say about trying to get the girls across the border and things like that.

Q: Did you practice any pimp slang?

Don't ask me why, but the "pimp slang" question was one of my favorites.

A: No.

Q: Now, in one of the versions that aired of the San Diego videotape, there's a picture of you wearing a fur coat. Am I right on that?
A: I believe in the produced version—I'd have to check the YouTube—the video walking up the stairs in a fur coat?

Q: Yes.
A: Yes.

Q: And where did you get that fur coat?
A: My grandmother.

Q: It's your grandmother's fur coat?
A: Yes.

Q: And can you tell me what is the fur that's on the fur coat?
A: I believe it's chinchilla.

I am not sure which law school Iredale attended, or whether he learned his interrogation techniques at said school, but you have to like the question that follows.

Q: And did you study to see whether chinchilla was the fur of choice of pimps at this time in the United States?
A: I did not. It just happens to be the material on the coat that my grandmother had and decided to give me.

Q: Did you tell your grandmother you needed it so you could look like a pimp?
A: I did not.

Q: What was the reason that you told your grandmother you needed the chinchilla coat?

At this point, Madigan objected on the ground of relevance. As to me, I just felt like singing, "You know it's hard out here for a pimp." Just through osmosis I was beginning to empathize with those guys. The questioning only got stupider from here. Iredale wanted to know about the hat I had borrowed from my grandfather, the Dollar General cane I carried, the footgear I wore—"Did you acquire any pimplike shoes?"—and Hannah's clothes to boot.

Q: **You didn't accouter her yourself?**
A: What does that mean?

Q: **Dress her.**

I had never heard the word *accouter* before. I looked it up. According to Dictionary.com, it means "to equip or outfit, especially with military clothes, equipment, etc." As I explained, Hannah accoutered herself in the hooker battle gear of her choice. As the conversation wore on, it got heated. Madigan had to restore order.

MADIGAN: Don't shout at the witness.

IREDALE: I'm not shouting at the witness.

MADIGAN: Yes, you are.

IREDALE: No, I'm not. I am not.

MADIGAN: Lower your voice.

It was great sport to watch these two old guys slug away at each other. Finally, we get to the action captured on the video. Close your eyes and imagine you were there:

Q: **But you're the nice pimp.**
A: Correct.

Q: Right? Because during the course of this, you raised the specter of the bad pimp who was abusing her, right?

A: I would argue that there was no such thing as a nice pimp.

As I explained, this "nice" pimp was "trying to get the [underage] girls across the Tijuana border." Not too nice. I presume Iredale was being paid by the hour as he continued to badger me with preposterous questions relating to my role as a pimp. The point he seemed to be making was that ACORN worker Vera was simply playing along with me.

Q: Did you ever think that maybe a person who came in and introduced himself as a pimp wearing an old hat and a raggedy old grandma's fur and carrying a one-dollar cane might not be regarded as the real thing by these people that you were talking to, that they might suspect that you were putting them on? Did that thought ever cross your head?

A: That thought did not occur to me because I was not wearing that costume inside the office.

In a TV legal drama, this is the moment when the camera zooms in on the attorney's bright red face. What a colossal screwup. Trying to recover, Iredale asked me in detail what I was wearing, as though that somehow mattered.

Q: But you felt with this manner of yours that you were accurately portraying a character that a person in the United States in the year 2009 would really believe was a real true-to-life pimp?

A: I don't think the pimp protocol requires the wearing of a chinchilla. Pimp protocol requires the whoring out of underage girls.

Q: I see. And your study of pimp protocol is based upon—

A: Common sense.

Q: What? Common sense?

A: Yes.

Q: Ever read a book on pimps?

Iredale was scrambling. He seemed to want to prove that Vera had done nothing inappropriate. After I elaborated on the specifics of what Vera had done, Iredale got bizarrely political.

Q: [Y]ou said [to Vera] you were really big in the Democratic Party down here. That's what you said, correct?

A: That's correct. I'm not actually . . . in real life big in the Democratic Party.

Q: No. You hate the Democratic Party.

A: That is incorrect.

Q: Incorrect?

A: Yes.

Q: You like the Democratic Party?

A: I don't hate them.

Q: I see. You're not a Democrat in any event.

These weren't exactly questions, and Madigan objected at this point. "Well, I wouldn't want to pry into your political beliefs," said Iredale, concluding his inquiry into my political beliefs. And remember, this was the guy who was painting *me* as a liar.

To clarify, given what has been said about me, the reader may wish to know a bit about this right/left dynamic as it applies to my work. Although my enemies seek to portray me as a polarizing figure, our work is more about systems and intentions than it is about politics.

If my targets seem to skew "left," it is for a reason. The left makes huge claims about government and its capabilities. Those who manage the government and other publicly funded social services all too often persuade themselves of their virtuousness, even if their virtue is subsidized with other people's money. Given their idealism, they refuse to cast judgment on their mission and tolerate almost no judgment from others.

Our target has never been the people who *consume* the benefits, whether they be unwed mothers or crony capitalists. Our target is the system that *provides* the benefits. In our work, we force the providers to make judgments about the nature of altruism. Should their generosity extend to people who don't deserve it? Should it even extend to those who trash the rules of the society that makes this generosity possible? In short, we plant moral trees in an amoral universe and turn the cameras on. There is nothing the media or political establishment can do to stop us. This is Alinsky's Rule #4 on steroids: *"Make the enemy live up to their own book of rules." Veritas!*

For years, the major media have chosen not to scrutinize the welfare state. You need proof? They let a thoroughly corrupt organization like ACORN sail through the first forty dubious years of its existence with impunity. In fact, so vulnerable was ACORN to the light of day that it took a pair of twentysomethings with a Sony Handycam a few days to pull the whole damn thing down.

San Diego was no exception. In court, Iredale tried every gambit imaginable to get his client out of trouble, but he instead put Vera in check time after time. "I asked you what specific assistance he gave you," he said repeatedly to me while I thumbed through the video transcript looking for specifics. Madigan winked at me. As he and I knew, there were dozens of instances. I found one and read it right into the official court record:

So I say to him, "So I don't know if this is something you can help us,
provide some type of guidance to. For the girls to get a house, profit
off—to help the prostitution business."

And he says, "Yeah, for the houses we're going to start to have the
seminars there. That's a program for first-time buyers."

"I want," I said, "I want assistance in the community to prevent
anyone from knowing about this. And guidance and advice that you
have not let anyone know. I don't want you to tell anyone if ACORN
assists me with this house of underage prostitutes. I don't want anyone
to know that we're doing this."

This conversation was all on video, and it was hard to mistake its meaning.
Vera later told me that I could trust him and that he wouldn't let anyone
know what I was up to. I consider that to be guidance and assistance. At
the end of the conversation, Vera and the pimp, me, exchanged personal
cell phone numbers. A week later he called me, the pimp, and invited me
to a housing seminar, telling me that ACORN had five hundred houses
under its jurisdiction. He advised me to be careful, not to talk about our
business in public. "Trust me," he repeated. "Trust the Mexican people."

In the course of the deposition, Iredale implied that Vera knew it was
all a scam and reported us to the police that night. The story that the ABC
affiliate in San Diego released after our video aired suggested otherwise. Apparently, Vera originally told ABC that he merely offered "to help the prostitute get away from a bad life," referring here, I suppose, to the "bad pimp."
As 10News later reported, however, "New video released contradicted Vera's
earlier statement." When Vera's supervisor saw the uncut video, he fired Vera.
As we later learned, Vera had apparently called the police but for some reason
failed to tell his supervisor for more than a week. At the time we produced our
piece, we had no reason to believe he had contacted the police for any reason.

That much said, 10News gave ACORN the final word, and its
execs were, of course, outraged by what they had seen. Said the ACORN

spokesman all too predictably, "Undercover stunts are wrong." Much of the mainstream media felt the same way. Vote fraud, housing scams, and helping pimps with their underage prostitutes might not be commendable exactly, but "undercover stunts" were wrong.

After three years of fighting this suit, we settled for $100,000. It would have cost us five times as much to continue to fight California's dubiously constitutional Invasion of Privacy Act, a law that seems designed to protect the powerful from video exposure.

The beauty of video, especially as amplified by the Internet, is to allow a handful of citizen journalists working on a shoestring to end-run the biggest news organizations in the world. When the American people saw our videos, they responded. Here is how the *New York Times* summed up the results of our investigation:

> *After the activists' videos came to light and swiftly became fodder for 24-hour cable news coverage, private donations from foundations to Acorn all but evaporated and the federal government quickly distanced itself from the group.*
>
> *The Census Bureau ended its partnership with the organization for this year's census, the Internal Revenue Service dropped Acorn from its Voluntary Income Tax Assistance program, and Congress voted to cut off all grants to the group.*

There would be no Pulitzers waiting for us at the end of the day, no speaking engagements at prestigious J-schools. Instead we would face a continuing blizzard of legal challenges, a swarm of snippy media crickets, and a tsunami of insider outrage at the slightest accusation of impropriety. Still, we would not be deterred. We had a mission at hand, and that was to save the 2012 election. It can be brutal along the way, but in the end there is something incredibly beautiful about shoving the facts down the throat of the mainstream media and watching them gag on the truth.

THE YES MEN

Veritas Rule #12:
If you're creative, you can always make the news.

It was October 2009, and I happened to be strolling through lower Manhattan when I stumbled across one of my idols. His name is Jacques Servin, but he goes by the name Andy Bichlbaum, or maybe it is the other way around. Andy is a mischievous, creative genius.

He first made his mark by inserting code into the video game SimCopter that, when triggered, would show groups of men in swimming trunks kissing each other. His employer, Maxis, published the game before anyone noticed. As you might imagine, Maxis was not pleased and promptly fired Bichlbaum. On the upside, the media furor that followed inspired him to cofound a creative activist group known as the "Yes Men."

From the beginning, the Yes Men were high on my eclectic list of inspirations. They identify their mission as "identity correction," or, more specifically, "impersonating big-time criminals in order to publicly humiliate them, and otherwise giving journalists excuses to cover important issues."

One video of theirs from 2006 that I particularly liked featured a Yes Man pretending to be a representative of corporate giant Halliburton. In that role, he gave a presentation at a "Catastrophic Loss" conference in Florida. Another of his colleagues quietly taped it. The impersonator did a wonderful deadpan imitation of a droning, uninspired insurance executive. As the talk went on, however, it became incrementally more absurd and culminated in the introduction of a ridiculous new bubble suit called "the Survivable." The suit would allegedly protect against climate change, but it made the person who wore it look like a Teletubby. The audience bought the whole concept. A couple of the insurance guys even tried the suit on.

I watched that video and others countless times and adapted many of the Yes Men techniques: the deadpan impersonations, the increasing levels of absurdity, the use of props, the hidden cameras, the fake websites, the public shaming of culpable parties.

If I had a gripe with their work, it was that their targets were too obvious. In 2006, a Halliburton executive couldn't cheat at solitaire without the *New York Times* writing an exposé on it. Besides, we were never quite told what it was that Halliburton was doing wrong other than being large, profitable, and once run by Dick Cheney. In reality, the Yes Men were not covering underreported stories as promised but overreported ones. America's newsrooms were filled with people who shared their worldviews. Still, they were very skilled at what they did.

Their fans appreciated them at least as much as we did. "Damn they are good," wrote one fan in the comment section of the Halliburton video. "MORE YES MEN PLEASE—GET RECRUITING—THE MSM SHOULD BE FLOODED WITH THIS," wrote another. "These guys are fucking amazing," wrote a third, showing that even when happy our progressive friends feel compelled to drop the F-bomb.

In none of the comments or media coverage did I see any of their fans scruple about their technique.

Speaking of attacks on Halliburton, I have seen painfully few critiques of Michael Moore. Yet Moore has been routinely guilty of what we were accused of, namely, selective editing to distort a speaker's intended meaning—and he doesn't dare release the unedited tapes. Let me give you an example. Like all major national organizations, the National Rifle Association schedules its annual meeting and trade show years in advance. In 1999 that meeting was scheduled for Denver. Unfortunately, ten days before the meeting, two kids went on a shooting rampage at Columbine High School, in nearby Littleton. By law, the mandatory NRA members' meeting could not be put off, but NRA president Charlton Heston, sensitive to the environment, canceled the massive trade show that accompanies the meeting as well as most of the presentations and speeches.

In the gospel according to Moore, as revealed in his 2002 movie, *Bowling for Columbine,* the cold and calculating Heston decided to hold "a large pro-gun rally for the National Rifle Association" in Denver as a direct response to the shooting. There Heston brandished a musket and shouted, "I have only five words for you: 'from my cold, dead hands'!"

Moore's editing here went way beyond improper. He took the "cold, dead hands" remark from a speech Heston made in North Carolina months later and spliced it into the Denver footage. The speech Heston really gave at Denver was conciliatory. And the Denver segment was just one of many equally egregious deceptions in the movie.

The ethical puritans of the government-media complex chose not to notice the fraud even after it was exposed. Moore won the Academy Award for best documentary and sat next to former president Jimmy Carter at the 2004 Democratic National Convention. In Washington, flocks of political worthies attended the premiere of Moore's next movie, *Fahrenheit 9/11.*

Back to Bichlbaum. I got to see him and his guys punk the Bank of America by depositing fake deposit slips into ATM machines. When finished, in pure groupie mode, I approached him, introduced myself, and told him the truth: he had helped inspire me to do investigations on Planned Parenthood and ACORN. He looked at me like I was a child molester.

"I didn't inspire you," he spit out. "What you did hurt people. Why did you do that?" At first, I thought he was just punking me, and I was prepared to join in the gag. But the look in his eyes gave away the game. There was no irony here at all. I was forced to confront one of my heroes, in the flesh, actually *hating* me. Thrown unexpectedly on the defensive, I explained to him that I didn't defund ACORN. Obama had. Bichlbaum wasn't buying. He looked at me with total contempt, then turned and walked away without the slightest recognition that I was worth even a "so long."

Instantly, I knew how Dorothy felt when she pulled back the curtain. The Yes Men were not true Alinskyites, not at all. Nor were they tacticians or even natural pranksters. They are agenda-driven ideologues. The media were watching their backs, and they knew it. They could sting Halliburton or Dow Chemical with impunity. They may have faced threats of arrest, but the media would not mistreat them as long as their intentions were "good." No one was going to investigate what their fathers did for a living or track their financing or dig through their diaries for usable dirt. What they did was safe and utterly, totally inconsequential. I can see that now, but at the moment, I was crushed.

An article in the British newspaper the *Guardian* two years later confirmed my impressions. "A lie itself isn't necessarily bad," the Yes Men's Mike Bonanno told reporter Sahil Kapur. "It's why you're lying and who's gaining and who's losing as a result." Although he conceded that our tactics were similar to his, Bonanno scored some more cheap points by calling Breitbart and me "sad, pathetic assholes." He explained his reasoning: "We lie in order to criticise people who are abusing their power. They lie in order to humiliate and take out people who are at the receiving end of power." All this goes to show that Bonanno had no idea how power works and less interest in learning. As to ourselves, we were about to find out what the power structure is capable of doing when you actually do "afflict the comfortable."

THE NEW ORLEANS 4

Veritas Rule #13:
Safely extract the tape. If you don't, they'll say anything and be believed.

None of us—me, Basel, Flanagan, and Dai—were seeing any too clearly this Monday morning in January 2010. We had partied a little too hard the night before. This was New Orleans, after all. The Saints had won the NFC Championship in the Dome. We were young and foolish. What were we supposed to do?

The streets flew by. They looked trashier than usual, almost as trashy as the inside of Ben Wetmore's beat-up Pontiac G6. Wetmore overslept. Lucky boy. He got to miss the hell that awaited us. So too did our Nigerian-American friend Shaughn Adeleye. He was back at Ben's little brick house by the trolley tracks, where we all had crashed. He was practicing his drug lord shtick for our planned action of the day, a sting on the easily stung Housing Authority of New Orleans.

This was to be our warm-up act. We planned to test the truth of Senator Mary Landrieu's claim as to why Tea Party members could not get through to her office. "Our lines have been jammed for weeks, and

I apologize," Landrieu had told the *Advocate* of Baton Rouge in December, but her constituents were not buying it. They wanted to discuss her vote on Obamacare and were convinced she was dodging them. From what we heard, they had no trouble getting through to the office of the other Louisiana senator, David Vitter. We figured the best way to find out where the truth lay was to pay Senator Landrieu a visit.

We found a space on Magazine Street near the Hale Boggs Federal Building and parked. We had improvised this one on the fly. It wouldn't take too long. Stan Dai, with a little intelligence training in his background, assigned himself the perimeter. Joe Basel, Bob Flanagan, and I would do the inside work.

At the security checkpoint, the three of us showed our driver's licenses, the real things. We would be accused of entering the building under "false pretenses," but unlike a certain percentage of the American electorate, the IDs we presented were our own. Sure, Basel and Flanagan were wearing hard hats, but the three beefy U.S. marshals in blue blazers did not ask us why, and we did not volunteer. We gave no false information. Besides, it is the right of any American to enter a federal building for almost any reason. For journalists, it is more like a duty. We had no sense that we were doing anything illegal, because we weren't.

The guys put their hard hats on the conveyor belt, and I did the same with our cameras. I don't recall seeing any signs that said, "No cameras in a federal building." These obscure Taiwanese cameras looked like MP3 players or iPhones. In fact, one of the cameras was modeled after an old cell phone but with a pinhole lens in the bottom that would record as it lay flat on the table.

Once through the metal detector, we headed for the bathroom. There Basel took off his hard hat. He taped a wire to the brim and fixed a pinhead camera to the lip. You'd have to look hard to see it. We walked out of the bathroom and headed to the elevator. I gave them the go sign. Everything was cool.

I pushed the button for the tenth floor. No problem. I got off first and walked into the reception area of Senator Mary Landrieu's office. It was an open office with no screening or security. I sat on the leather couch against the wall and took out my cell phone. It was, in fact, the video surveillance recorder with the pinhole camera on the bottom, and it was running.

"I'm just waiting for a friend to arrive," I said half truthfully to the staffer, an indifferent thirtysomething strawberry blonde. I looked innocent enough, your basic young Democrat type in a button-down shirt and khakis. She just shrugged. A few minutes later, in walked Basel and Flanagan. They were dressed in jeans and denim shirts. Over that they wore the yellow and green striped reflector vests and hard hats they had bought that morning at Home Depot. Basel also wore a tool belt, but without tools in it. No one seemed to notice.

They had to notice that Flanagan, at six foot five, was way too big for the vest he wore. The reflecting vest rode his shoulders like a small child. I tried to hide my smile. If they looked carefully, as I did, they could see that Basel's tape was coming undone. Not good. "We're looking to fix the phones," said Basel. The staffer seemed surprised. So was I. We should have role-played this one a little more. A lot more.

Basel was supposed to say, or at least I thought he was, "We've gotten complaints that the phone lines were tied up, and no one can get through." The phone tie-up was true enough. Tea Partyers were convinced the senator's office was stiffing them. The staffer might then respond, "It's those tea-baggers tying up the lines." Basel, a clever guy, was supposed to tease out of her that the office was purposefully ignoring their calls.

In an even more fruitful scenario, a staffer would tell us how their allies were flooding the offices with calls to shut out the Tea Partyers. If we recorded a member of the senator's staff *saying* the office wanted to take down its own system, that would have been huge. Of course, we never would or could assist them with the technical part—we did not have a clue how—we just wanted a confession out of them. I was supposed to shoot it all, then promptly leave without doing or saying anything.

"Can we check the phones to make sure they're working?" Basel added. I didn't like where this was going, but I had no way to intervene. I had already established I was just some guy waiting in the office. Basel picked up the receiver as if to listen. He continued to BS the staffer. They talked about whether there was some sort of central telephone closet that might provide clues as to why the phones weren't working properly.

Telephone closet? "Basel, my man," I wanted to say, "you don't have any tools. They're going to catch on." This felt very wrong. Although Basel was doing nothing illegal, his offer to fix phones was not really scripted. I couldn't sit by any longer. I needed to get everyone back on message and jumped in. "You know, with all those tea-baggers calling in all those complaints," said I, the ever-helpful eavesdropper, "maybe that's the reason the phones aren't working, right?" Flanagan and Basel just looked at me like I was an alien.

It quickly got weirder. Out walked another staffer, a tall lady with big shoulders and a bad attitude. She was annoyed. You could see her thinking, "Why are these telephone repairmen trying to solve a problem we don't even have?" She directed Flanagan and Basel to talk to someone in the hallway who might be of more assistance. This someone just happened to be from the General Services Administration; in other words, he was the guy in charge of maintenance for the whole federal building. If Basel and Flanagan could not fool the lady at the front desk, they weren't going to fool the guy with all the keys on his belt.

"Beat it, guys," I thought. "Just keep walking." This moment would inspire a new Veritas rule: *If it feels wrong, abort and get out safely.* Unfortunately, we had not thought this rule through just yet. As we would learn, even the suggestion of an impropriety in a federal building is like saying "bomb" on an airplane.

Now I was all alone in the room again with the staffers, just sitting there, my heart beating, knowing I was in the moment. I always get a little nervous in the moment, living on the edge. But while I knew we had gone way off script, I didn't think it was catastrophic. I waited a minute, looked up, and saw the rest of the staffers giggling at each other.

"They're not telephone repairmen," the receptionist said to a balding bureaucrat type in the next cubicle. They both laughed about it. I remember thinking, "If it was so obvious, why didn't you speak up when they were inside the office?" But, hell, if they weren't going to take it too seriously, there was no reason for me to.

Time to move on. I was a fly on a wall in a room that the party had just left. I got up and headed out. I did not know where Basel and Flanagan had gone. I took the elevator down, walked past security, and found Dai walking the perimeter outside.

"Have you seen Flanagan and Basel?"

"No," said Dai. "Should I have?"

"I don't know. I think they're inside, but I am not sure." We had no sooner turned down Magazine Street to get the car than we got our answer.

Basel and Flanagan were sure as hell outside. There was no missing them. They stood on the sidewalk, stripped of their gear, surrounded by serious men in dark suits with large guns pointed right at them. If you were passing by, you'd think the feds had just nabbed John Doe Number 2.

The guys' hands were in the air. Their belongings—hard hats, vests, credit cards, wallets, cell phones—were strewn every which way, as if they had just taken a nasty spill on a ski slope (where I was supposed to be the next day but would not quite get to).

I heard the one suit yell out something about "false pretenses." I heard Basel say in his Marge Gunderson accent, "It wasn't false pretenses!" I had confidence in Basel. He was cool. He could straighten this out. We were videographers. This was just a misunderstanding.

Dai and I walked calmly across Magazine Street. Kevin Kane had an office right there. His organization, the Pelican Institute, a libertarian research organization, had brought me to New Orleans to speak on the subject of "Exposing Truth: Undercover Video, New Media and Creativity." Kane is a smart guy, an attorney, a native Long Islander. If anyone could help, he could. Dai and I took the elevator up to the nineteenth floor and popped in unannounced.

I told him what had happened. Then I took the miniSD chip from my camera, plugged it into my laptop, and showed him. Kane didn't have much to say. He kept this icy cool demeanor as he weighed the risk/reward ratio of our action. Dai and I pretended everything was okay and left to get lunch. Everything wasn't okay. We headed for the car and got in. I pulled out my laptop and inserted the chip with the camera file and watched again. At Kane's office, I should have uploaded that file to sendspace.com. It would have been available online. The world would have seen what happened inside that office. That would have changed everything. But at the time I had no idea the feds would seize the chip and a district judge would later order the video file destroyed. This inspired a useful Veritas rule: *Safely extract the tape. If you don't, they'll say anything and be believed.* But once again, this was a lesson I had to learn the hardest way.

Dai and I sat in the car for a few minutes. We reassured each other that everything was cool. Dai had a way of doing that. Soon enough, we talked ourselves into getting some pizza. I remembered that I left a water bottle on top of the car. I opened the driver's-side door to reach up and grab it. As I did, I saw a black blur screaming down Magazine Street twice as fast as the traffic. It was an SUV, and it was coming our way.

I thought at first it was just some crazy-ass drunk of the sort you see routinely in a New Orleans morning. In a second, I knew otherwise. The flashing strobe on top was a giveaway. Siren blaring, the SUV screeched to a stop so close it almost knocked our car door off. Two men in dress shirts and khakis jumped out. They pulled out guns that Dirty Harry would have envied and pointed them right at me and Dai. These were feds, and they weren't messing around.

"Freeze! Hands up!"

I don't know why, but I wasn't scared. This was America, New Orleans maybe, but America. We could talk. We could sort this out. This was just a misunderstanding. Then one guy grabbed my arms, yanked them behind my back, and handcuffed me.

"Wipe that fucking smirk off your face," he said as though he owned me. He was a scary dude with a Deep South drawl, an acne-scarred face, and a soullessness that could chill Satan himself. My bravado started melting away. Scarface pulled my phone out of my pocket and put it on top of the car. It started ringing. I could see it was my friend Christian Hartsock calling, and I couldn't answer it. I felt heartsick, helpless. I had just lost my freedom. That was the first thing they took away from me, one of many to come.

I knew the meaning of the word *dread,* but I had never experienced it before. Now I did. It swept over me unannounced and unexpected. All our equipment was in the car, all my caroms, all my files, all my CDs, all my hopes, all my plans. An hour ago I had been on top of the world. The media were still buzzing about our ACORN sting. More than thirty members of Congress had cosigned a resolution honoring Hannah and me as citizen journalists. Better still, my buddies and I had an RV rented in California. We were heading there to go skiing between speaking gigs. I had it all lined up. I had it all figured out. I was riding so high. We were traveling vagabonds, doing good work, living the dream, and 2010 was just beginning.

No more. The phone continued to ring, and I couldn't answer. The cowboys directed us to the curb. Dai kept his cool. He stood at parade rest and referred to them as "sirs." His Chinese looks and professional bearing checked them for a moment.

"Former military?" Scarface asked.

Dai answered ambiguously. He had taught people in the military, he told them. The cowboys quickly lost interest in his patter and started rummaging through the car. The second one, a mild-mannered guy in a beige shirt, pulled out a brown wig.

"Mardi Gras?" he asked.

"We're just filmmakers, comedians," I told him. "We were making a YouTube video."

"You were making trouble, boy, and now you're in a world of it."

I could feel the darkness descend on me like a storm cloud. This was getting grim. It began to occur to me that these marshals thought I did something much worse than I actually did. But what, I wondered, could they possibly get me on? As I would soon enough learn, it didn't much matter. This was New Orleans. Scarface lifted me by the arms and shoved me into the back of the SUV, his left hand on my head. He did the same to Dai. They drove us back a block to the federal building we had just left. This time I noticed its drab, brutalist architecture, a hint of East Germany. A special gate opened, and the SUV descended into the bowels of the building. We were getting to know this place inside out.

Ben Wetmore had once said to me, "No one can call himself a freedom fighter until he's been arrested and processed." When you're arrested on the federal level, those words ring true. One thing you lose when you lose your freedom is control of time. That was no longer ours. It was theirs. The "authorities" make you wait and wait some more. Wait in the car, wait in the hallway, wait at the door.

When they had taken all the time they felt like, the black-shirted marshals who ran this jail escorted us to small holding cages. The black shirts were all white men. Excluding the four of us, the prisoners were all black. As I soon learned, they weren't in for DUIs or missed child support. One guy kept telling me he had robbed a bank, and even he was scared of the other characters in this joint.

In the cages we met up with Basel and Flanagan. The two of them were still wearing their costumes, hard hats and all. They had been instructed to leave them on. Who knows why. We had also lost our right to ask questions—or at least to get answers. I was happy to see Basel. He smirked gently as if he had just taken a whiff of nitrous oxide. Maybe it was his defense mechanism. Each of us responded differently. Mine was worry, and Flanagan I worried about. This wasn't his thing. We had recruited him at the last minute. His old man was the acting head of the U.S. attorney's office in Shreveport, Louisiana—a fact that would actually end up hurting us, not helping us, because that office wanted not to be seen as having a conflict of interest. He was anxious. I didn't blame him. Basel, I knew, would be okay. We were about to go through hell, but at least we would go through together.

We just sat in the holding cell. An hour passed. Nothing. Basel, Dai, and I talked to each other reassuringly. "Everything is going to be okay once we get to explain," we agreed. We talked loudly. We hoped someone would hear us and get curious. I had no idea how this process worked. I thought maybe they watched us through the black oval cameras attached to the corner of the room. I was beginning to feel like a character in a science-fiction movie.

"We're just filmmakers," we repeated to each other as much for our own morale as for the cameras. We could hear the other inmates in holding cells around the corner. We couldn't understand what they were saying to us. We weren't sure we wanted to. Flanagan didn't say much of anything. He looked down, despairing. He had to be thinking I had done this to him. I continued to feel bad for him.

An hour went by, two hours. I was scared, but not so scared as to forget I hadn't eaten anything all day. I never did get that pizza. It was

2 p.m. now, 3 p.m., 4 p.m. Finally, the black shirts brought me into a room by myself and took my handcuffs off. It is hard to explain, but I felt a sudden surge of freedom, which made what happened next all the more painful. After taking off the cuffs, they chained my hands together and attached those chains to a band around my waist. They chained my legs and attached those, too. This was not funny any longer, if it ever had been; not at all.

With my legs chained together, I could only shuffle. With each shuffle the chain pulled painfully against my legs. The black shirts took me now to a holding cell, a small, windowless box. From time to time, for no reason I could figure, they moved me to a different box. After one move, they put a young tough in an orange jumpsuit outside my box. He just sat there on the hallway floor and stared at me for an hour without looking away. I suspect he had seen skinny white prisoners before, but I doubt if he had seen one wearing khakis and a button-down shirt.

For the guy in orange, this outing was a diversion, a field trip. If he was like the rest of these guys, he was headed to some other hellish way station in the penal archipelago, and I was something to look at on this stopover. Just another day in the life for him, but for me, the world had totally turned upside down. It was about to get worse.

For no reason we could figure, the black shirts took Dai and me out of our cages and instructed us to sit down in the hallway on the floor. Among the many things that worried me was the fiendish delight my media foes would take in my predicament. There would be no stirring op-eds about First Amendment rights violated. There would instead be snickering diatribes and evocations of "Bubba," the nightmare prison rapist.

I was biting my nails. I do this sometimes when nervous. Dai saw they were getting to me. He began to speak to me softly and with assurance about the need for fortitude and decorum. I respected Dai. Though only twenty-four, he owned a home. He was professional, courteous, serious, a guy with more to risk than I had. He had followed me here, found himself in this absurd pickle with me, and was turning it all into a teachable moment. It was bizarre, sitting there on the floor, handcuffed, being lectured by my colleague about my leadership qualities. "Stan," I said as nicely as I could, "now is not the time. This is not my fault."

Some other random guy in a black shirt with the U.S. Marshals Service logo on it came and ended the discussion. He picked me up and left Dai behind. I shuffled along with him to an elevator. We boarded it, got off a floor or two above, and made our way to still another windowless room. Here the same two cowboys who had arrested me were waiting for me.

"Can you behave yourself?" asked Scarface.

"Yeah," I answered. I am not sure I had a choice. They took off the chains and shackles and left the handcuffs on. Pure Stockholm syndrome—I was beginning to feel grateful.

"You're in trouble. You know that, right?"

"It seems that way."

"You're in very serious trouble."

I nodded. I was not about to challenge their authority. I tried to explain that I had gone to the federal building to expose corruption, to uphold the law, not to break it. My motives were patriotic, I told them. I might as well have been telling him why we parked the car on Magazine Street. My words simply did not register. His indifference was frustrating, unnerving. I could see how easy it was to break a prisoner. I was close.

Scarface passed me a consent form. It was a waiver of my Miranda— "Everything you say can and will be used against you"—rights.

"You're a smart guy," he said. "You spent some time in law school. It's in your best interest to sign this." They did not tell me the form was a Miranda waiver, and in my emotional state, I did not think to ask. Hell, I could not even understand what was written on that document.

Looking back, I should not have said anything. I should not have signed anything. I had studied this very issue in law school. Even if I hadn't, I had seen enough TV cop shows to know it was a bad idea. But this was no TV show, and I didn't think well in chains. No one does. A nightmare day in windowless cages had shrunk my will to nothing. Plus, I had a plane to catch. I was supposed to go skiing at Tahoe. I just wanted out. Signing the document was my plea for mercy. I had done nothing wrong. I had nothing to hide. If I could talk, I could clear this up and be out on the slopes pronto. The truth would set me free, wouldn't it?

No, I learned, it would not, but I signed the document.

"I just wanted to make a YouTube video," I told them. I held nothing back. They weren't buying.

"Tell us the truth," they kept saying. "You know how we got Martha Stewart, don't you—lying to the FBI."

I thought to myself, "I'm trying *not* to lie to you, but if you keep asking me the same questions over and over again, I may trip over my words and sound like I am." We were flirting with tyranny here. I had never seen it up close.

"Tell us about your LLC," the short agent asked. "Where do you get your money from?"

"I do speaking engagements."

"How much do you get paid?"

"Objection, your honor!" I wanted to shout but didn't. I'm not that stupid.

"What else do you do?"

"I make YouTube videos," I repeated. "We expose corruption."

"Like what?"

"Like ACORN. Did you see those videos with the pimp and the prostitute?"

"That was you?"

"That was me."

"I know about you, man," Scarface said with a smile but without enthusiasm—definitely the reaction of someone who was not a fan. He was writing down my words and said something about matching them with those of my friends. I wondered if the others had signed away their Miranda rights. They had, I would learn, and for the same reasons I did. "Education is the period during which you are being instructed by somebody you do not know," said Chesterton, "about something you do not want to know." If so, this was Injustice 101.

After a while, the cowboys led me back into a larger room, almost like an office. I was encouraged. The mood had lightened. The other agent, the nicer one, stood next to me now, and talked to me almost like a friend.

"Oh yeah, right, the ACORN and Planned Parenthood videos. I kind of remember those." A lot of people had seen those. It was just dawning on him that he had, too. Scarface was on the phone with someone. I didn't know who.

"Yeah, he did the ACORN videos and Planned Parenthood, put them up on YouTube. Says he was making YouTube videos here."

I breathed a little easier. They were getting it. If I knew then what I learned later, I might have told them how in 1949, Edward O'Neill of the *New York Daily News* dressed as a telephone repairman, entered Brooklyn Borough Hall under that guise, was ushered to the telephone terminal box, and was promptly lionized by the media for his efforts in exposing the ease of tapping government phones. But that was 1949. This was 1984. We were in the slammer and didn't even fake tapping anything.

"All right, yeah, yup, all right." Scarface continued talking into the phone. The voice on the other end was assuring him that this was all a misunderstanding, that we would be set free. So I thought.

Wrong again. The black shirts came back for me. They chained me up, took me down in the elevator, and led me shuffling to a place I had not been to before and never want to go to again. Have you ever seen *Midnight Express,* the movie about the young guy who gets busted for smuggling drugs in Turkey? Okay, this federal holding cell in New Orleans wasn't a Turkish prison, but it was close. The room was long and narrow, with a wire cage for a front. Benches ran the length of it. They had been carved on for decades, then pissed and shat on until you could just about see the bacteria growing in the grooves. The wood actually stunk. As to the toilet, it was so gross even the hard core did *everything* standing up, and just about everyone here was hard-core, the baddest of the federal bad.

On the plus side, all the other guys were there. They weren't hard to find. Dai was hanging tough. Basel still had that wry smile. Flanagan was brooding, and who could blame him. To Basel, I made a skiing motion with my legs, swinging them back and forth. We both laughed out loud. I was trying hard to convince myself that in less than thirty-six hours, I would be on top of the world again. We'd be cruising California in our rented RV, heading for the slopes, and joking about our misadventures in the Big Easy.

Or not. Nothing was happening. We waited in the cage an hour, two hours. Time was their property here, not ours. Other inmates came and went. They didn't look a bit like us.

"When are we getting out of here?" Basel asked a black shirt.

"Beats me."

We kept asking, but they didn't know. The hours passed, 8 p.m., 9 p.m. Through an interior window, we could see down the hallway. At one point, I could make out what looked like U.S. marshals and some men in suits, FBI agents maybe, or prosecutors, sitting at a wooden table in an office with a reinforced glass front, chatting away in comfort as though this were just another day.

We couldn't hear, but we could see them. The discussion was

animated. We thought they might be deciding our fate. The negotiation continued longer than made sense. What could they possibly be charging us with? Did they know about my previous work? Would my ACORN stuff redeem us or hurt us? Had the Yes Men ever found themselves in this kind of jam? Doubt it!

I was not a citizen journalist any longer. I was a prisoner, a nobody like all the other nobodies sealed off from the world in the concrete caverns of a federal building in New Orleans, of all places—Claustrophobia 'R' Us. Another hour or so passed, and a black shirt came back.

"Hey, what's up?" said Basel. "We have a plane to catch tomorrow morning."

"That ain't likely to happen," a different U.S. marshal said almost sympathetically. "We spoke to the senator's office. They're pretty shaken up over this. You messed with a high-ranking federal official. I think you just earned yourselves a night in the parish jail."

Damn. We had screwed the pooch. The issue was no longer whether we would get freed tonight. The issue was whether we would ever get our freedom back the way it was that morning. This had the potential to be a life-changing event, and it was a change I hadn't counted on.

We didn't have much time to think about it, in any case. Some unsmiling black shirts took us into a booking room. While we were being processed, one of them casually played with my phone as though it were his. It buzzed. I saw the name Kevin Kane flash on the screen. He wasn't about to let me take that call. Once processed, the black shirts led us outside and down to a small prison transport bus. It was getting cold, but we had more pressing issues to worry about.

"Can we get some food?" I asked when I saw where we were going. I had not had anything to eat or drink all day. I was beginning to feel like the guy trapped between rocks in the movie *127 Hours*. A few more hours of this, and I'd have been tempted to saw off my right arm for a Coke and pizza.

"Don't know," said a guy in a puffy down-filled jacket and black ski cap. He didn't look like a federal employee. He looked like a gangster or a rapper—Puff Daddy—but he now seemed to be in charge of us. We climbed into the bus as best we could. This is not easy to do shackled. The other cons had an easier time. I suspect they'd had more practice. Once we found our seats, the black shirts looked in on us as if they were checking out cattle for hoof-and-mouth disease.

"Take 'em over to the parish prison," said the one gum-chewing agent. "I don't think they've eaten yet. See if they got any food. If they don't, don't worry about it."

Don't worry about it? We had been detained for eleven hours without food or water and had not even been charged with a crime, and this guy is saying, "Don't worry about it." Hell, if this were Guantanamo, the readers of the *New York Times* would be crying for us over their cappuccinos.

With that, Puff Daddy nodded military style and slammed the doors shut. In almost complete darkness now, we rolled down the New Orleans streets, chained to a rail in a prison transport bus, the bus jostling up and down, the shackles bruising our wrists and ankles. Just twenty-four hours ago we were partying in these very streets. This was not exactly how we expected to end the day.

Through the tinted windows, the streets of downtown became the suburbs, which became industrial parks, which became a postindustrial no-man's-land of unpainted buildings and exhausted factories.

"Watcha' in for?" said Puff Daddy, glancing over his shoulder. "You all carjackers or bank robbers or what?"

"We're journalists," I answered.

"Journalists!" he burst out. "What on earth they got you on?"

"We have no idea. We haven't been charged with anything yet."

"You haven't been charged?" He was dumbfounded. Puff Daddy had seen everything, but, as he told us, "I ain't never seen anything like this before."

Never seen it before. This was the story of my life. I used to joke about it with friends. My doctor examines a strange condition of mine: "Well, James, I've never seen that before."

A technician tries to fix my computer glitch: "O'Keefe, I've never seen that before." A TV producer checks out my ACORN videos: "Interesting, kid. I've never seen anything quite like this before." And now my federal chauffeur/gangster rapper wannabe with puffy jacket and ski cap listens to the tale of our outrageous incarceration and says, "Never seen that before." That was the story of my life, and it would only get stranger.

LOUISIANA WATERGATE

Veritas Rule #14:
*No journalist can speak truth to power unless they are
willing to be slandered and arrested.*

After a sleepless night in the St. Bernard Parish jail, Stan Dai, Joe Basel, Bob Flanagan, and I, chained hand and foot, resplendent in our orange McVeigh suits, shuffled into a small cage, there to meet the public defender. A slovenly, uninspired guy, he reminded us only that we had done something very bad.

"It is important you understand what I'm about to tell you," he told us through the Plexiglas that separated us. "You are being charged with a felony that carries ten years of a prison sentence. Please be advised that if you do get your own attorney, he should have federal experience."

As paranoid as it might sound on the free side of the Plexiglas, on the unfree side we felt like political prisoners. If we expected support from the First Amendment champions in the major media, we were fooling ourselves. As we would soon enough see, the same journalists who would one day defend David Gregory's illegal ammo-waving "stunt" on *Meet the Press* were then celebrating our imprisonment. I thought my life was shot, my career over.

I consider myself a strong enough person, someone willing to take risks and accept consequences. But after the first federal bureaucrat left that morning, and we were shuffled off to a new cage with a new bureaucrat, and he began probing my medical history, I was sinking fast. This guy quizzed me about my extended family. He asked questions whose answers I did not know and scolded me for not knowing them. He extracted secrets from me I did not intend to yield, secrets that would later be used against me, and wrote them down in front of me as seeming proof of both my weakness and my guilt.

I had read my Orwell, my Koestler, my Whittaker Chambers. I knew this stuff could happen, but I did not think anything like it could happen here, not in the present anyhow. Now I could see a little of what Chambers had seen sixty-some years ago. In accusing establishment golden boy Alger Hiss of espionage, Chambers brought upon himself a hell that I thought was a relic of the past. It wasn't.

"Tragedy occurs when a human soul awakes and seeks, in suffering and pain, to free itself from crime, violence, infamy, even at the cost of life," Chambers wrote in his masterwork, *Witness*. "This tragedy," he added, "will have been for nothing unless men understand it rightly." That is what worried me in New Orleans and still worries me today, the fear that what we were attempting to do would be misunderstood, not so much by our antagonists as by our allies, those who actually do fight for government accountability and human freedom.

Just as in Chambers's time, most political journalists, especially those who are well paid, live in fear. They fear being wrong. They fear the ridicule that might follow being wrong. They fear ultimately for their careers. Too many of them, conservatives especially, will abandon allies when that alliance threatens their reputation or self-image. A single misstep, a single misstatement, a momentary misunderstanding is sometimes all it takes. I would be painfully reminded of this truism over and over again in the few short years of my self-defined career.

"It is the role of a good journalist to take on powerful abusers," wrote WikiLeaks founder Julian Assange, "and when the powerful abusers are taken on, there's always a bad reaction." How bad a reaction was becoming much too clear. Shaking up society and reforming government through the practice of real journalism, I was coming to see, requires more moral and physical courage than most of us have. And no one comes away unscathed.

That afternoon we were taken back to the scene of the crime, the Hale Boggs Building. We were marched into a courtroom and positioned on an elevated side bench overlooking it. To my right were three tough-looking guys in orange jumpsuits, all facing bank robbery charges or worse. To my left were my three buddies, all facing the unknown. Here we were arraigned before Magistrate Judge Louis Moore Jr., who spoke in a soft and slow southern cadence with long pauses and alarming non sequiturs. He reminded me of Fred Gwynne's judge character in *My Cousin Vinnie,* but without the charm or wisdom.

"You boys are first-time offenders," he drawled. "What's this? Eagle Scouts? College educations? Graduate educations? Law school even? Hmmm."

At the time, I was thinking these were good things to be hearing at our arraignment, things that would somehow factor in our favor. After all, who could possibly think ill of an Eagle Scout? Well, as Mike Madigan would later tell me, Judge Louis Moore could. In his mind, the fact that we had solid educations meant that we must have known what we were doing when we were committing this heinous crime—whatever that crime was.

As Moore carried on, I scanned the courtroom looking for journalists. I knew we were edging up against the public domain at this point, and I suspected that at any moment we would be found out.

Among the people sitting in the rows behind the prosecutor, one got my attention: a scruffy, curly-haired young guy in jeans. Sure enough, when I saw him pull out one of those pocket-size, Office Max memo books and a laminated badge, I knew there was at least one reporter in the room. His name was Patrick Semansky, and he was from the Associated Press. For a story that would go international in an hour, he was at that moment the only human being in the media who knew I had been arrested.

Once I made him, I tilted my head and stared down at him like one of those gargoyles on the Chrysler Building. I wanted him to know that I knew he was there, and I wasn't afraid of his nonsense. I had no doubt that he and the rest of his profession wanted to serve me up as tomorrow's breakfast. If so, I wasn't going to let him see me looking depressed. I wasn't going to allow the media to think they had me, even if they did. I knew I was innocent and wanted to prove it to Semansky through my stare. No matter what was happening in that courtroom, I had it all under control—such, in any case, was my unspoken message.

As the judge talked, in walked a harried-looking lawyer apologizing for being late. I didn't know Eddie Castaing at the time, did not know he was a local white-collar criminal defense attorney, and I certainly didn't know Madigan sent him, but Madigan had. He had heard about what was going on through Ben Wetmore, at whose house we had been staying. Apparently the feds impounded Wetmore's car. That kind of got Ben's attention. Wetmore didn't know the details but knew we were in deep. He sent an email to a guy named John Burns, with the subject line "I think James just got to DEFCON 1 in NOLA."

Burns didn't know the name of my attorney, but he did know Breitbart associate Mike Flynn, who did. Flynn emailed Madigan, and Madigan called my cell phone, which, unfortunately, was in the possession of the U.S. Marshals Service. Knowing how things likely went down, Madigan left the message "James, this is your attorney. Please call me. If U.S. marshals are listening to this call, you must let him make a phone call to his attorney, and I urge you to let him make that call."

Castaing arrived at the defense table just in time to represent us. By then, I thought this must have all gone public, but it had not yet done so. That was the first small miracle. Castaing argued that we were first-time offenders with pristine backgrounds. In the absence of publicity, Moore released us on personal bonds of ten thousand dollars a head. Madigan would later inform me that this was another mini-miracle. To walk out of this kangaroo court in a hostile jurisdiction and see the light of the day meant either that God was watching us, or our enemies hadn't gotten their act together; or it meant both.

As eager as I was to sign the bond, I discovered it's not easy when you're shackled. I had to contort my body and just about rip the skin off my wrists to get my hands high enough above the table to sign the yellow carbon paper, but these were complaints no one was going to listen to.

We were escorted out of the courtroom and onto the prison transport bus. We were going back to the jail to get our clothes. The same guy—the federal chauffeur/gangster rapper wannabe with the puffy jacket and ski cap—was driving. He was listening to CBS Radio News, and just a few minutes into the trip, I heard something about telephone repairmen in New Orleans.

"Turn the radio up!" I shouted. Puff Daddy looked back at me, incredulous that a prisoner would make special requests, but he turned it up anyway. "Four men were arrested this morning in New Orleans after entering the office of Mary Landrieu and posing as telephone repairmen," said the newscaster. Hearing this, we all shouted out spontaneously. It wasn't the attention we were celebrating. It was the fact that now the world knew of our plight. We had been shackled, stashed away, and falsely accused. For two days we felt like characters out of Koestler or Kafka, and now we felt like we had returned to America. We would not have to suffer alone. Maybe we would attract supporters, who would hear us out and send assistance.

As the bus pulled into the jail parking space, we could see a dozen reporters milling outside. The word had obviously spread. That was fast. Ours was the kind of story these guys loved to report. "Here we go," I muttered. Semansky, the AP reporter, continued to badger me. I gave him a one-word quote, *veritas,* and that was that. "Ve-ri-tas?" he asked. "Is that Latin for truth, James?" We didn't say anything else. I just stood there, as local TV cameras scanned me up and down. I was glad that viewers couldn't smell us through their TV sets. We hadn't changed or showered in forty-eight hours, and we looked it. "VERITAS??!!" echoed hundreds of information-hungry blogs, having no idea what on earth I was trying to say through that message.

We walked briskly out the door, bond papers in hand, my pants falling down because I had offered Basel my belt. As I was getting into the cab, I said, "The truth shall set me free," and I meant it. Hannah Giles would later tell me she knew we were innocent when she heard this response. The problem was getting the truth out there. As Stan and I pulled away in the cab, a posse of journalists chased us down the street to a red light. Once stopped, I adjusted myself in the seat to allow the photographers to snap a photo. One of those who did appeared to have cropped it in such a way to make it look like I was in a police car, not a taxicab. I was still learning.

Before the ink had dried on our signatures, the media were calling the affair the "Louisiana Watergate." In deference to our ages perhaps, MSNBC was calling it "Watergate Jr." The fact that my attorney, Mike Madigan, served as counsel to Senator Howard Baker on the Watergate Committee did not go unnoticed, at least not by the Associated Press.

True, Watergate was a massive abuse of power by a sitting president that included several burglaries and break-ins. Landrieu-Gate, on the other hand, was an attempt by a crew of unaffiliated young guys to shoot a YouTube video in the course of which they entered an office showing their real IDs and asked staffers some innocuous questions. Otherwise the phenomena were very much alike. Each, after all, had something to do with telephones, and the "victims," in either case, had influential friends in the media, now giddy with delight.

The message was this: 4 ARRESTED IN PHONE TAMPERING AT LANDRIEU OFFICE. So trumpeted the *New York Times* on the front page, a spot previously denied our adventures. The editors may have been slow to report our ACORN sting, but they made up for it reporting our arrest. They had the story posted online the same day we were arraigned. In those brief hours, they managed to track down ACORN's chief executive, Bertha Lewis, who gloated that the arrests were "further evidence of Mr. O'Keefe's 'disregard for the law in pursuit of his extremist agenda.'" In the way of mixed blessings, many Americans would find out about the corruption at ACORN only through our arrest.

ACORN has some experience of its own in the area of entering federal buildings under false pretenses. In 1991, its operatives seized the House Banking Committee hearing room and held it for two days. Of course, they did this without reproach from the same media that were now libeling me as a thug and a felon.

"It was not clear precisely what the men were trying to do in Ms. Landrieu's office," admitted the *Times*, but that did not prevent the editors from captioning the photo of Senator Landrieu "Four people were arrested for trying to tap the phones of Senator Mary L. Landrieu, Democrat of Louisiana, at left, on Capital Hill on Tuesday." It was not until the twelfth paragraph that the patient reader learned that "The affidavit did not accuse the men of trying to tap the phones, or describe in detail what they did to the equipment." Bob Flanagan's attorney, J. Garrison Jordan, confirmed the same in the thirteenth paragraph. "There is no wiretap allegation." Details!

Greg Marx, writing in the *Columbia Journalism Review*, would trace the Watergate angle to the *New Orleans Times-Picayune*. The paper began its original story on the bust, "Alleging a plot to wiretap Democratic Sen. Mary Landrieu's office . . ." Carol Leonning had a much more prominent podium—front page of the *Washington Post*—and seemingly a greater responsibility to get the story right. She did not.

Leonning may still have been miffed about the correction she had to make after her ACORN misreporting. Whatever her motive, she came back misfiring both guns this time.

ACORN Foe Charged in Alleged Plot to Wiretap Landrieu, screamed her January 27 headline. One detail she did get right was this: "Democrats gleefully pored over the details of the criminal charges Tuesday." She did not mention that this glee infected just about every newsroom in America, including her own.

Leonning returned the following day on page four a bit less gleefully. Wiretapping? What wiretapping? Now, Leonning was reporting, "O'Keefe, 25, waited inside the office and used his cellphone to record his two colleagues saying that the senator's phone was not receiving calls." Her source for this was "charges unsealed Tuesday." Tuesday was January 26, the gleeful day after our arrest. Her initial article was January 27. There was no excuse for making so massive an error.

This error prompted still another Leonning correction on page two of the January 28 edition, admitting that the "Jan. 27 Page One article misstated the nature of the charges recently filed against four men including James O'Keefe." Swell, but who reads corrections? "Hopefully you'll be a bit more careful with your reporting in the future," I emailed her. "Remember, good government accountability means investigating government, not just other investigative journalists." I cc'd her editors; haven't heard much from her since.

"Any story that results in multiple corrections is troubling," Andy Alexander, the *Post*'s ombudsman, admitted to Breitbart TV's Larry O'Connor. O'Connor wanted more than a faint apology. "What is the

Washington Post's policy regarding a reporter's repeated use of falsehoods when writing about the same individual?" he wrote back. "Is it wise to continue to assign Ms. Leonning stories that involve Mr. O'Keefe considering the appearance is now that Ms. Leonning is not capable of reporting only the truth with regard to him?"

Nothing came of this. Last I looked, Leonning is still bumbling along at the *Washington Post*. Instinctively, the media, Leonning included, went trolling for conservatives to denounce us. This is part of their shtick. They did not have to troll too hard. Our presumed allies were volunteering their distaste without prompting.

You would think that conservatives would have learned to distrust the media narrative, that they would wait until facts were in before piling on. Not so. "If this is true, this seems like an absurd act," said Pat Buchanan. "If that's what they're doing, bugging her—the New Orleans office of a United States senator? What in heaven's name do they think they're going to pick up?" "If"? C'mon, Pat! The higher up the conservative food chain, the more likely the commentator was to attack us. Hannah Giles, after an initial hesitation, nailed the problem: "[A]fter the ACORN videos everyone and his conservative dog was aboard the new-media campaign bandwagon. Yet, the moment an unsubstantiated report on James was leaked, the rank and file of our movement exposed themselves as vulnerable to the MSM as anyone."

Breitbart, as always, knew best how to respond—attack! "Mainstream Media, ACORN, Media Matters (all the supposed defenders of due process and journalistic ethics) are jumping to conclusions over the arrest today of James O'Keefe," he wrote, "with the clear intention to smear and, if possible, convict O'Keefe and his alleged co-conspirators in the court of public opinion in order to taint the 'jury of their peers.'" Andrew concluded that "until I hear the full story from James O'Keefe, I will not speculate as to what he was doing in Louisiana. . . . I predict much egg on your J-school grad faces."

★   ☞   ★

In the now-century-old "Journalist's Creed," Walter Williams insisted that a successful paper is "self-controlled, patient, always respectful of its readers but always unafraid, is quickly indignant at injustice; is unswayed by the appeal of the privilege or the clamor of the mob; seeks to give every man a chance." Andrew understood that if this creed ever held, it no longer did. If today's reporters found themselves in revolutionary France, they would be endorsing the head choppers, and their audience would cheer each head as it hit the basket. Here is a sample of the comments posted upon my arrest. Many of those posting proudly used their real names. *Reader discretion is strongly advised.* My critics have developed an unsavory interest in prison rape:

"Enjoy prison sex, because it's all you're gonna be getting for a while."

"O'Keefe will soon be spending 10 years in a federal pound-me-in-the-ass-prison."

"I can't wait to see O'Keefe's next hidden video project of him getting assraped in prison."

"I'm elated he got caught. Now that I know what he looks like physically. They are going to love him in prison."

"You didn't see FAUX News didn't mention his arrest. I hope this little bitch get fucked up the ass in prison. Now he's going GET pimped."

"Well you should by him a box of KY Jelly when he is sentenced. It will hurt less if you do."

"Irony is a bitch James . . . especially when its a 300 pound cellmate on Viagra."

"I guess the party is over at Fox. Jimmy's going to make a nice prison bitch for a black Daddy for the next 10 years."

"Just think . . . little white boy goes into a black ran organization trying to bring it down while dressed like a black pimp . . . oh shit . . . this is a made for pay per view story with an anal raping! LMAO LMAO."

I'd like to be able to tell you that I "laughed my ass off," too, but I could not laugh at all. None of us could. As Mike Madigan made us aware, the U.S. Attorney's office handling our case, headed by Jim Letten, was much too tight with Senator Landrieu. Just the year before, Landrieu had personally lobbied President Obama to allow Letten to keep his job. Madigan was sufficiently concerned that he wrote to assistant attorney general Lanny Breuer and asked that Letten's office not be involved with our criminal prosecution. Letten had already recused himself, but his leadership team stayed on that job. On that team were Jan Mann, his first assistant who was now handling our case, her husband James Mann, and Landrieu's own brother, Maurice Landrieu.

Scarier still, we had every reason to believe that leaks from within the U.S. attorney's office were keeping the crazies worked up. In a March 3, 2010, letter to that office, Madigan put his concerns on record. As he observed, the arresting officers had confiscated my computer and cell phone from Ben Wetmore's car without my permission or his. They both contained multiple private communications, a few of which had fallen into the hands of at least two of the journalists who had contacted Madigan. "The information that I have confirmed was disclosed to the media appears to be intentionally calculated to foment negative public opinion against Mr. O'Keefe, presumably in an unethical effort to prejudice any criminal proceedings against Mr. O'Keefe," wrote Madigan prophetically. He got no response to his letter.

In retrospect, that does not surprise. Madigan was protesting to the very people we believed were responsible for the leaks. In December 2012, Letten resigned after two of his top lawyers admitted using aliases to post comments critical of their investigative targets on the website of the *Times-Picayune*. One of the two was the woman managing our case, Jan Mann. As the *New York Times* noted dryly, "The exposure of Ms. Mann, months after Mr. Letten's avowals that Mr. Perricone had acted alone, raised doubts about the effectiveness of an internal investigation by the Justice Department." Although it was hard to believe that the corruption ended there, Senator Mary L. Landrieu promptly commended Letten's "record of rooting out public corruption," and Attorney General Eric H. Holder Jr. called the now-disgraced U.S. attorney a "valued partner, dedicated public servant and a good friend." The old expression "thick as thieves" was beginning to make sense to me.

Sources would later tell me the feds wanted the case to go away. In an extended trial, our motives would be front and center. The public would learn that we merely hoped to catch Landrieu staffers on tape talking about how they were neglecting their constituents. This would make neither Landrieu nor the prosecution look good.

Contrary to the word on the street, I did not "plead down" to a misdemeanor. The charges were refiled to a misdemeanor—18 U.S.C. § 1036, "Entry by false pretenses to any real property, vessel, or aircraft of the United States or secure area of any airport or seaport"—because the feds had no evidence of a felony. We had showed our driver's licenses upon entering the federal building. Had we gone to trial, the prosecution would have had to argue that I committed a crime by telling the Landrieu staffers I was waiting for someone when I really wasn't. It was for this innocuous act, in fact, that the federal government would harass me for the next three years.

When Mike Madigan called me two months later, in May 2010, I was in Rhode Island, celebrating Maureen Wagner's graduation from law school. It would prove to be my last weekend as a free man for three years. Madigan didn't waste time with niceties. "They got you by the balls," he said. "They assigned a district judge to a misdemeanor. This is highly unusual."

And not just any district judge. A Clinton appointee with a name straight out of Faulkner, Judge Stanwood R. Duval, had once gotten national press when he ruled in favor of Planned Parenthood and against the state of Louisiana on the issue of special-design license plates that bore the message CHOOSE LIFE. Given my own record with Planned Parenthood, I think Duval should have recused himself. He obviously thought otherwise.

Madigan forwarded to me the perfectly arbitrary court "order" Duval had just filed. "This is obviously not good and is in fact outrageous," said Madigan. Duval was now claiming that our "crime" was "extremely serious and may have lasting ramifications." In a scary bit of sophistry he linked our "unconscionable" deception to those "acts of violence" that resulted in the deaths of other federal officers. Ratcheting up our threat potential, the *New Orleans Time-Picayune* ran with the headline HANDLING OF MARY LANDRIEU CAPER CASE CALLED "VERY UNUSUAL." Dane Ciolino, a professor at Loyola Law School, told the *Time-Picayune*, "Usually in misdemeanors, district judges don't get involved in any respect."

If we saw ourselves as Woodward and Bernstein, Duval saw us as Nichols and McVeigh. "Perceived righteousness of a cause does not justify nefarious and potentially dangerous actions," he thundered. He could make these outlandish comments and get away with them only because I could not show the video shot in Landrieu's office that demonstrated how unthreatening our presence there was. Madigan had asked for that video file pre-trial, and the court refused. Finally, after my plea, the feds returned our equipment, including the video chip, but the file in question had been removed. This was acknowledged during my sentencing hearing on May 26, 2010, with ABC News and Fox News in attendance, but no one saw fit to report this destruction of critical exculpatory evidence.

With this evidence suppressed, the court felt free to throw out "the Final Factual Basis" both sides had agreed to earlier. That one talked about engaging in "political speech," presenting "real driver's licenses," explaining to the U.S. marshals that we were "journalists," admitting to being "imprudent," and other such truths.

The new one was not nearly as forgiving. For our dubious misdemeanor we received not the six-month probation we were expecting but three years with full travel restrictions, and all I was allowed to say was "I'm sorry."

"What could be more important to the preservation of a free society than laying out the truth on the table?" asks a character in Canadian writer Michael O'Brien's *Eclipse of the Sun,* an apocalyptic novel set in the near future. As the character learns, and as we too learned in New Orleans, to the state there are any number of things that are more important, self-preservation being high among them. We had offended the gods of the government-media complex. They were keen on getting their revenge, and they got it.

My well-wishers would not get to see me raped by Bubba, but they would enjoy many of the gratuitous indignities dished out punitively by Duval over the next three years through the agency of Daniel Knowles, a magistrate judge who worked under Duval. No, this wasn't the Soviet Union. As much as he might have wanted to, Duval could not send me to prison. What he could do, what he did, was just walk me right up to it and ask me to be grateful for not pushing me in. I was his boy. I was his bitch. He had me, as Madigan kept reminding me, by the balls.

I ask the reader to forgive us for not knowing the law. It is very rarely enforced. Two months before our arrest, for instance, I had watched with interest the nervy bluff of Michaele and Tareq Salahi. They had finessed their way through several levels of White House screening and managed to confront the president of the United States at a reception, a more dangerous security breach than ours in anyone's book. Do you remember reading about their being arrested? No? Well, you wouldn't because they weren't. Instead of jail, they got a slot on *The Real Housewives of D.C.* I guess that was punishment enough.

I should note that a year earlier, on behalf of the fictional "Taxpayers Clearing House," we had run a sting on Maine U.S. senator Olympia Snowe in her office without any formal complaint from that office nor any negative media coverage. As the scheme worked, we delivered a comically oversized bailout check to any number of organizations, AIG, Citibank, and Goldman Sachs among them.

We had gone to Senator Snowe's Capitol Hill office under the pretense of being students from Bates College, located in Lewiston, Maine. Although we never got near Senator Landrieu, we actually met with Snowe and presented her with an oversized check payable to Amtrak worth $1 billion. "It's for the one billion dollars for the new stimulus package, on behalf of the taxpayers," I told Snowe, and asked her to sign it. "I'm a good supporter of Amtrak," she answered. We taped her without her knowledge and posted the edited video on YouTube as the "Bailout Prize Patrol." Did I mention that Snowe is a Republican?

ABC GOES FOR THE JUGULAR

Veritas Rule #15:
Stick to the facts.

When you trail-blaze, when you hack your way through the jungle—excuse me, rain forest—you sometimes stumble, and that is what I very loudly did in New Orleans. In the months that followed, it was all about picking myself up and pursuing a path that almost no one thought worthy of pursuing, a path made doubly difficult because I could not travel.

Before the New Orleans fiasco, Joe Basel and I had been working on a sting of federal Department of Housing and Urban Development. The HUD staffers lived up to the low expectations we had for them. In Detroit, we went to the HUD office testing the Obama administration's 10 percent tax credit for first-time homebuyers. Once there, I asked a staffer if I bought a place for $50,000 but got the seller to agree to say it was $80,000, could I get my 10 percent credit on the $80,000.

"Flip it any way you want," the staffer told us.

I pushed the fraud factor up a level. What if I really paid only $6,000? "Yup," he said, "you can do that." Basel and I pulled the same sting at HUD's Chicago office and at several independent housing offices, with pretty much the same results. Andrew liked what we had done. Once the dust settled in New Orleans, he and I started shopping the video around.

Andrew wanted to release the video through ABC News. He had an in with the Emmy Award–winning senior producer for ABC's *Good Morning America*, Chris Vlasto, the same guy he would eventually go to with the Anthony Weiner story. At the time, I was wary of the whole deal, but Andrew kept encouraging me. "Have you ever seen the movie *The Incredibles?*" he asked me. (Even if he didn't have four kids, I suspect he would have still watched cartoons anyway.) "You're a superhero, too," he continued, "and you don't even know it. Yes, you're down, but so were the Incredibles, and they bounced back. Just act confident."

Given my travel restrictions, Vlasto came over to New Jersey, and we met at P. J. Finnegan's, an Irish pub in Westwood. He reminded me of the dogged Al Pacino character in *The Insider*. He had all kinds of good things to say about me and my work, and I began to think Andrew knew what he was talking about. Although I could never be sure, I would even go so far as to say that Vlasto's intentions were solid. Afterward, I sent Vlasto a copy of the HUD video, and he seemed excited, almost too excited. He wanted to air it as soon as possible. "I do really think you are making a difference," he told me, "and that is the most important thing." He called me weekly to keep me posted on the progress of our project within ABC.

Vlasto's intentions could well have been sincere, but I had my misgivings. ABC was an incestuous place. Vlasto is the son of James Vlasto, press secretary to former New York governor Hugh Carey. His brother, Josh Vlasto, has worked for current New York governor Andrew Cuomo, whose brother, Chris Cuomo, had recently been the news anchor for *Good Morning America*. Andrew Cuomo had spent eight years at HUD, four of them as secretary. Chris was to interview us on the HUD sting. I had already been arrested once on that bogus "entry by false pretenses" charge. We were vulnerable here as well. Vlasto "just liked a good story," Andrew insisted, but his colleagues and bosses were deeply entrenched in the government media-complex and had a legacy to protect.

While waiting for final word from ABC, my friend Shaughn Adeleye and I did some undercover work on the U.S. Census Bureau. First a word about Shaughn. To know him is to understand the American potential for self-creation. Born in Nigeria in 1974, he did not settle permanently in the United States until age fifteen. After graduating from the University of Louisiana and unable to find work as a designer, he took a real job in a place where fine arts majors rarely venture: the oil fields.

That work strengthened his conservative instincts, which had been on display even while in college. Flashing her biases, one professor had openly written him off as "the waste of a perfectly good black mind." Shaughn simply refused to live his life as a stereotype. In 2009, he started attending Tea Party events, where he met a friend of mine, and the friend recommended me to Shaughn. In this business you need to find people who can make decisions and take action. Shaughn fit the bill. He was with us in New Orleans, but fortunately he did not accompany us on our ill-fated adventure.

What Shaughn and I had done was simple enough. We signed up to be among the six hundred thousand temporary Census 2010 workers, he in Louisiana, me in New Jersey. Without looking hard, we both found supervisors who couldn't care less whether we reported our work hours honestly. At the time we were negotiating with Vlasto, I made him aware that I had footage of these census scammers as well.

Then things started getting a little strange. One evening I finagled a hall pass from my probation officer, and I met Andrew and Vlasto in New York at Molyvos, a pricy taverna in Midtown overripe with artifacts from the Greek islands. There Vlasto dropped the bombshell on us that anchor George Stephanopoulos, who was Greek himself, wanted to interview not Shaughn and me, but Andrew and me about the census footage. I soon enough found out why.

The first of our census pieces went up on May 31, 2010, and Andrew and I went into the ABC studios the next day. Stephanopoulos barely faked an interest in the census footage. After introducing us, he said, "I do want to get to the new project, but, first, let's set the record straight. You did commit a crime, correct?" In the unedited interview, I said I was cleared of a felony. That never made it on air. After reviewing my arrest in New Orleans and all the bad things my critics had been saying, Stephanopoulos moved in for the kill:

STEPHANOPOULOS: I want to get to the census. [No, he didn't!] But, one other point your critics make is they say you're animated by resentment over race. They point out that you've attended at least one conference where white nationalist literature and speakers were promoted. And they point to a time in college at Rutgers when you were kicked out of a dorm for using racist slurs.

O'KEEFE: That's outrageous. I mean, that's been completely disproven on the Internet. I'm not even going to address that. . . .

BREITBART: This is the type of journalism we do is to counter the false narratives and the slurs that happen from political operatives, like Max Blumenthal, like Joan Walsh at *Salon,* who use journalism as a platform, to slur James O'Keefe. It's not true.

O'KEEFE: When you take on corruption—

STEPHANOPOULOS: But this is your diary that points it out.

O'KEEFE: When you stand up . . . when you stand up to institutions, people are going to come after you. They're going to use character assassinations. Well, we're going to rise above that. This is not about me. I'm creating a movement of investigative journalists across the country. And they're not going to stop us with character assassination and innuendo.

I saw Vlasto in the studio afterward. "Chris, I can't believe what they just did," I said in undisguised disgust. "How could you allow them to do this?" He understood our chagrin and conceded we had a right to feel the way we did. "You thought you were playing ball before," said Andrew later. "This is Disney. This is the big leagues." He suspected that Vlasto had been stepped on by his own bosses. I at least felt grateful that I didn't give in on the HUD sting.

A young woman waiting in the greenroom overheard our exchange with Stephanopoulos. "Well, what did happen at Rutgers?" she asked accusingly. That was her takeaway. I was some sort of white supremacist. If the Nigerian-born Shaughn had been with me, of course, Stephanopoulos would not have dared that line of attack. But he is a sly little character who learned from the sliest of them all, Bill Clinton.

In the Clinton White House, Stephanopoulos played the role of media fixer. As Andrew pointed out in a satirical piece posted that same day, it was Stephanopoulos who forced his way onto ABC's *This Week* and savaged White House whistle-blower Garry Aldrich. "Someone should have to pass a bare threshold of credibility before they're put on the air to millions of viewers," raged Stephanopoulos. "A thirty-year record in the FBI in and of itself is no proof of credibility." But a few years under Clinton is? Aldrich's book went on to sell a million copies.

Impressed apparently by his media savvy and/or his good hair, ABC hired Stephanopoulos after he left the administration in 1996. As they say, you can take the boy out of the White House, but you can't take the White House out of the boy. In 1998, Stephanopoulos tried to sidetrack the Clinton/Lewinsky story by demeaning Bill Kristol's sources on ABC News' *This Week*. And now he was attacking me for a diary entry from my freshman year in college? This is what journalism looks like in America today.

We posted two Census Bureau pieces, one narrated by me, one by Shaughn. What they showed wasn't damning, just depressing. Bureaucrats in both locations had no compunction at all about shaving an hour here and an hour there off our workdays. The case we made was that if six hundred thousand employees each fudged an hour per diem, that represented more than $10 million in waste each day.

Not surprisingly, the Census Bureau responded with a heavy hand. "The Census Bureau obviously does not condone any falsifying of or tampering with time sheets by its employees," said spokesman Stephen Buckner after our video was posted. Then, playing to the media's biases, Buckner reminded the media that our video was "selectively edited" and that I was "an admitted criminal." The media did not need reminding. They had been tagging me as a would-be criminal and trick-shot editor even before New Orleans. We citizens may pay the salaries of our federal employees, but the folks at the Census Bureau have not gotten the memo.

Some of our allies were not happy, either. I was forwarded a petulant email from Stephen Morse, a guy roughly my age who had been awarded a Phillips Foundation journalism fellowship to work on a project called "My Two Census." Although he had never talked to me, he felt comfortable telling his fellow young conservatives in the Phillips programs that he was "majorly irked by the recent 'journalism' activities of one James O'Keefe."

Morse rattled off my shortcomings as though he had gotten his talking points from *Media Matters*. He seemed particularly peeved that my census work had netted much more publicity than his own. "Is this guy really worthy of a *New York Times Magazine* profile?" he whined. Morse was referring to a lengthy and shockingly fair article by Zev Chafets in July 2011. Whatever his politics, Chafets understood our work better than Morse did. This experience and others like it prompted another useful Veritas rule: *Know who your friends are and be loyal to them.* As G. K. Chesterton once said, "The Bible tells us to love our neighbors, and also to love our enemies; probably because generally they are the same people."

BEAUTIFUL SWIMMERS

Veritas Rule #16:
Know who your friends are and stay loyal to them.

It can come anytime from the last week in October to the first in December. There will be a fickle day, unseasonably warm, during which two or three minor rain squalls blow across the Bay. The sun appears fitfully in between; sometimes there is distant thunder. A front is passing. The first warning that it is more than an ordinary autumnal leaf-chaser comes near the end. The ragged trailing edge of a normal front is nowhere to be seen. Ominously absent is the steady procession of fleecy white puffball clouds that usually presages two or three days of fine weather. Rather, the front picks up speed and passes so rapidly that it is stormy at one moment and unbelievably clear and cloud-free the next. Then it comes.

The wind rises in a few minutes from a placid five or ten knots to a sustained thirty or forty, veering quickly first to the west and then to the northwest. The dry gale has begun. . . . When at last it stops, the water is gin clear and a new cold creeps over its surface. The grays and green of summer's discoloring plankton blooms have been banished. Canada geese that rafted lazily far from shore on Indian summer days move closer to land and the hunters' guns. To be sure, sparkling days may yet come. But there will be more "bluebird weather" during which the yachtsman sails in his shirt-sleeves or the hunter sweats uncomfortably in his blind. Autumn, a charmingly indecisive time on the Chesapeake, has given way to winter.

—FROM WILLIAM WARNER'S PULITZER PRIZE–WINNING
Beautiful Swimmers.

On one of the fickle autumn days of the kind described by William Warner, as the trees lining the Chesapeake Bay revealed their first early hint of color, CNN producers and photographers were manning speedboats and bearing down on my boat slip on Solomons Island. The CNN armada had one mission: an amphibious photographic assault on yours truly.

The CNN crew pulled up close to where my old, twenty-seven-foot Catalina sailboat was docked. I am told their producers actually jumped into the water and waded in to within feet of my boat. The man who told me was the eighty-year-old owner of the property where the boat was docked, Robert Anderson, aka Captain Ahab. He walked toward the dock while they were shooting and observed silently.

A cantankerous old fart with a New York accent and a beard like Santa's, Ahab was a perfectionist when it came to things nautical, and he would not hesitate to point out to me my many flaws and imperfections. As I recognized, I still had as much to learn about sailing as I did about life.

Like most of the mentors in my life, Ahab had his own imperfections. As willing as he was to impose his seafaring views on me, he once told me that pro-lifers should be shot and killed for "imposing their values" on others. He may have just been giving me a hard time. I am not even sure he knew how I made my way in the world, though he did admit having "heard" about the ACORN videos. You never knew with Ahab.

Ahab was a master of the dry, ambiguously comic email. A few weeks earlier he wrote, "James, please secure your boat for the hurricane by doubling your lines, wrapping the mainsail with line, and putting the jib below. You also need lots of slack in the lines to the dock to compensate for the surge."

Given the limits of my knowledge, I thought "double your lines" had to have some tricky technical meaning, like maybe tying the lines with a unique knot or a different cleat configuration. Confused, I asked a clarifying question: "Robert, I'm not sure what you meant by double your lines. I provided a bit more slack away from the dock on the starboard side."

Ahab replied, "Double your lines? This means if you have one line from the port bow to the piling, add another line. That makes two lines from the port bow to the piling, which is double what you had previously." I laughed at this response until I, literally, cried.

I first learned about the CNN armada from one of Ahab's trademark emails. "James," he wrote, "Two men in a power boat were circling the dock this morning. When Dawn [his wife] went down, they asked if this was James O'Keefe's boat? They said they were from CNN and were doing a story. They were taking pictures of your boat. They did not go aboard your boat. And then they left, Bob." Ahab wrote this as casually as if I had forgotten to double a line.

This time, I didn't laugh. I looked at the email in something close to horror. I knew what this meant. It meant that CNN was gearing up for a major hit piece, the mother of all hit pieces, in fact. But what did they know? How did they know it? I was afraid they knew just about everything.

A little background. A producer named Scott Zamost had been shooting a documentary titled *Right on the Edge*. It focused on young citizen journalists like Jason Mattera, Hannah Giles, Lila Rose, Ryan Sorba, Christian Hartsock, and me. In the final product, Zamost described me as "the most secretive of them all." What made me "secretive" is that the others all agreed to be interviewed by CNN's attractive young on-air personality, Abbie Boudreau, but I chose not to. I hesitated because, of all the people CNN might have talked to, they focused almost exclusively on those who worked closest to the Planned Parenthood and ACORN videos. O'Keefe "does not trust CNN," Boudreau would say in the documentary. She got that right.

Boudreau had wanted to interview me in Los Angeles, where I was shooting a spoof music video about the Landrieu operation with Hartsock, a serious producer and director. I presumed her goal was to bait me into saying something that offended the CNN gods of race, gender, and/or orientation. I had experience with CNN. I had watched its spokespeople defend ACORN from day one and trash me along the way. They had continued to harass me at every opportunity since. I had no reason to expect anything but another smear, and so I turned Boudreau down. Unfortunately, it didn't end there.

Tired of the incessant media attacks, my media mentor Ben Wetmore and I schemed of ways to turn the tables on CNN. Ben, I should add, has an outlandish sense of humor. He and I would often bat around crazy ideas until they settled into some semblance of sanity. If this were a longer book, I would tell you about Ben's Minor Animal Action Group, the proud sponsor of Operation Squirrel Nuts.

Once we agreed on a plan, Ben sent me a thirteen-page outline that became known as the "CNN caper document." In it, he suggested the following script for me: Boudreau "wants to lull me into thinking she's my friend so that she can use me and hurt my career. Instead, I've decided to have a little fun. Instead of giving her a serious interview,

I'm going to punk CNN." For those who did not understand our goofy creative process, the thirteen-page public document made us look considerably sleazier than we actually were. There were suggestions in the document that would have made me cringe if I had taken them seriously, but I knew Ben's sense of humor, and he knew my limits. Unfortunately, no one else would.

For better or worse, we decided to stage a fake, over-the-top seduction scenario with Boudreau. Think the yacht scene in *Some Like It Hot.* Despite everything that would happen, I still find the humor in Ben's stage direction "Use Alicia Keys because the oeuvre of Marvin Gaye is too cliché." This may be the first time "oeuvre" and "Marvin Gaye" were used in the same sentence.

Why would I ever even consider discussing such an outrageous plan? I saw it as a form of ridicule. The idea was to send a message to the corporate media. As I would later tell CNN's media critic, Howard Kurtz:

> *The message would have been that the media is not doing the job. And they want to do documentaries on James O'Keefe and company, and they don't want to do documentaries on malfeasance in society, as evidenced by, you know, the questions you're asking me right now. . . . If the media won't take us seriously, we won't take them seriously.*

Boudreau agreed to interview me on Solomons Island. As planned, when she arrived at the property, the Project Veritas executive director, Isabel Santa, greeted her. "Izzy," as we called her, was supposed to walk Boudreau down to the boat to meet me. Instead, she nervously asked if she could get into Boudreau's car. There she warned Boudreau that she was about to be "punked." Izzy told Boudreau that I was going to greet her with strawberries and champagne and hit on her once she got on the boat, cameras rolling the whole time. I was, of course, going to tell her that I was recording her because we were in Maryland, a two-party-consent state.

Once warned, Boudreau came down to the dock but refused to board the boat. I refused to leave it. She did not get her interview. Miffed, she returned to her car and breathlessly recorded herself on a video camera relating her adventure. I was told she made that recording later on, driving around Atlanta. I can't be sure. At the time, I did not know Izzy had intervened.

I respect Izzy for warning Boudreau. She showed good judgment, better than mine, and proved willing to act on it. What I do not quite understand is why Izzy then shared with CNN the caper document and a rash of emails between me and her and other people, including CNN. She must not have understood, for instance, that my proposed intro line to the would-be video, "We got the bubble-headed-bleach-blonde who comes on at five," was straight out of a Don Henley song. She must have believed that I was actually planning to seduce Boudreau.

To get a sense of the temptation that the right faces when dealing with the mainstream media, Google "Izzy Santa courageous whistle-blower." To get a sense of how little temptation the media offer reformers on the left, Google "Anita MonCrief courageous whistle-blower." After exposing the corruption of ACORN's Project Vote from within, MonCrief caught a two-barreled blast of unreported grief. Says Mon-Crief, "I have been blacklisted by ACORN, fired from my new job for bogus reasons, and threatened daily." You would not know that listening to CNN. They had littler fish to fry.

After the CNN armada returned to port with B-roll in the can, CNN began to put its sensational story together. I was eating mani-cotti at a fine Italian restaurant in New Jersey with my parents when the messages started rolling in. Zamost, Boudreau's producer, asked me for comment. Before I could even read his message, I got a text from a publicist friend, who wanted to know how the hell they got in touch with him. The assault was coming from all directions: ground, air, and sea.

I didn't eat anything that night, and didn't sleep, either. As I tossed fitfully in bed, Breitbart, who never slept, called and asked what was going on. He had heard it had something to do with recording Boudreau on a sex boat. I assured him that it wasn't as bad as it sounded. They were reporting on plans I never intended to execute. After we got off the phone, Andrew sent an email with links to more articles about dildos, sex toys, and rape accusations. "She's a bunny with ears, James," Breitbart wrote. "She wasn't out to get you. She wanted to do a nice profile on all of you. Christian, Ryan, Lila, Jason, Hannah." I disagreed then and still do now. As with Ahab, Andrew knew his stuff, but his conclusions were not always right.

Then came the CNN hit piece, eight minutes of pure torture on CNN's *Newsroom*. It began with the kind of twisted reporting that provoked me in the first place: I was best known for my "antics" with the innocent and now-exonerated ACORN. I had deceptively edited my tape. I was arrested. I was still on probation.

Then came Boudreau relating her frightening exchange with Izzy and me. "Imagine what would have happened if she hadn't tipped you off," said the show's female anchor to Boudreau. The audience was asked to imagine the worst. CNN reported the incident as though I had planned to blindfold Boudreau, bind her, record the seduction on video, and—then what?—post the video on YouTube? I was not sure where the satire here began and ended, but the joke was clearly on me.

In its online version, CNN headlined this misadventure as "Fake pimp from ACORN videos tries to 'punk' CNN correspondent." To CNN I was not the guerrilla journalist who just brought down what AP called "the once mighty liberal activist group ACORN." I was a "fake pimp." Zamost, the article's author, felt compelled to qualify my success. In a string of half-truths masquerading as news, he alerted his readers "that prosecutors in New York and California eventually found no evidence of wrongdoing by the group, and the California probe found the videos had been heavily and selectively edited."

No evidence of wrongdoing? The press release posted by the California attorney general's office on April 1, 2010, suggested otherwise. "A few ACORN members exhibited terrible judgment and highly inappropriate behavior in videotapes obtained in the investigation," said then–attorney general Jerry Brown. "But they didn't commit prosecutable crimes in California." If Brown went a little easy on his people, it may have been because his spokesman had recently been caught secretly recording conversations with at least five reporters—that whole "glass house–throwing stones" thing.

Still, Brown knew what he saw. And even after covering for his political allies—"Sometimes a fuller truth is found on the cutting room floor"—he knew that what he saw was "highly inappropriate." Not having police powers, we were in no position to show illegal behavior. And in that our underage prostitutes were fictional, the ACORN workers could not be charged with aiding and abetting an imaginary crime. That much said, the Brown report "uncovered 'likely violations' of state law" that were "referred to the appropriate authorities."

The *New York Times* had pulled the same shell game on its readers as CNN had. In a terse statement on March 1, 2010, Brooklyn district attorney Charles Hynes said only that "no criminality has been found" in the Brooklyn ACORN office. In *Times*-speak that translated into "cleared of wrongdoing." Maybe I went to the wrong schools, but instructing a pimp to bury brothel profits in a tin can has always struck me as "wrong." For any number of reasons, all of them bad, CNN and the rest of the media had been rehabilitating ACORN right before my eyes, and I felt powerless to do anything about it.

As dependable as a rush-hour backup on the George Washington Bridge, my sometimes allies on the right queued up to denounce me.

Even Andrew took the bait. "From what I've read about this script, though not executed, it is patently gross and offensive," he said in a tone too lawyerly to have come out of his own keyboard. "It's not his detractors to whom he also owes this public airing. It's to his legion of supporters."

Andrew was being cautious. His sources in media—and he had dozens—were telling him that the failed sting was merely "the tip of the iceberg." He was acting on bad intel, but even I did not know at this point which intel was good. At this time I was still unaware who had provided CNN with the emails and documents. After twelve months of trying, the media finally got their divide-and-conquer moment. Soon after, Boudreau got promoted to ABC News. I suspect she impressed her new bosses with her ability to "take O'Keefe down."

My shirtsleeve days were over, but as chilling as these betrayals were, they did not break me. It was my probation officer, Pat Hattersley, who did that. For the first few months of our relationship, he had been largely sympathetic and hands-off. That changed with the Boudreau story. "James, what happened?" he asked me anxiously over the phone. "I got everyone up my ass—reporters, supervisors, judges. Come see me." I drove to Hattersley's office expecting the worst, and I got it.

Hattersley was all business. "You lied to me, James. You said you were not working in Maryland."

"I wasn't, Pat," I protested. "I was just meeting with a reporter." In fact, much like the New Orleans trip, the Boudreau meeting was not even the sole purpose of my trip. I gave a speech on the same trip. As I told Hattersley, I did not realize I had to disclose every single human interaction when I traveled.

"That was working," he countered angrily. "You could have at least given me a heads-up about the media story."

"Pat, I can't control what the media say about me, and I didn't know about the hit piece until the day before they ran it."

Then came the moment of truth. "James," he asked solemnly, "were there dildos on that boat? Were there? Were there dildos on your sailboat? TELL ME IF THERE WERE DILDOS ON THAT SAILBOAT!"

I wasn't quite sure what his fixation on dildos was, but I was dealing with a federal officer whose control over me, if not absolute, was pretty close. I did not know what my rights were. I did not know what fabrications CNN had up its sleeve. I did not know what "iceberg" Andrew was referring to. I had already suffered through one legal circus for a crime I didn't commit. I did not know what was and what wasn't violating the terms of my probation. With my world turned upside down, I was afraid to say anything at all that could just be used against me. And then came the bombshell.

"You are restricted from traveling outside New Jersey for a year, James. You can do your investigations. But they must be in New Jersey." New Jersey, remember, isn't exactly California. San Bernardino *County* is more than twice the size of the Garden State. I felt the knot instantly. There is something soul-killing about being confined anywhere, especially given the political nature of that confinement.

I told Mike Madigan. He believed I had made a mistake with Boudreau—I knew that—but he called Pat unprompted in any case. "We're all Catholic here," he told him. "What are you going to do—put James in limbo?" Yes, he was. Pat has a family, a summer home in Pennsylvania, a comfortable life. He was not going to let my circumstances jeopardize his.

On the darkest day of my life to that point, I found myself in a pew at St. Gabriel the Archangel Church in Saddle River, New Jersey. To get there, I drove a car that didn't even have a starter in it. I had to park on hills and pop the clutch to get it running. That's how wrong it had all gone: twenty-six years old, living at home, stuck in Jersey, mired in debt, abandoned by my allies, estranged from my friends, unable to sleep, unwilling to eat, my career in tatters, crushed by the weight of it all, and praying not for a miracle, but just some relief.

Felon! Terrorist! White supremacist! Racist! Pervert! Was this really worth it? If you work for a big news organization, you have all kinds of support systems to see you through even a major screwup, and at the end of the week you get a paycheck. I had none of that. My successes had made me more enemies than friends, and recent events had cost me my friends, not all of them, but many. Beyond my sister and my parents, I was not sure there was anyone I could count on. A year that had started badly in New Orleans had just taken a major turn for the worse, and it was still only October.

I brought to St. Gabriel's Church a book that Ben had given me days before. It was written by a former communist turned Catholic named Douglas Hyde, and titled *I Believed*. I read it intently. I focused on his struggle and tried to find glimpses of inspiration. I browsed the chapters about Hyde trying to find peace with God. I thought about the risks involved with what I did and the failure that always seemed to loom. I wondered whether the results justified the grief.

As I pondered these things, I read about Hyde sitting in a pew like mine, years ago, watching a young girl pray the Rosary. As she prayed, he could see in her very face the trouble pass and the weight of the world lift off her shoulders. As a recovering communist and atheist, he wondered what strange power had brought him there, but he understood right then where real solace lay. He knelt down and looked up, but he did not know how to pray. Searching, he suddenly found himself humming a 1920s dance song: "O sweet and lovely lady, be good, O lady be good to me."

I knew that I too had to surrender to God. If I did so, I could withstand the powerful forces aligned, fairly or not, against the citizen journalist. In my possession I had a series of tapes showcasing corruption at the New Jersey Education Association, a teachers' union. I asked myself whether I could justify taking the risks anymore, whether I could endure the lies of my enemies and the defamation of the machine. But

I knew then that as long as I had my family and my faith in God, I was going to be okay. I immediately felt renewed. It was out of my hands now.

I was going to expose the New Jersey teachers' union, and I was going to survive. My media colleagues did not think it was a worthwhile project. I thought otherwise. Soon enough, so would Governor Chris Christie. The thing about getting into hot water, Chesterton once wrote, was that "it keeps you clean."

TEACHERS GONE WILD

Veritas Rule #17:
Never let your guard down.
You are always behind enemy lines.

I had seen a lot in my short life, but what happened on this gray October day stunned even me. After refusing an interview with me in the parking lot of her condo complex, teacher Alissa Ploshnick got in her blue Toyota, pulled up right behind me, and tailed me all the way to Interstate 80. When I got on the interstate heading east, so did she. I sped up and so did she. She stayed right on my ass for miles, flashing her high beams. Occasionally, she would pull up alongside me, wave her stubby middle finger at me, or rage away on her cell phone.

I pulled my video camera out, held it over my shoulder, and shot behind me as best I could, but I had violated one of the Veritas rules—*Don't work alone. Tell someone your plans.* And I was paying for it.

When I veered abruptly off at an exit, so did she. There I was driving through suburban neighborhoods with a crazed member of the New Jersey teachers' union in hot pursuit. I stopped for a stop sign. She stopped behind me, honking and screaming. I swerved through neighborhoods as kids playing basketball stopped and stared. I jumped back on I-80. So did she. Now I was getting a little nervous. I could see she was on her cell phone screaming and gesturing again, probably talking to union bosses, because my dad was getting strange phone calls at home from some of them. This was New Jersey. Things happen here. Ask Jimmy Hoffa.

I had called ahead to meet my father at the Fireplace, something of a landmark restaurant in Paramus. At this stage in my career, I had few people I could depend on other than my family. Even Andrew had gone cold. I was operating at my own risk, with only God and my video camera as witness. I had to find a way to lose this heat, fast. We were coming up on a sharp exit onto McLean Boulevard in Paterson. Ploshnick was pulling up beside me, gesturing for me to stop the car. I quickly swerved onto the exit ramp, very nearly fishtailing in the process, and lost my car amid the traffic on Route 20 along the Passaic River. Ploshnick couldn't stop. She zoomed past the exit ramp and continued on.

This all started back in late summer 2010, when some two thousand local and state leaders of the New Jersey Education Association (NJEA) met for their annual leadership conference at the swank East Brunswick Hilton. The conference wasn't about students, and it wasn't really about education. It was about making sure that teachers could continue to get theirs even as the state was going broke. By the way, the *starting* salary for a teacher in New Jersey is roughly $55,000, about $10,000 higher than the *median* salary of an average New Jersey worker, and the worker wasn't getting three months off each summer and two weeks off each Christmas. This was a gig worth fighting for. The teacher following me was making nearly $100,000 a year.

"When schoolchildren start paying union dues, that's when I'll start representing the interests of schoolchildren," reportedly said union honcho Albert Shanker some years back. There was no doubt about whose interests were being represented at this conference. Its theme was as bel-

ligerent and self-interested as Shanker's at his peak: "In Enemy Territory—Defending Your Rights in a Hostile Political Climate."

I was able to get a crew together to scout the location and plan our
own sortie into "enemy territory." The teachers' point of vulnerability
was the hotel bar. Union people like to drink. As some old Roman once
said, *In vino veritas*. The teachers supplied the vino, and we supplied the
Veritas. Our crew came with hidden cameras and mikes and cast a wide
net. All in all, the teachers seemed to be having a good time. "That is
why we were laughing here," one young teacher joked. "We are playing
video games on [the taxpayers'] dime." Then, as if to address those taxpayers, she shouted, "Screw you!"

The Project Veritas crew was also treated to some sing-alongs. "Let's
have a whiskey and get a little misty. Join me now and slander Chris
Christie!" sang a well-watered chorus of teachers. They followed that with
"Read, write, and arithmetic. Here comes Christie with a whipping stick!"
After a verse that I could not quite make out, they continued, "What are
we gonna do? Kick him in the tool box!" That I could figure out.

One teacher who proved particularly forthcoming was the villain in
the car chase, the unfortunately named Alissa Ploshnick, a thirty-eight-
year-old special educator in the Passaic City Schools system. If you have
watched HBO's *The Sopranos,* Ploshnick might remind you of Tony's
sister Janice, a little hefty, a little unkempt, but still in the game.

"It's really hard to fire a tenured teacher," Ploshnick told the young
man with whom she was flirting. "It's really hard—like you seriously
have to be in the hallway fucking somebody." Ploshnick then told her
new friend about a case in her own school system in which a teacher
yelled "you nigger"—her words—at a student. That person, she continued, "is still teaching." Ploshnick would come to regret sharing this
little insight.

Shaughn Adeleye was our man for this job. Shaughn's best moment
was yet to come, but he rendered an essential service in the teachers'

union project. He called Lawrence Everett, assistant superintendent of Passaic City Schools, pretending to be the father of a boy whose teacher had called him the "n-word." In his response, Everett was pretty straightforward. Yes, using racial slurs was "definitely unacceptable," but no, the teacher who used them was unlikely to be removed from the class. "We can't just walk in and fire a tenured teacher," said Everett. The best solution Everett could suggest was to transfer the student to another class, but even that hinged on there being room available in the other classroom. The district, after all, had "contract stipulations" to consider.

To make my teachers video work, I knew I had to talk to Ploshnick, and I knew that would not be easy. The message may have gotten to her that she had said one word too many at the union gathering. To initiate contact, I went to the high school where Ploshnick taught, found a photo of her posted on a bulletin board, took it with me, and taped it to my steering wheel.

My friend Ryan agreed to keep me company on a stakeout of her condo development. Ploshnick was proving elusive. We had waited for hours when finally Ryan broke down and sneaked off to the bushes to pee. No sooner did he let loose than some older woman spotted him from a window and started screaming. Ryan ran back to the car, and we hightailed it out of there. The last thing I needed was an indecent exposure rap. I came back alone a couple of days later, a Sunday, October 24, and my patience paid off. I caught Ploshnick walking to her car. I approached her, mike in hand, a journalist on a mission but without a home or a salary.

"Are you Alissa Ploshnick?" I asked. "What do you have to say about students being called the n-word in your district?" I wish I could tell you that this kind of confrontation came naturally to me, but it did not. The lack of a "CNN" or "NBC" on the mike made the act all that much harder. As always, I had to will myself to do it. Ploshnick looked stunned, but she said nothing. She held a newspaper in front of her face, climbed into the car, and within minutes began her wild chase down the interstate. Fortunately, I caught stretches of it on video.

With the Ploshnick footage in hand, I would be able to finish my two-part "Teachers Gone Wild" video that night and have it ready for posting the next morning. After New Orleans and the CNN debacle, however, no one wanted to post it and promote it, not even Andrew. I was a media orphan, with no home other than YouTube. And then, while still at dinner, I got a call that seemed seriously providential. I walked away from the table and picked up. It was Vince Coglianese, senior editor for the *Daily Caller*. He wanted to run with the story. Thank you, God. I was on my way back.

The story hit on Monday, October 25. I called part 1 "Teachers Gone Wild" and edited it with the same flashy graphics and dumb pizzazz as the "Girls Gone Wild" video series:

Uncensored

Unprincipled

Unhinged

You get the picture. Part 2, which I released that same day, was a lot more sober. It included Shaughn's discussion with Assistant Superintendent Everett and my confrontation with Ploshnick. Together, they stirred up, if you'll excuse my Irish, one major shite-storm in New Jersey.

True to form, the NJEA aimed right for my tool box. In an article posted the day after the video's release, October 26, NJEA spokesman Steve Baker tried to convince the readers of NJ.com, the *Star-Ledger's* online presence, that there was nothing to see here, just keep on moving. Baker conceded that I had sent people to the conference but he left the impression that I dubbed the audio after the fact, using actors and not real teachers. In short, I was "completely and utterly discredited."

The article made no reference at all to Ploshnick or her unhappy choice of words. It focused instead on my crimes and misdemeanors, real and imagined, and gave Baker the final say. After telling the reporter that NJEA was not planning to take any action against me, Baker said, "He's not really worth the effort. This is not somebody that's going to get a lot of our time or attention." Like so many of our subjects, he forgot that content is king.

On October 26, I released a new NJEA video. I had acquired an audiotape of Wayne Dibofsky, the associate director of the association, talking casually about the voter fraud that took place inside the union's Jersey City office in a tightly contested 1997 mayoral race. On the tape, Dibofsky claimed that he called the city clerk's office after two voting machines were dropped off at the union office and was told to "leave well enough alone." Said Dibofsky, "I knew enough to be quiet." This being New Jersey, where everyone has a vote fraud story, this video got little traction. Unlike with Ploshnick, I was unable to get Dibofsky to comment about this offense on the record.

I had spent a week in a Hudson County library corroborating Dibofsky's comments, reviewing old election races from 1997, looking at ward maps in the archives until even the librarians starting asking questions. "What's to investigate?" one woman said to me sharply. "I've been a member of the NJEA for years." She then turned to a colleague and yelled, "Hey, Jacob, this young man wants to make copies, but I don't know why he wants to do it." First a teacher chasing me, now a librarian challenging me about making copies. This prompted a new Veritas rule: *Remember, you are always behind enemy lines.*

I did any number of interviews for New Jersey media on that transformative day, October 26, most of them taped. The one I did live was most memorable. To record it, I went to the My9 TV studio in Secaucus. Through the magic of an interruptible feedback loop, or IFB for short, I was able to speak with Jeff Cole, an investigative reporter for Fox 29 News in Philadelphia. I was hearing Cole through an earpiece and talking directly into a camera. It is the hardest kind of interview to do.

Cole looks like the kind of guy who would play a TV anchor in the movies: white, square-jawed, middle-aged. Think Jeff Daniels in *Newsroom* or Will Ferrell in *Anchorman*. As I suspected, Cole couldn't have cared less about the NJEA. It was me he wanted to skewer, and he started where I thought he would:

JC: First question I have for you. Give us some context here, James. Who funds you and who made the choice for you to go and do this piece on the education association? First the funding, if you would.

I had to be the tool of someone, didn't I? I had heard this line before and would hear it over and over again.

JO: We have a 501(c)3 nonprofit organization called the Project Veritas, theprojectveritas.com. And we are equipping citizen journalists to go out there into the states, in New Jersey, and investigate.

JC: I know what a 501(c)3 is, friend. Who puts the money in the 501(c)3s? Who are your contributors?

JO: Public donations, solicitations . . .

JC: Could you name one for us, could you name your biggest contributor for us?

JO: A one-hundred-dollar contribution from a grandmother down the street. We get funded by people sending money to us on the Internet.

At the time, in fact, I was getting contributions from almost nowhere. Hell, I had to borrow my sister's old Mercury Marquis to stake out Ploshnick, but that I kept to myself. Cole and others seemed to think I was much more powerful than I actually was. I was adopting another Alinsky rule: *"Power is not only what you have, but what the enemy thinks you have."* Cole would not let up, and he kept getting angrier and angrier.

> **JC:** I got it. I got it. I got it. Let me ask you something, first. . . . These actors, these citizen journalists that you send in, did you pay these folks to go in and do this? Did you pay folks for the union investigation that you did?

> **JO:** Sir, are you paid?

This question really set him off—"don't go there!" If Cole were a cartoon character, smoke would have been coming out of his ears. I still do not understand why the reporters at Fox 29 should get paid but ours should not.

> **JC:** Did you pay these people to go into this investigation—don't go there! Answer the question. Did you pay these people to go in and do this?

> **JO:** No, these were citizen journalists. These were volunteers, who volunteered their time to investigate an organization that, frankly, the establishment media is refusing to investigate.

> **JC:** That is absolutely false.

Cole then repeated the NJEA claim that we had manipulated the audio. "Of course they are going to say that," I replied, "because there is no way they can defend calling a black student the n-word and talking about having sex with people in the hallways of the schools." Getting nowhere, Cole complained that he was losing his IFB feed and cut the interview off. Bull. After the abrupt ending, I said to the producer about the whole deranged interview, "Sir, I can't believe that just happened."

In the way of occupational hazards, Cole himself had been hit with racism charges two years earlier. His Fox 29 video crew had been secretly following and recording Philadelphia city councilman W. Wilson Goode Jr.'s attractive young legislative aide. Apparently, the crew found her in some compromising places when her time sheet said she was at work. Cole reported on this aggressively. In response, the aide pulled the race card on him. Sitting at a public meeting, she held up one sign saying FOX 29 IS RACIST, and another that said KKK, all of which was caught on video.

Cole cornered Goode after this incident at City Hall. "Don't you ever disrespect a black woman like that again," Goode told him, wagging a finger in his face. Cole asked reasonably, "What is racist about me asking you about your publicly paid employee?" Cole reported on the race angle himself. The station's black anchors were supportive. So were the rest of the local media. Cole was one of their own. "Fox 29 reporter Jeff Cole isn't a racist (despite what a City Council staffer says)," read the subhead of an article in the magazine *Philadelphia*. "He's just obsessed with busting liars, cheats and bad guys."

To his humble credit, Cole did not accuse me of racism. Others in the media did. One even dragged up the Rutgers dorm incident as though that had something to do with the NJEA. These well-paid shills felt the need to subvert my work, and there were two good reasons why. One, as outsiders, amateurs even, we made them look bad. We were breaking stories they were not. Worse, we were breaking stories about their allies—the liars, cheats, and bad guys they routinely protect. Wilson Goode was easy. He carried no political weight. He was just one more uninspired pol in a city of uninspired pols. The NJEA was a different matter. Its mother ship, the National Education Association, was arguably the single most powerful force in the Democratic galaxy.

By this time, though, I had attracted at least one powerful ally of my own, the governor, Chris Christie. Earlier that same day, he had been asked about the video at a town hall meeting in South Brunswick. "Nothing on it surprises me," he said angrily. "If you need an example of what I've been talking about for the last nine months—about how the teachers' union leadership is out of touch with the people and out of control—go watch this video. It's enlightening, it's enraging."

I immediately dashed off a note to Pat Hattersley, my probation officer. He had allowed me to do my job only in Jersey, and now I was master of that domain: the governor of New Jersey had my back. "Do you see the value of what we do?" He did not respond. I still could not leave the state. I may have been the first guy in New Jersey history to get a commendation from the governor while living in his parents' basement and serving federal probation. "I don't like supervising you any more than you like being supervised," Hattersley would tell me. He may not have been keen on his job, but I was keen on mine. I'm a journalist. I had work to do.

Gov. Christie Shouldn't Cozy Up to Muckraker of "Teachers Union Gone Wild," read the headline of a *Star-Ledger* editorial three days later. This was self-parody at its purest. The *Ledger*'s editorial board zoomed past issues like tenure abuse, admission of voter fraud, public intoxication, indifference to taxpayer dollars, and the casual use of the n-word, and zeroed in on the state's real problem, me. After reciting my past misdeeds—now compulsory for my media critics—the editorialists warned the governor, "Yes, politics makes strange bedfellows, but Christie should check for fleas." Didn't they mean "bedbugs"? Someone should have been fired here just for cliché abuse.

The same day Christie weighed in—no pun intended—I reconnected with another powerful ally. He called while I was still at the studio. "I just saw the Jeff Cole interview," said Andrew Breitbart. "You smoked him. Totally cool." Andrew told me even Vlasto was impressed by how I handled Cole.

Reporters were asking Christie what he thought of the video. Breitbart was first to transcribe the governor's comments and post them:

> *This is another exhibit as to what I've been talking about. The arrogance, the greed, the self-interest, the lack of introspection, the lack of standards. And it hurts the great teachers just as much as it hurts the kids. I think that this video makes the distinction better than I ever could.*

Even more important than allies, though, I had content. Remember Veritas Rule #1: *Without strong content, nothing else matters.* Content is king. It empowered me. As I was leaving, Sharon Crowley, a reporter for My9, approached. She wondered if I could do a quick interview. Sure. She got right in my face. "A lot of people say you don't have any credibility," she said. "Who's behind you?"

"Sharon, the American people are behind me," I answered. I had had enough, and I was feeling the power. After all the crap these people had thrown at me, I dumped some share of it back on Crowley. She immediately turned the camera off and retreated back inside My9. I had given her a taste of Alinsky—*"Go outside the experience of an opponent, cause confusion, fear, and retreat."* Retreat she did. Channeling Breitbart, I yelled back at her: "You, Sharon, are just a branch of the establishment. You defend unions. You curse the citizen journalist. You ought to be ashamed of how you treat the people you're supposed to be representing." It won't surprise the reader to learn that this interview never aired.

Speaking of Alinsky, I understood something about my content that the media kept missing. The early articles focused on the jibes at Governor Christie or teachers "cursing, discussing voter fraud and laughing about how hard it is to fire tenured teachers." Almost none of them mentioned Ploshnick's unfortunate use of the word *nigger,* a word she used in its raw, unvarnished state. Taking Alinsky's advice, we were about to make the enemy live up to its own book of rules.

Over the use of this one word, even though she was merely quoting its use, Alissa Ploshnick's head was on the chopping block. This made little sense. Everyone was pulling for her: the media, the NJEA, her colleagues. The governor was indifferent to her fate. So were conservatives. No African-American organizations were protesting—the NJEA was their ally.

So why then did Passaic schools superintendent Robert Holster feel compelled to punish her? According to the *Star-Ledger,* he "took particular offense to the racial epithet." He had to. In his world, once the incident became public, taking offense was mandatory. Of course, some black rappers and comedians can't even say grace without using the n-word, but Ploshnick wasn't black.

On November 10, 2012, Holster came down with his verdict. He admitted he could have been harsher, but in the blame-free precincts of the NJEA, a nine-day suspension and a void on the next pay raise had the ring of capital punishment.

"Passaic is multicultural and everyone has to be extremely sensitive in their thinking if they're on our payroll," said Holster. Ploshnick was on that payroll to the tune of the "high 90s," good work for a nine-month position in a down economy. No wonder she was so pro-tenure. As she told Project Veritas, "Once you get that third year, it's like, 'Schwing!'" Although Ploshnick took the fall, the media refused to blame her. Forget about the drunken racial slurs, the crude language, the cynical praise for a corrupt tenure system, the reckless ninety-mile-an-hour chase down I-80. She could play the victim because they had me to play victimizer.

"I felt like I was raped," Ploshnick told the *Star-Ledger*'s Bob Braun. By extension, I, a "pretend journalist and admitted criminal," was the rapist. My accomplice, according to Braun, was "a 'nice' young man who bought her drinks." In reality, none of our guys bought anyone drinks, but this falsehood, which was picked up widely, made Ploshnick seem all the more a victim. Consider the headline of an *Atlanta Journal-Constitution* article the following day: JAMES O'KEEFE'S LATEST VICTIM: A SPECIAL ED TEACHER. Ploshnick's ultimate victimizer, of course, was Governor Christie. His role in the metaphorical gang rape was to praise my video.

Eighteen paragraphs deep into his weepy article, Braun shifted gears and cited the actual reason why this "heroic N.J. teacher" was punished. He called it by its name, "political correctness," a phrase that sounds benign until you have been whiplashed by it. "That is, after all, why she was suspended by the Passaic superintendent," he wrote. Exactly. Union corruption is no big deal in New Jersey. Ditto for tenure abuse, vote fraud, and the waste of taxpayer dollars, but say the n-word, if only indirectly, and you can kill your career. Even a pretend journalist can figure out those rules.

The NJEA got the message. One of its representatives sent out a blast email shortly afterward about the upcoming annual teachers' convention. "NJEA is concerned about the security for our members at this event," wrote Jan Witmer. "We are advising all members to be cautious when speaking with strangers at the convention and when out and about the town. Please watch what you say and who you speak with no matter where you are." We were apparently getting a little more of their time and attention than Steven Baker had promised.

Witmer also attached a document identifying some of those allegedly involved with the videos. "We can only protect ourselves if we know who these 'journalists' are. But beware, they may also have others working with them to catch unsuspecting member in conversation." Well, at least this union boss got one thing right. We weren't out to rape people, just catch them in conversation. The attachment was hilarious. It was a picture of me, Shaughn, and producer Christian Hartsock from years before. None of us had gone undercover in New Jersey. I was beginning to see that I would have to train others to do what the U.S. government no longer allowed me to do, and that wasn't such a bad idea.

GUERRILLAS IN THEIR MIDST

Veritas Rule #18:
Obsess over getting your subject in frame.

On February 22, 2011, a stretch limousine pulled up in front of the National Public Radio offices in the heart of Washington, D.C. Two NPR executives, Senior Vice President Ron Schiller and Betsy Liley, director of institutional giving, climbed in and headed off, as arranged, to an upscale Georgetown restaurant called Café Milano. There they were to meet two representatives from the Muslim Education Action Center (MEAC) Trust, Ibrahim Kasaam and Amir Malik, who had already arrived in their own stretch limo.

Of course, there was no MEAC, and Ibrahim and Amir were not really Ibrahim and Amir. They were, respectively, our Nigerian-American friend, Shaughn Adeleye, and "Simon Templar," a literary pseudonym adopted by one of the undercover reporters whom I met on Facebook. We had been working on this score for months. There were a lot of wrinkles, and we were ironing them out through instant messaging:

ST: James, I checked with the NPR main office, and they require ID to enter the building for the development office.

JO: Close to the day we want to meet with him, but at a nearby posh hotel. We get him a limo and pick him up at NPR headquarters and bring him to a hotel.

ST: I just got an email back. . . . Ron Schiller might be able to do the 22nd.

JO: You can't go into that building. Fake IDs are too dangerous, and he needs to be taken out of his official corporate zone.

ST: Lunch is good though. We can book it at a really ridiculous place, provided [you are] willing to spring for this. . . . Is there any kind of max budget for this? Lunch will run at least 300. Not sure what the limo would be.

JO: That will be fine.

What I didn't tell Simon Templar was that the cost of all this would *not* be fine. I was fronting the equipment, flights, limo, and meals on my credit card. This was a seven-thousand-dollar gamble, my riskiest and most elaborate to date. Thanks to New Orleans, I'd have to do it by proxy.

ST: It'd be a huge power move if we just tell them we'd like to send our limousine to pick them up. I think lunch is the way to go. Only way to get him out of the office.

JO: Maybe that place in Georgetown, what's it called? Milano? You'll have a limo and five million dollars. They will dance for you.

ST: It might be good to give them money as well. . . .

JO: I am uncomfortable actually wiring them money.

ST: Why?

JO: Because we are there only to get stuff on conversation. That's always been our only purpose.

ST: The scandal though would be these guys accepting Muslim Brotherhood money.

JO: Just trust me on this. I walked into a building and was accused of wiretapping. You cannot give them an inch. High risk, low reward.

ST: I can't imagine what they would try to suggest we're doing—conspiracy to finance NPR?

JO: The scandal will be in NPR's comments. Just trust me on this.

ST: That sounds like bullshit to me, but okay.

JO: Upon further reflection you will agree with me.

I typed those words hoping and praying Simon would follow my lead, but nothing was forcing him to. It wouldn't be the first time I almost lost my temper with Simon, but I was at his mercy. Even though I barely knew him, we were a team. We needed each other. People think you need talent to do what we do. No, what you really need is the will to act and the resolve to follow through. Willpower and courage—these are the most important qualities in recruits. Simon had both.

This was the first major investigation that I had to improvise by proxy, and I needed someone brazen enough to do the things I could not do myself. Taking a lesson from Douglas Hyde on the way communists organize, I recruited from outside the existing power structures. In this case, that meant from beyond the Beltway. After finding someone with the will and the resolve, the rest was just conversation.

Actually, many, many conversations. Simon, Shaughn, and I talked constantly. While we did initially meet in New Jersey, most of our interaction was through instant messaging. We discussed, debated, cajoled, compromised, and planned every conceivable aspect of the sting. Shaughn wanted to focus on NPR's controversial firing of Juan Williams. Simon wanted to focus on the Muslim Brotherhood. As to myself, I wanted to investigate the media directly. It was difficult trying to share my insights and experience through a computer screen. Sometimes I found myself pounding the keys as I typed and pleading for consensus, but in an operation without hierarchies, I could only persuade, not demand.

Our media critics would later squeeze as much negative juju as they could about disputes between the guys and me, but citizen journalists are by nature headstrong, independent people. I cannot hold them with promises of a big salary, a New York office, or a network golf shirt they can wear to their next high school reunion. If Ken and Shaughn's tactics varied from mine, they felt free to go their own way, much as I felt free to come and go with Breitbart.

The sting took three months to pull together, and the guys put their all into it. Simon grew out a beard, dyed his hair, and started tanning. My "all" was limited to my guidance and my credit card. But, as Alinsky said, "Tactics means doing what you can with what you have." Simon did not always understand.

JO: Your camera will arrive. I sent you a bag camera.

ST: You've got to be kidding me.

JO: I've run out of tie cameras.

ST: A bag?

JO: A purse/bag camera. But it's androgynous. You'll have to make due. It's black and normal looking.

ST: There's no such thing as an androgynous purse/bag.

JO: I didn't want to buy another tie camera.

ST: Yeah but how did I end up with the bag. . . . I mean out of all the people you work with. . . . I'll just assume your reasoning was that I was the only one masculine enough to pull it off.

That was a battle I let Simon win. I bought another tie camera to go with the bag camera. He had an incredible attention to detail, almost obsessively so, and I had to respect that. Simon brought that same intensity to our collective creation of a website for "MEAC of America," the apocryphal Muslim Brotherhood front group with the mission of "spreading the acceptance of Sharia across the world." Ben Wetmore assisted us in helping write the prose for the site, which contained all manner of progressive catnip for the media:

> *Bigotry arises from misinformation. . . . The influence of corporate media cannot be discounted either and is of increasing interest to MEAC. . . . Corrupt entities such as Roger Ailes' Fox News have demonstrated the need for an increased focus in the responsibility in journalism and reliable sources of news.*

Better still, the website had the kind of three-step postmodern action plan that would make the apparatchiks at PBS swoon:

- INFORM
- INVOLVE
- INCLUDE

A stickler for comic detail, Ben had written in the "curriculum" portion a run-on sentence rich in malapropisms to show that English was not exactly our first language:

> *Quran History Islam in America Religious history, religious truth Islamic Discrimination through the ages Historical oppression of followers of Allah Women and Feminism in Islamic countries Islamic Biology, Genital and/or bodies modification. (greater detail on our curriculums offering coming soon)*

The website proved so perfectly outrageous that a month before the sting it evoked the wrath of Pam Geller, one of the nation's leading voices against Islamic extremism. MEAC's mission to promote sharia law apparently troubled Geller a whole lot more than it would Ron Schiller. We also created a series of fake associates with email addresses coming from the server meactrust.org. These associates began to reach out to PBS and NPR officials seeking a meeting, ideally with the top brass. Although the luncheon with the NPR execs would get all the subsequent attention, we had, in fact, set up a lunch meeting at Café Milano with PBS's senior vice president for development, Brian Reddington, the day before.

Of the two, PBS's Reddington proved to be the tougher nut to crack all around. Still, in his Café Milano luncheon with Ibrahim and Amir, Reddington shared an animus against Christianity with such conviction that I had to believe it was both real and readily accepted at PBS.

As Reddington interpreted the world, Christians "have done far worse" than what Muslims have been accused of. He did not seem to be referring here to some distant past, either. As he told our fake Muslims, "I've seen the crimes committed in the name of the Christian religion that I don't support at all." On more than one occasion he attributed his insight to the fact that he "was raised as a Christian." As such, he could see that there were many elements of Christianity that "frankly are really strange and intellectually don't make sense."

Given this perspective, little about Islam or sharia law particularly troubled Reddington. When Ibrahim lamented that critics interpreted MEAC's promotion of sharia law to mean "we want to take over the world," Reddington came to his defense: "Anyone can take anything anyone says and twist it because they have their own agenda." Fox News, of course, was one of those entities that did the twisting. Sensing an opening, Amir asked if Fox News' claim to be "fair and balanced" was true. Reddington freely answered, "No, not at all." He compared Fox unfavorably to PBS, where programmers "really, really try to be unbiased and be not liberal, or not conservative—not anything but fair." Reddington seemed bewildered that anyone would think otherwise.

From the beginning, NPR was the easier score. One of our fake associates, "Raja Zogbi," engaged in a series of emails with Beckie Cairns, executive coordinator for development at NPR, seeking a meeting on behalf of his superior, "Mr. Kasaam," a member of MEAC's board of trustees. Cairns could not have been more helpful. When she suggested a meeting at NPR's offices, Raja countered with a better deal. "If Mr. Schiller is pressed for time," wrote Raja, "we can arrange to have Mr. Kasaam's limousine pick him up and return him and I can make reservations for a quick lunch." We figured that lunch at a high-end restaurant had more show-off potential, especially if we could escort the NPR execs there in style. The NPR execs had no objection:

> Hi Raja,
>
> Thank you for setting this up. Café Milano is a delicious
> choice. Please have the car pick up Ron and Betsy at the

front entrance to our main headquarters, 635 Massachu-setts Ave., NW at 12:15pm.

Beckie

Given that Simon was in his twenties, we needed to create a scenario that made sense of his age. As much fun as this was to conceive, we knew we risked undoing what we had established.

Dear Ms. Cairns,

> *Unfortunately due to recent events, Mr. Kasaam will have to extend his trip to the Middle East through the weekend. Mr. Kasaam regrets his absence as he was especially looking forward to establishing a relationship with NPR. Fortunately I have arranged for his son, Ibrahim, to travel to DC as he has agreed to handle his father's MEAC appointments for the beginning of the week. He will be joined by Amir Malik. Both are trustees, and I will ensure that they are properly briefed. The arrangements for lunch at Cafe Milano are unchanged as are the arrangements for transportation. Please send Mr. Kasaam's sincerest regrets to Mr. Schiller and Ms. Liley.*

Regards,

Raja

If nothing else, the PBS luncheon proved to be useful as a training exercise for both Simon and Shaughn. After reviewing the video, I suggested some refinements in approach.

JO: You almost had him agree with you when you told him that Jews control the media. All you had to do was stop talking and let him talk. Make sure he's allowed to talk after your catalytic moments.

ST: Shaughn and I talked about tweaking some things for tomorrow.

Tweak they did. That next day, I was on the phone with them until the moment the NPR execs walked into Café Milano. "They're here, got to go," said Simon. I sat by the phone anxiously waiting for news—for an hour, two hours. Finally, they called. Success! Simon and Shaughn were at least ten times as excited as they had been after the PBS lunch. When I listened to the recording, I understood why.

The lunch had indeed gone swimmingly. Schiller and Liley left with big grins, confident of their score. "Pretty unbelievable meeting," Schiller was overheard saying as he got back in the limo. "If they're for real, we can make this happen." In fact, the next day Beckie Cairns was already hooking us up for a potential meeting with Vivian Schiller, then CEO of NPR.

The stretch limo obviously helped. Through a botch in the planning, however, we ordered two of them. To make the best of the second one, we used it to take Simon and Shaughn, still in their Muslim garb, to the Anacostia section of D.C. for a Medicaid sting. Anacostia is not your best neighborhood, not by a long shot. Drive through in a stretch limo with a camera sticking out the window, and you get people's attention. Inside, the guys did a skit claiming their desperate need for Medicaid before heading back out to their stretch limo. Simon says they attracted some seriously bizarre looks. I don't doubt it for a minute.

Ken, Shaughn, and I had a difference of opinion on what to do next with the NPR footage. They wanted to nurse the concept, to milk it in other contexts, to make a larger statement about the infiltration of the Muslim Brotherhood. As much as I respected their opinion, there was a central reality I had to contend with. I had financed those limos on my credit card. To maintain any kind of organization and income flow, I needed successes. As Alinsky reminded us, "Tactics means doing what you can with what you have."

When, however, Simon went to his computer to upload the footage, we realized that not everything had gone as planned. "Ohhh," wrote Simon. "Shaughn may have a problem with his video. We're not sure why, but Shaughn's video is completely blurred."

I hated the tie cameras for a reason. The satin fabric often shifted over the lens. If the subject said something rash but did so out of frame, the impact was lost. "Yep," confirmed Simon. "Shaughn didn't get any video. This is unbelievable. Schiller's facial expressions were priceless." Simon turned next to the bag camera, but he was not optimistic. That camera had been centered on Liley. Ten anxious minutes passed as we waited for the bag footage to upload. Then this: "The waiter actually bumped the bag camera OFF of Betsey Liley ONTO Ron Schiller. Previously it was picking up only Liley."

This was truly remarkable, maybe even divine. Still, I had my production work cut out for me. I had to sync more than two hours of footage from three recording devices—one just audio—find the relevant parts, and add subtitles to make comprehension easier. It took me four days just to go through and sync. The results were worth it.

What the world saw were two Islamic gentlemen expressing their interest in giving some $5 million to NPR, partly to offset the threat of Republican defunding. The NPR execs were all ears. They resented the federal government for the $90 million they had to beg from it each year. Yet, as Schiller conceded, without that money, "We would have a lot of stations go dark."

Ibrahim (Simon) would have hated to see that happen. He was particularly interested in keeping NPR on air for one specific reason. Although "the Jews do kind of control the media," he said, they had less influence at NPR than they did elsewhere. He even joked—to laughter all around—that, among his crowd, NPR stood for "National Palestinian Radio." Responded Liley, "Oh, really! That's good. I like that."

When Schiller suggested that the Republican Party had been "hijacked," Amir (Shaughn) had a good idea who did the jacking, namely, "the radical, racist, Islamophobic, Tea Party people." The Tea Party people were not "just Islamophobic," interjected Schiller, "but really xenophobic." He called them "scary" and "seriously racist." He said this so casually you could imagine him saying it unchallenged around the NPR water cooler.

The fact that Schiller had not a clue about what the Tea Party stood for did not stop him from sounding off. "The Tea Party is fanatically involved in people's personal lives and very fundamental Christian," Schiller added solemnly. "I wouldn't even call it Christian. It's this weird evangelical kind of move." This was nuts. I have spoken to any number of Tea Party groups, and I can assure you, they are not the ones banning smoking, demanding free contraceptives, or regulating soda intake. The sign you see at just about every Tea Party rally kind of sums up the movement: DON'T TREAD ON ME.

What Schiller said next was heartfelt. From my own experience, I can tell you that the great majority of people taking up space in America's newsrooms share his opinion. What disappointed him most about America, he explained, was that "the educated, so-called elite in this country is too small a percentage of the population." As a result, a "very large uneducated part of the population" controls America's destiny.

By the "elite," of course, Schiller meant the people who staff NPR, the other friendly media outlets, and the universities. The "ideas" that the "uneducated" could not quite grasp included the notion that the Muslim Brotherhood was a force for good in the world. To show she was down with her Muslim brothers, Liley compared America's treatment of Muslims to its treatment of Japanese-Americans during World War II, a mainstay in the media self-flagellation arsenal.

At lunch, Ibrahim openly endorsed MEAC's mission to spread sharia law. "We must combat intolerance," he said, "to spread acceptance of sharia across the world." Schiller did not blink. The fact that sharia law advocates openly endorse the death penalty for homosexuality seemed to trouble no one at lunch. What did trouble Schiller were the sentiments of his former colleague Juan Williams, who had been dropped by NPR for sharing his anxiety about flying with people dressed in Muslim garb. Said Schiller, "What NPR did, I am very proud of."

"Now, I'll talk personally, as opposed to wearing my NPR hat," Schiller said, digging his hole deeper still. "It feels to me as though there is a real, anti-intellectual move on the part of a significant part of the Republican Party. In my personal opinion, liberals today might be more educated, fair, and balanced than conservatives."

In my favorite line of the day, Ibrahim answered, "I like it when you take off your NPR hat."

THE EMPIRE STRIKES BACK *AGAIN*

Veritas Rule #19:
*When the content is strong enough,
the publicity will take care of itself.*

I did not underestimate the potential of the NPR sting. The *Daily Caller* helped us roll out the finished eleven-minute video on March 8, 2011. To its credit, NPR responded that same day, accurately for the most part, and appropriately. It quoted at length several of Schiller's comments, linked to our unedited two-hour video, and concluded, through a spokesperson, "We are appalled by the comments made by Ron Schiller in the video, which are contrary to what NPR stands for."

A day later, the NPR board forced out CEO Vivian Schiller, no relation to Ron. If he had not already accepted a job elsewhere, Ron Schiller would, I assume, have been booted as well. Our video was one screwup too many for Vivian. The first was her mishandling of the Juan Williams termination six months earlier. So far so good. I knew it would not last.

Unlike other video news producers, Project Veritas posts the unedited video online. This inevitably leads to headlines like the one from *Time,* "Hatchet Job: The Video Hit Piece that Made Both NPR and Its

Critics Look Bad." The article author, James Poniewozik, made the case that, yes, "Schiller did say some bad things," but "the short video took them out of context."

Of course, Poniewozik could make this case only because we put the entire conversation online. He was sophisticated enough to know that when you whittle two hours down to eleven minutes, more will be cut than kept. But he was partisan enough to point out misleading nonsense like the video "left examples of [Schiller's] complimenting Republicans on the cutting-room floor."

Here, Poniewozik missed the point, likely on purpose. As was evident in our short video, Schiller was not targeting all Republicans, just the Tea Party conservatives who were driving the Republican agenda. I am convinced that the unnamed Obama-friendly Republicans to whom Schiller alluded were a rhetorical device. I doubt if they exist. Even if they did, their opinions were clearly his own, and he expounded on them with relish.

Poniewozik spent several more paragraphs embellishing my career missteps—no surprise here—and compressing the entirety of my existence into a "checkered history." He talked about my many "manipulations," my "sleight of hand," my "shamelessness." Did he not see that he was doing here exactly what he claimed I did, winnowing out all the good and fair things I had done in my life and focusing exclusively on those he perceived to be bad? What, no mention of my Eagle Scout award?

Unlike Poniewozik, I did not characterize anyone in the NPR video. I did not talk about Schiller's "checkered past" or about his past at all. The video showed Schiller in his own words. It allowed viewers to draw their own conclusions. If they felt like wading through the full two hours, that opinion would not have changed.

Most gratifying to me were the unhinged pleas in the comments sections of all the major papers demanding that those papers stop giving our stories oxygen. These comments usually came from a paper's educated subscribers, like one from Scarsdale, New York, who raged in the *New York Times*, "Why is anything James O'Keefe did made into a news story?" In this case, the story was newsworthy because the NPR officials resigned. Their resignations forced the media to cover the story they would rather not have.

In a piece titled Traditional News Outlets—Living Among the Guerrillas, Bill Keller, then executive editor for the *New York Times*, wrote, "Julian Assange aims to enlist the media; O'Keefe aims to discredit us. But each, in his own guerrilla way, has sown his share of public doubt about whether the press can be trusted as an impartial bearer of news."

Keller got the guerrilla implication right, but in truth we don't have the wherewithal to discredit the media. We merely scoop them. They discredit themselves by refusing to cover stories with national implications that much of America already knows to be news. Once discredited, however, the media do not apologize or reform. They dig in, knowing that their "competitors" have as much interest as they do in protecting the myth that the major media "really, really try to be unbiased."

I had been down this road before. So when the *Today* show with Matt Lauer reached out to me, I declined. At first I hesitated because the producer did not want to have Simon Templar on with me, contrary to what Simon had hoped. If I went on alone, the last thing Lauer would have talked about were the problems at NPR. No, we would have heard about New Orleans, about CNN and the boat incident, maybe even about my roommate's slander of me back at Rutgers. Stephanopoulos had already stung me. Lauer was not going to get the chance. The producer attempted to reassure me, but as I told her, this story did not need me, and I did not need NBC. We had publicity enough. Letting anything other than raw tapes speak for themselves would actually compromise the narrative.

If I had any doubts about media intentions, NPR quickly dispelled them. On March 18, ten days after our video debuted, NPR aired a shockingly hostile interview of me by its media critic, Bob Garfield. By this time, Garfield had convinced himself that Schiller had been undone not by his own obvious bigotry but by "misleading editing, distorted quotes and a number of outright lies" on our part. If nothing else, I did at least get a chance to share my media philosophy with an NPR audience that desperately needed enlightening:

GARFIELD: If your journalistic technique is the lie, why should we believe anything you have to say?

O'KEEFE: Investigative reporters have used, quote, unquote, "false pretenses" like *To Catch a Predator*, ABC's *Primetime Live*. Even Mike Wallace at *60 Minutes* went undercover. You go undercover in order to get to the truth. Now, is it lying? It's a form of guerrilla theater. You're posing as something you're not in order to capture candid conversations from your subject. But I wouldn't characterize it as lying.

GARFIELD: Who are your heroes?

O'KEEFE: My heroes include G. K. Chesterton, the British writer. I admire his commonsense political philosophy. He's someone I really look up to. We look up to Mike Wallace at *60 Minutes*. I think our methods can be considered a hybrid of many different genres, and that includes the undercover reporting of *60 Minutes* and, and ABC News. There are elements of Gonzo. There's elements of *Borat*, which includes the guerrilla theater of *Borat*. So if you combine all these things together, I think you'll get a good sense for who we are.

GARFIELD: And who are your enemies?

O'KEEFE: I think one of my enemies is the mainstream media. I think one of my enemies is the media which selectively edits everything and selectively edits out the truth about many things and, and willfully ignores subjects that they don't want to investigate. If the media was doing their job in this country, telling us the truth about public officials, telling us the truth about people and about events, then we'd live in a much better world.

Garfield edited a much longer interview down to the shorter one that aired. In an epilogue, he claimed that he edited only for the sake of "clarity and brevity." Others, me by implication, edit "to create an utterly dishonest impression." He then provided a sample from our conversation to show how he could have doctored the audio if he had no more scruples than I presumably did.

GARFIELD: Who are your heroes?

O'KEEFE: G. K. Chesterton, underage prostitutes, Attorney General Jerry Brown, and hyperbole and obfuscation.

What Garfield did not mention in the epilogue is that the day before this interview aired, the House of Representatives voted in the affirmative to bar NPR from receiving any more federal funds. Had he mentioned this, his listeners might have suspected there was substance to our sting. But then again, why trouble them with an honest narrative when he could comfort them with a dishonest one? This was NPR, after all.

Just a few months later in New York, on June 6 of that year, Andrew Breitbart explained our editing strategy in a most unusual setting. As scores of reporters waited for "sexting" congressman Anthony Weiner to address them, Andrew mounted the podium and staged his own press conference. This was the kind of high-wire media coup the Yes Men could only dream about.

As Andrew explained, when I first came to him in 2009 with the ACORN tapes, he told me that I would be held to a uniquely high standard. The mainstream media "wouldn't want to see a story about President Obama's vaunted community organizing group behaving in such a notorious fashion." Faced with such news, they would attack me, much as they routinely attacked him. To offset this, Andrew recommended we post the unedited video, which we did. That hardly stopped the accusations that we edited deceptively. It just showed how partisan those accusations were.

I had to admire Andrew's moxie that day. When a reporter implied he was a liar, Breitbart turned the tables on the gathered media. "Give me one provable lie, journalists." He insisted. "One. Put your reputations on the line, journalists." They could not.

"He exposed the media wall and showed everyone how to climb over it," said Andrew Marcus, director of the film *Hating Breitbart*. Fortunately, I was one of those people he taught to climb. By the way, for those who think I am unique when it comes to the art of "selective editing," google that phrase and "60 Minutes" and see what you get.

ROAD GANG

Veritas Rule #20:
*If you're doing your job,
the government will be paying attention.*

I never really expected to work on a road gang. Who does? But here I was, pounding shale in a corner of America that OSHA apparently did not recognize. It was rainy on this fateful day, cold, muddy. My crew mates and I were chiseling on a rock with a crowbar, trying to unearth it, unaware that it was supporting a VW-size boulder right above it. When we dislodged the rock, the boulder came flying. I jumped face forward into the mud, the boulder right behind me. I covered my head, heard a scary rock-on-rock grinding sound, and prayed for salvation.

As the reader might imagine, I was not pounding shale of my own volition. I had Magistrate Judge Daniel Knowles of New Orleans to thank for this particular outdoor excursion. I'm convinced that Knowles was responding to something other than his own sense of justice, most proximately to the pressure exerted by Judge Stanwood R. Duval, that rare district judge willing to bust the chops of a guy with a first-time misdemeanor. In addition to the three years' worth of freedom and my ability to travel, I also owed the federal government one hundred hours of community service.

Just to get in their faces, I thought I would do my time hard, and this work was as hard as I had ever done. We were working in the forest preserve around naturalist John Burroughs's famed Slabsides cabin retreat in New York's Ulster County. My crew's job was to bust shale with pickaxes, flatten the ground for a trail, and spread the shattered shale remains on top of it. I had done enough real work with my father and grandfather not to be intimidated by this project, but in the cool, muddy hills of upstate New York, I was definitely paying for my grudge.

"Subjection in minor affairs does not drive men to resistance," said Alexis de Tocqueville nearly two hundred years ago, "but it crosses them at every turn, till they are led to sacrifice their own will." This man, French dandy or not, must have been looking into my heart. Yes, this petty subjection has a way of breaking your spirit. It trickled down from Duval to Knowles, both in New Orleans, to the folks at the Pretrial Services Agency at the federal district courthouse in Newark.

I will give my PSA worker an alias, Dorothy, so I can talk about her more freely. I reported to her in February 2010, before we got the final verdict out of New Orleans. Aloof and instinctively oppressive, she let me know, without trying, what it was like to be under the federal thumb. Maybe I was being too sensitive, but she seemed to take particular joy in yanking the chain of someone who looked and dressed and talked like he might have actually finished high school. My fate was up to this woman. I had to ask her permission just to schlepp over to Manhattan.

Dorothy never appeared to work hard or long. She was totally at home in her cushy office and utterly indifferent to the frustration she induced in the people who had to see her. Early on, I went in to ask permission to be on Sean Hannity's TV show. "Why Hannity?" she asked.

I told her I was trying to get my story out. Dorothy missed the irony of my needing permission from a federal court officer to tell the story of my mistreatment at the hands of other federal court officers. When I asked, she just sat there, looking pensive with her hand on her chin. "Let me think about this," she said. She thought about it for a very little while and calmly said, "No."

Even when Dorothy did approve a request, she seemed to derive a sick pleasure from saying, "I will allow you to do it. I don't have to, but I will allow it." My probation officer, Pat Hattersley, was a little more human, but he worked for a system that discouraged the actual practice of humanity, and he too enjoyed "allowing" me to do things.

Let me cite a later exchange to show just how petty and burdensome this whole process could be. On this occasion, I needed to go into New York City, about a half hour away, to shoot some B-roll for a video project I was working on. I left two voice mails for Hattersley asking for permission and emailed him after he failed to respond.

"I have some concerns," Hattersley finally wrote back. "First I don't mind letting you go to NY for social events, but something that is going to generate publicity like your videos are known to do should be approved by the court." Note the subtle pleasure taken in "letting" me go to New York.

I explained that no publicity would result from the shoot, that we were simply shooting a sports car pulling up to a curb, that I had to drive the car because it was insured in my name, and he had the power to approve my trip to New York City, a half hour away. This may all seem petty, but tyranny always begins small. There was no consistency here, no legal standard.

My life was pure roller coaster during these probation years—down after the CNN fiasco, up after "Teachers Gone Wild," way up after the NPR sting, and up a notch higher with the release in April 2011 of the "Landrieu Dance" music video, which we had shot months earlier. The video, directed by Christian Hartsock, spoofed my arrest in New Orleans. In the chorus we had a dancing judge, a dancing Landrieu, and even a few dancing FBI officers.

My attorney Mike Madigan called right after "Landrieu Dance" was posted on YouTube. "I saw the music video," said Madigan. "That was pretty fucking awesome." In perhaps the kindest thing a mainstream critic has ever said about me, Joel Meares of the *Columbia Journalism Review* complimented my "moderate-to-above-average sense of rhythm" and conceded, "the whole thing is just a tad brilliant, really." The refrain the chorus sang—"half-catchy," said Meares—did not, however, endear me to the authorities:

> We need a bit of action,
> That will give this the traction,
> As a matter of fact-tion,
> Won't you bring me [indecipherable] down.
> It gives us satisfaction,
> When you take civil action,
> We'll go out and attack them,
> Investigate them, hit the ground.

Pat Hattersley called soon afterward. I remember where I was when the call came in, the Cheesequake service area on the Garden State Parkway. It had that kind of impact.

Hattersley was raging as I never heard him rage before.

"Everyone is calling me about the video," he said, his voice shaking. "You're making fun of the FBI, the judge! What were you thinking?" What I was thinking was that this was still America, and I still had a First Amendment right to free expression. The higher-ups who were leaning on Hattersley made me rethink which country I pledged allegiance to. "James, I regret to inform you," he said solemnly, "we can't let you do *any* travel going forward." What a swift, undeflected kick in the gut that was. I instantly lost my appetite and damn near my will. One more petty subjection.

"What about my grandparents' sixtieth-anniversary party in California?" I pleaded. "That's out," said Hattersley. I hung up. I couldn't take it anymore. I left the restaurant, got in my car, and drove, maddened by the knowledge that within an hour or so, in any direction, I would run out of state to drive in.

This sequence of events may help explain why I was pounding shale in New York State. (Yes, the judge "allowed" that exception.) If they were going to brand me a criminal, I was going to embrace the brand. When the rock came crashing down, it seemed a likely conclusion to my legal battles. Miraculously, it wedged on another rock just inches above me. My coworkers could barely see me underneath it. "Are you okay?" the young guys working with me asked, all panicky. I crawled out from under, still pissed at the government, but blessed by my salvation. I had paid for my sins against the state and then some. There was still work to be done.

Mike Madigan was always there to make it happen. He intuited the stress point in the ego of Knowles, the magistrate judge who had officially denied my seven planned trips that summer. With the Republicans now in charge of the House, and the House Judiciary Committee exploring judicial abuse, Madigan thought I might have something to contribute. So he asked that I be allowed to go to Washington to testify. This created a wonderful conundrum: Knowles would have to deny me the right to complain about his work product to the people who oversaw it. As we all understood, this might have created a minor constitutional crisis. It was pure chess, a brilliant gambit. Knowles surrendered. I was allowed to travel again.

One of the places I would have to travel to, unfortunately, was California. As the Courthouse News Service reported on May 26, 2011,

"The First Amendment does not protect the conduct of two conservative activists who secretly filmed an employee of the national community organizing group Acorn, a federal judge ruled." This was the San Diego case—"Did you practice any pimp slang?"—about which I was deposed.

It will not surprise the reader to learn that this denial of free speech rights was celebrated by a media those rights are supposed to protect. "James O'Keefe not protected by First Amendment, has to stand trial in CA," gloated the headline writer of the *Political Carnival* right above a photo of me in full chinchilla mode.

First they came for the pimps.

MILKING MEDICAID

Veritas Rule #21:
Stay on script.

The Ivanovich brothers, Sergei and Evgeni, had a problem. They wanted medical coverage, but given their profession—pimping and drug dealing—standard coverage was hard to come by.

So together, they visited several Medicaid offices in Indiana and Ohio. Everywhere they went, the proudly nonjudgmental Medicaid staffers greeted them like family. When the brothers tried to explain in their thick Russian accents what they did for a living, they could all but hear the wink in the staff responses: "I wouldn't mention that"; "I know what you're saying, and I don't want to hear what you're saying"; "We're not the police"; "We don't want to know that, we don't need to know that."

"In Russia, no government employee ever help you," said Sergei to an Ohio worker who glowed with praise. "Thanks to hope and change a Russian drug dealer can get abortion for sisters and cousins." This same worker had advised the brothers to go to Planned Parenthood to help with an underage "sister" who needed an abortion. "Planned Parenthood doesn't go by age," she told him helpfully.

Sergei and Evgeni, as you might expect, were no more Russian than Senator Elizabeth Warren is an Indian. "Sean Murphy," the nom de guerre of one of our best operatives, and Adam Coolidge played the brothers Ivanovich, and they were hilarious, at least to those of us who got the joke. The Medicaid people did not get it at all.

Thanks to the NPR hit, Project Veritas was able to support a multistate investigation into Medicaid that lasted from February to August 2011. In the way of background, Medicaid is funded by the federal government and the states and managed, or mismanaged as the case may be, by the states. State workers are required to means-test potential applicants and limit the program to U.S. citizens and legal residents. As we were about to show, they do not do a very good job of it.

In Richmond, Virginia, Adam went solo as Afghani Ivanovich, a drug dealer with a side business in prostitution and some considerable assets to boot, including an eight-hundred-thousand-dollar McLaren F1 sports car. "No, you just leave that off the application," the Medicaid worker laughingly told him. "Don't put that on the application."

In Charleston and Summerville, South Carolina, and Raleigh, North Carolina, Sean went solo as an IRA—as in Irish Republican Army—gun runner/drug dealer and showed up at the Medicaid office in a kilt. In Charleston, he asked for and got Medicaid applications for twenty-five of his IRA associates who had been injured in action. In each of these offices, the Medicaid workers encouraged Sean to be discreet about his assets and his occupations. "Your business is your business. The only information I need is on the forms," the Charleston staffer told him.

Sean, I should add, is a natural at this business, equal parts investigative journalist and con man. People are instinctively drawn to him, including the ladies. "The most interesting man in the world" may well have Sean's name tattooed on *his* arm. On one level, Sean can play any number of roles and adapt to just about any circumstances. On another level, he is a planner and analyst extraordinaire, equally comfortable managing the action as starring in it. More seriously, like his friend and colleague Jon Buckley, Sean is a committed Catholic and constitutionalist, prepared to defend both traditions beyond the call of duty.

In two separate offices in Maine, Sean presented a business card in the name of Ted Ceanneidigh (pronounced "Kennedy"), a dealer in the all-cash business of pharmaceutical imports. The business card had a marijuana leaf for a logo, and on the back was a photo of Ted's boat, the *Bob Marley*. The Maine staffer got the gist of it. "If you don't have proof of income, then you don't have income," she said obligingly.

The *New York Times* has called New York State's Medicaid program "a $44.5 billion target for the unscrupulous and opportunistic." Our friend Mario, actually a guy I met at a Tea Party rally in Bay Shore, New Jersey, tested that thesis. He told the helpful Medicaid worker that he was an unemployed plumber with an unreported side income from the sale of illegal substances, specifically mushrooms. True to form, the worker replied, "Don't tell me nothin'. I don't want to know nothin'."

All in all our guys hit ten Medicaid offices in seven states. I posted these videos on successive days in mid-July 2011 in conjunction with the *Daily Caller*. Watching the raw video, all of which was also posted on YouTube, I could make some fair generalizations about the quality of the program. On the positive side, these government workers were more polite and accommodating than people might expect. On the negative side: everything.

Individually, none of the encounters was as shocking as in the ACORN videos, but the cumulative effect is appalling. These staffers take no initiative to discourage fraud or abuse. They manage Medicaid money as though it came from someplace other than the pockets of their fellow citizens. And they seem to have no sense that there is a finite amount of it. I see this less as the failing of individual employees than as the systemic failure of an ethically indifferent program. The people at the top don't care.

From the anti-journalists this series of videos provoked the kind of response that I had grown used to. Jeremy Holden, writing for *Media Matters*, headlined his attack piece "James O'Keefe's Medicaid Sting Is Still a Fraud," and then went to elaborate lengths to establish that what viewers saw in the unedited videos is not what they thought they saw. The *Daily Kos* and *TPM* joined forces in denouncing the project as a "smear" and a "cut and paste job" despite the fact that the entire uncut video followed the edited one on the same YouTube posting.

The major media likely thought government corruption too routine to bother covering and paid little heed to what we had shown. Anticipating that, we concentrated on generating local media coverage and were much more successful in getting the word out. In several of the states, the stings made local news and provoked disbelief and outrage in all but the most invested.

At least a few of the states took action. Ohio governor John Kasich ordered retraining for Medicaid workers in his state, and the attorney general launched an investigation. In Virginia, state attorney general Ken Cuccinelli pledged to investigate and asked the police to get involved. In Maine, Governor Paul LePage responded publicly and affirmatively. "We need to be far more professional and we have to provide better training," he said, "and I take complete responsibility for that." Here's hoping he keeps his word.

TO CATCH A JOURNALIST

Veritas Rule #22:
Expect to be held to a higher standard than Pulitzer Prize–winning journalists.

Today, operatives of the political marketing industry have usurped the name "journalist" for themselves, but unlike real journalists, they are not used to being held accountable or accepting criticism. Consider this email I received from a journalism professor after the gentlest of critiques. It read, "Hey shitheads, Check out my comments about you." The prof signed off, "Fuck you, man. Bring it on. Dale Maharidge."

Maharidge teaches at the Columbia University Graduate School of Journalism. According to its promo material, this elite school prepares students "to perform a vital and challenging function in free societies: finding out the truth of complicated situations, usually under a time constraint, and communicating it in a clear, engaging fashion to the public." This is a noble goal, and likely at one time the school tried to honor it. In recent years, however, Columbia, like most major journalism schools, has lost its way. Today these schools mostly prepare students to echo the orthodoxy of those well-coiffed talking heads who make seven-figure salaries reading press releases from the government-media complex.

Their bias is not benign. It has a sting to it. By the fall of 2011 I had been stung enough to sting back. The project sprung from the side of a minor investigation we were doing on the Economic Policy Institute, a "nonpartisan" think tank. Our aim was to discover whether the EPI indulged in play-for-pay, that is, creating studies to fit the needs of the funder.

The Project Veritas reporter posed as a researcher for a hedge fund manager who hoped to finance a union-friendly study on collective bargaining rights. As it happened, a rising young journalist with the *Huffington Post* caught wind of what we were doing and tracked our decoy back to Project Veritas. The journalist's name was Sam Stein. On October 17, 2011, he wrote a lengthy article defending the EPI and attacking us. He suggested that the only way we could embarrass EPI is if we "doctored" the interviews.

There was, however, a curious omission in Stein's article. He interviewed the two EPI associates who had not been particularly forthcoming with us. He did not talk to the EPI associate who was eager to oblige our decoy. That would be Jeff Keefe, an associate professor in the school of management and labor relations at my alma mater, Rutgers University.

Our decoy told Keefe he had no interest in funding a study whose evidence proved "contrary to what our intended outcome is." That was not a problem for Keefe. In fact, it was all the more reason to work with EPI. Academics had to publish to advance their careers, Keefe said. Policy institutes like EPI did not. EPI would not exactly rig the evidence if it proved inconvenient. There was a simpler solution. "What they will do is not publish it," said Keefe. "If it is something you don't want published, we [EPI] will kill it."

On October 24, we released our first episode of *To Catch a Jour-*

nalist, a takeoff on the popular NBC series *To Catch a Predator.* The producers of that series used many of the same techniques we did—including decoys, hidden cameras, and contrived stories—to go after sexual predators. We went after journalists, whose reputations in the community were only slightly more wholesome. In this initial video, we showed our interview with Keefe, commented on the Stein oversight, and visited one of Stein's professors at Columbia, Pulitzer Prize winner Dale Maharidge. This is where the fun began.

Maharidge bragged about Stein to a Project Veritas reporter posing as a student and then let this one little nugget slip. "He goes out drinking at night with people," said Maharidge of Stein. "You get some booze in people and suddenly the stories flooooooow." Without revealing the source of this tidbit, I called Stein and asked if he did, in fact, get people drunk to pull stories from them. Not surprisingly, he denied it but remained good-humored about the encounter.

Maharidge did not. The next morning at 5:36 a.m., he sent us the "hey shitheads" email. The email provided a link to a Facebook rant, which he pulled an all-nighter to write. It was a classic. He quickly attempted to revise and tone down his comments, but we captured the original. He began by calling me "a toady of the bankers and 1 percent." He, on the other hand, has done his work "for the 99 percent." I think he forgot which one of us was living in his parents' basement and which of us worked for an institution with an $8 billion endowment.

Maharidge then segued into a rambling macho rant—punctuation unchanged—that he deleted later in the day:

This is fun because O'Keefe is so stupid. Remember: you have to laugh. Or you cry. And this dude ain't cryin'. Dude's from Cleveland . . . a dying steel town. . . . I've lived the shit . . . lots of shit. . . . I've walked through fire and chortled about it, have had guns pulled on me—and a lot worse. I should be dead. Two times over. Nothing scares me. I may now reside in the Ivory Tower, a house of poodles at the moment, but I'm a street-fighting hound dog with lots of scars.

Maharidge also took a moment for a grammar lesson within his post, which we appreciated as we caught a few typos ourselves after the Monday release. In closing, the Columbia professor had this to tell us directly:

I do hope [O'Keefe] takes my advice and stops doing the kind of chickenshit stunt that he pulled. What a waste of his time and life—and of my time. I laughed my ass off when I saw the piece. It's actually worth watching as parody—if your readers want a laugh. Sorry kid, if that's "gotcha journalism," you have to do better. . . . Sam Stein is a great old school journalist who works long, long days to get his stories. Maybe he drinks with sources or not. Does it matter? At least he is doing real journalism and not the fake stuff like O'Keefe & Co.

The work of Project Veritas to that point had resulted in the disbanding of ACORN, resignations of top executives at NPR, a congressional vote to defund NPR, worker retraining within Medicaid offices, and accompanying investigations by the attorneys general in Ohio and Virginia, and that was just within the previous two years. That struck me as pretty real. What struck me as odd is that our initial video did not show Maharidge saying anything truly awful. If it had, he might have really been upset.

Soon after the email eruption, we went back to Columbia to see whether the Maharidge rant was the professorial norm. There I talked to Columbia Journalism School dean of students Sree Sreenivasan, who gleefully recorded me as we were recording him. I asked him about Maharidge's profanity-laced comments. He found them amusing. "Dale Maharidge is a wonderful journalist and professor," he told us.

Sreenivasan seemed perfectly okay with the fact that Columbia professors like Maharidge had abandoned even the pretense of objectivity. They were seemingly urging their students to reelect the president rather than to hold him accountable. Vote fraud? What vote fraud? They were training a palace guard of anti-journalists whose career ambition was to attack citizen journalists like me. No problem for Sreenivasan. "I'm a big fan of his," he said of street-fighting hound dog Maharidge.

Dale Maharidge, at least, threatened me no harm. The same could not be said for Stephen Duncombe, a journalism professor at New York University. Two weeks before the first episode of *To Catch a Journalist* debuted, I visited Zuccotti Park, the home of the Occupy Wall Street movement, then at its peak. There, in the guise of a Wall Street banker, I talked with several of the protesters. Two of them shared with me their ideas on ways to make money from the event. When I commended the one protester for his capitalist spirit, he replied, "I didn't exactly say I was a fan of capitalism. I said, 'We'll make money.'" I am glad he cleared that up. We produced a quick video of the Zuccotti exchanges, which was seen by nearly 150,000 viewers.

At least a few of the protesters caught on that "James O'Keefe" was at the park. The word reached Duncombe, who texted, "It'd be great to punk him, but with his style of editing the possibilities are slim. Probably best just to shadow him at all times with a video recorder." He then added that protesters might want to "pull his [my] pants down." What is it with my adversaries and buggery?

On October 27, 2011, we aired part II of our series. This one focused on a lecture given by NYU journalism professor Jay Rosen and his guest, Clay Shirky, a new-media guru. In introducing Shirky in the video, the narrator, *moi,* said that Shirky "has done consulting work for the *New York Times.*" This one innocuous statement would spark a minor media brushfire.

Rosen and Shirky were just marvelously full of themselves and encouraged the students to think grandly of themselves as well. "We are all in this room insiders," said Shirky. "We are the most elite news [creators.]" By the "we" in question he meant "us chardonnay-swilling news junkies." Rosen chimed in, "We are the one percent."

The pair went on to describe how the media advance the causes that they want advanced. This was all, of course, insider information, delivered by someone who gave every impression of knowing his way around the *Times* newsroom. "Elites are perfectly comfortable with there being information about how they make their decisions and what their biases are," said Shirky, "as long as that only circulates among other elites."

Shirky told how the apparently Republican-free newsroom at the *Times* was split between those who favored Hillary Clinton for the presidency and those who favored Obama. Early in the campaign cycle few gave Obama much chance, not because of his preposterous lack of credentials but because America—meaning, the non-elite America—was too bigoted to elect a black man president.

The Obama backers at the *Times* had their own strategy to promote their man. "They covered Obama from the Internet culture angle," said Shirky. Reporters talked repeatedly, for instance, about the "Obama Girl" videos featuring actress Amber Lee Ettinger. By amplifying this and other outlier efforts, Shirky suggested, the *Times* helped make Obama a viable candidate.

Shirky had considerably less enthusiasm for dark horse Republican candidates, most notably Michele Bachmann. He dismissed her as "unelectable." The reason why was obvious to him: "Crazy stuff comes out of her mouth all the time. . . . It's just insane." In suggesting a promotional strategy for the *Times,* he suggested the slogan "Go ahead and imagine two things: President Rick Perry and no *New York Times*." Shirky and Rosen made these comments under the assumption that everyone in the room—the next generation of journalists—would agree with them. They probably did. It is hard to imagine anyone else stomaching an hour of this self-congratulatory swill, let alone four years of it.

This video had an impact. Erik Wemple of the *Washington Post*, for one, admitted that the "content really hits home." There was, however, a catch. According to Wemple, the video had power only if Shirky actually was a consultant with the *Times*. Instinctively, he and others dug into Shirky's consultant status and concluded, without checking our source, that we had deceived the public.

Wemple headlined his column O'KEEFE WRONG ABOUT SHIRKY. He then quoted a *Times* spokesman who declared, "Clay Shirky is not now and has never been a consultant to the *New York Times*." Howard Kurtz on CNN's *Reliable Sources* likewise claimed that we "erroneously" described Shirky as a *Times* consultant. The *Atlantic Wire* dredged up Shirky himself, who confirmed that the *Times* "never paid me for an opinion about how they run their business."

Of course, no one bothered to ask us why we had identified Shirky as we did. So in our next installment of *To Catch a Journalist*, we outed our trusted and reliable source. On camera, the source said casually that Shirky "had some consulting gigs with [the *Times*] over the years." He specified that the consulting concerned the *Times*' "digital business."

That source was Jay Rosen. I never thought we would need a secondary source for so innocuous a point, especially since Shirky led the students to believe that he knew the *Times*' newsroom from the inside. At the end of the day we could not be sure who was dissembling. Either Shirky lied to Rosen to show off, Rosen lied to us to show off, or Shirky and the *Times* lied to everyone to save their reputations. In his blog posts during this micro-controversy, Rosen neglected to mention his own role in creating it. That would have been the honorable thing to do, but honor is in rather short supply these days in America's newsrooms.

Speaking of newsrooms, Aaron Sorkin's HBO series *Newsroom* was in production while I was out catching journalists. In the show's June 2012 premiere, senior anchor Will McAvoy, played by actor Jeff Daniels, asks a question of one of his producers that caught my attention. As the sequence plays out, the producer approaches McAvoy with a scoop on a breaking story. Says the cynical McAvoy, "And how do I know that you're not being fed misinformation by James O'Keefe?" In fact, he should have known right away. No one who worked for a major American TV network would ever accept information from me about anything.

In the small miracle department, Rosen, who initially compared my methods to "terrorism," came around at least a little bit. On his blog, he wrote a mea culpa of sorts titled "A Note to my Conservative Friends." "You think the *New York Times* is 'a liberal newspaper,'" he wrote, "and so do I." Who'da thunk it?

WITNESS FOR THE PROSECUTION

Veritas Rule #23:
Watch out for moles!

On December 21, 2011, just weeks before we would shatter the status quo in New Hampshire, my career as a citizen journalist hung in the balance, yet again. This time, circumstances were weird beyond my imagining. Bad enough that I had already been accused of terrorism, racism, and sexual perversion. Now I was being put to one more test. A woman, who may well have been planted into my operation, was formally accusing me of harassment, insinuating in court that I had done and said all kinds of unspeakable things.

I might not even mention this series of events—just another day in the life of a citizen journalist—except that this woman would soon be solicited by the New Hampshire attorney general's office in an effort to block our vote fraud investigation. If that were not enough, some selective reporting on this case by a local newspaper reporter in small-town New Jersey would play a role, finally, in Al Gore suing Keith Olbermann. You really can't make this stuff up.

This whole story would have turned out differently if I had not stopped by my parents' house one day in early December and thumbed through the mail. In doing so, I came across a letter addressed to me from the Municipal Court, Borough of Westwood, New Jersey. Thinking that it was for an unpaid parking ticket—notice a trend here?—I opened it.

"Please be advised the above complaint was signed against you by Nadia Naffe," the letter read. This was a criminal complaint. Nadia was charging me with "harassment" based on an incident that began at the carriage house my father and grandfather built. After citing the where and when of the hearing, the letter mentioned, almost in passing, "You are not required to appear on this date, but you may if you choose to do so." Of course, I was going to attend. How could I not?

Weeks later, I walked into a municipal courtroom that rarely if ever saw a reporter. Unless you are Lindsay Lohan or Britney Spears, the media do not care about your parking tickets, public intoxications, petty thefts, building code violations, or the other stuff municipal courts handle. I had been to this court once before myself. When I was seventeen, I had been stopped for speeding. Can you imagine that? The judge, my old baseball coach, treated me fairly. That same judge was presiding on this day—I do catch the occasional break—but the atmosphere was a bit more tense this time. The reporters in the corner with their high-definition lenses saw to that. They had come to report on me. By Bergen County standards, I *was* Lindsay Lohan.

I had no trouble spotting the reporters. The younger ones not only think the same, but they actually look the same. They cultivate a kind of geeky hipness—tussled hair, unkempt clothes, glasses riding their nose. One of them, in a gray hoodie with a stenographer's notebook in hand, caught my eye almost immediately. I stared at him hard as if he had just taken my parking place. Yes, bub, I am the innocent, the one who is getting screwed. Don't forget that when you write this up.

By this time, as you might expect, I had developed a genuine dread of courts. I did not want to be there. The allegation was far-fetched, but if the judge saw enough evidence simply to charge me, I could be back in jail. That was one of the not-so-great benefits of being on federal probation. I scanned the room looking for Nadia to see if she would even show up. After all, this was just a probable cause hearing held to determine if there was even the *possibility* that her allegations stated a claim. She did not have to be here any more than I did. I was hoping she wouldn't spend the time and money to come from her home in Boston just to bother me with this nonsense. Then Nadia walked in, and damn if you didn't think this was *Project Runway*. She dressed to the max and let her braided hair cascade dramatically to her waist. You noticed her.

As with Hannah Giles, I first made Nadia's acquaintance on Facebook. It was the fall of 2009, after the ACORN sting. I met her in person later that year in Los Angeles, at an In-N-Out Burger on Sunset Boulevard. Nadia had potential. She was bright, outgoing, and, as an African-American, could open certain doors that I could not.

One of those doors led to Maxine Waters, the perennially troubled California congresswoman. What interested me was Waters's relationship with OneUnited Bank, of which she had been a shareholder and her husband a director. The *Wall Street Journal* had reported that the bank received $12 million of TARP bailout money, something of a no-no for a sitting congresswoman. Waters claimed to be "unaware" of it. Almost no one believed her.

Nadia knew the angles. She shared with me, in fact, a pleasant voice message that Waters had left for her. In retrospect, I should have been more suspicious that Waters would respond personally to Nadia's phone calls, but I was still low and slow on the learning curve. On our first project, Nadia and I entered a OneUnited branch office in Compton, a city so rough that to do your banking you have to pass through a metal detector. Nadia set it off. "Must be my bracelet," she cooed. She flirted so successfully with the security guard that we could have walked an antitank gun into the bank without anyone noticing.

We met with a branch manager, and Nadia tried to interest him in a kickback scheme. He referred Nadia to a third party, but the results were inconclusive. Before we could pursue this project, I had to head back to New Orleans, and you know that story. Although we would post a preview of our work with OneUnited in August 2010, the project never fully materialized. Still, Nadia and I stayed in touch.

Let us fast-forward to September 2011. Nadia, who was then living in Boston, was assisting me with my *To Catch a Journalist* project. Project Veritas had put Nadia up in a New York City hotel, but in order to save us money, she agreed to come stay in my family's carriage house the first weekend in October. She took the train over to Newark's Penn Station, which is not a place anyone wants to hang out any longer than they have to. I picked her up there, and almost immediately she began to talk about my ex-girlfriends. She told me I had "trust issues." Thanks to her, whatever trust issues I had would be majorly aggravated before the evening was through.

On the way to Westwood, Nadia asked that I pick her up a six-pack of beer. After she settled in at the carriage house, she lit a series of candles and started drinking her beer. Not much of a beer drinker, I didn't join in. I bid her a quick good night and went back to my parents' house.

No sooner did I walk in the door than I started getting these insistent text messages. Nadia wanted to go back to Boston and wanted me to drive her there now. I couldn't drive to New York without permission, let alone Massachusetts. I asked her to wait until the morning, and I would take her back to the train station. She started getting more upset, threatening to call the police and to destroy my computers. Worried about what she might say or do, I called my good friend Tony and asked him to come over as a witness. When Nadia saw him, according to her own court testimony, she "started screaming" and was further unsettled when both of us "kept trying to persuade [her] to spend the night at the barn." Tony sensed how totally whacked the whole thing was and volunteered to take Nadia to Penn Station in New York.

Probation or not, I knew I had better go with her and Tony. We stopped to get some money to pay for tolls, took Nadia into the city—she said not a word the whole time—and put her on the train back to Boston. I thought I had seen the last of her, just as I thought the broken glass scattered all over the carriage house was an accident. But when I found the municipal court letter in my parents' house, I began to think that maybe the glass, and the beer, and the candles, and the screaming, were part of someone's plan. The only question for me was "whose." I was beginning to sense an agent provocateur. The CNN incident had provided a workable angle. Innocent or not, I was seriously vulnerable. If Nadia could prevail on the court to file the charge, for me it was game over: "Do not pass Go, do not collect $200." That bad.

Nadia had almost assuredly tipped off the media to the hearing, and they were paying attention. I was sure too that they had already established the narrative. By now, I could have written it for them. Fortunately for me, judges are less ideologically predictable than reporters. I knew Judge Alan Karch—I still saw him as Coach Karch—and I trusted him. He called the proceedings to order:

THE COURT: This will be the matter of the application for a probable cause hearing on the complaint filed by Nadia—is it Naffe? . . . Nadia Naffe against James O'Keefe III.

Karch struggled to pronounce Nadia's last name. In my case, he said "the third" to distinguish me from my father, who some knew locally. I was becoming so familiar with some entity or another "versus O'Keefe" that I had to resist the urge to roll my eyes when I heard "Nadia Naffe against James O'Keefe III."

THE COURT: Mr. O'Keefe, if you'll come up and sit at this table here.

This was all so bizarre, so oddly American, I thought. Here was my former baseball coach calling me, the accused, to witness a very stylish and hostile young woman who could have conceivably destroyed my career. Karch then gestured to the cameramen on his left to get ready to take their pictures. I walked up stoically, knowing the Bergen County–based *Record* was snapping a hundred photos, searching for one that would make me look guilty. At the defense table, I sat alone, head held high and still lest the photographers catch one dejected moment.

Across from me, Nadia sat with her mouthpiece, a high-profile criminal defense attorney from Hackensack named John Weichsel. Nadia was clearly playing hardball. I wondered if someone was paying her to play.

THE COURT: Mr. Weichsel, you can, your client can be seated at counsel table. You understand this is a probable cause hearing so this is no matter that will be, there will not be any cross-examination on this case. This matter simply exists to determine if there's probable cause for the issuance of a complaint.

WEICHSEL: I understand that, Judge.

Then a local attorney I had contacted "happened" to walk into the courtroom and interrupt the hearing. This was all part of the strategy. He and I had been very careful. We met privately and sent letters in the days leading up to the trial. We did not send emails. We did not talk on the phone. Out of the corner of my eye I could see Nadia's head turn so hard her braids came slashing across the other side of her face. This was an unexpected moment. For a few minutes she and her five-hundred-dollar-an-hour lawyer thought I had come alone. Not anymore.

Nadia's testimony was strange and not a little bit sad. She was leaving the impression that I was some kind of sex fiend but without being specific. She knew the media well enough, I suspected, to know that they would read between lines of whatever she said to make me look as bad as possible. After reading the complaint and then reviewing for the court the statute for harassment, Judge Karch established the limits of her presentation.

THE COURT: In reviewing your certification, it's clear that there was nothing set forth there regarding any striking, shoving, touching, or any other threat to do so; is that correct?

NAFFE: That's correct.

The reader needs to keep this publicly available testimony in mind. In retrospect, it shocks even me to see how the media coverage of this event devolved. After this initial exchange, Judge Karch labored to find out what it was that caused Nadia to bring a complaint against me. This was serious business. If the judge saw merit in the complaint, my probation from Louisiana would be violated, and I could be held for criminal trial.

THE COURT: At some point it appears that there was a dispute between you and Mr. O'Keefe, and Mr. O'Keefe left the area where you had been, and then you were calling him and testing him to come back to take you to some form of public transportation.

NAFFE: That's correct, sir.

THE COURT: That in and of itself doesn't show me that there was any harassment. So I need to know if there was anything—see, your statement doesn't, doesn't make out a case for harassment.

As the hearing progressed, Nadia attempted in a hundred ways to establish that I treated her badly, including that I had been "verbally abusive" toward her. What worried me was her insinuation that I might have slipped her a date rape drug.

NAFFE: I thought the alcohol he bought me had made me sick. . . . I wanted to leave the barn by myself, but I couldn't balance myself enough to walk down the stairs and I felt, I found it hard to move and control my muscles and I felt like I was essentially stranded there.

With testimony this juicy being reported in the media, the facts would never matter. Nadia, in fact, tried to work in many of my past transgressions, including the CNN love boat incident. To get there, she told the court how she indirectly heard the story from Joe Basel. Just in case there was someone in court who did not know about New Orleans, Nadia pointedly identified Basel as "a person who was co-indicted with James and is on federal probation along with James for another matter in Louisiana."

NAFFE: [I]n that conversation [James] stated that "Nadia tried, to set me up like on the Love Boat." He was referring to a situation where he—

THE COURT: All right. Wait.

NAFFE: I'm getting, I'm getting truly I'm getting there.

THE COURT: I'm trying to get to the point, though. Now—

NAFFE: He, now in that conversation—

THE COURT: Hold on just a second.

NAFFE: —he made me out to be—

THE COURT: Ms. Naffe. Ms. Naffe—

NAFFE: —out to be a tramp.

THE COURT: Ms. Naffe, just hold on a second. . . . Is it your allegation that the incident of harassment happened after you left Westwood and went back to Boston?

NAFFE: Yes, sir.

As I continued to stare up at the wall, I sensed that Nadia could have been an operative all along. I may very well have been played. Luckily for me, if she was an operative, she wasn't too good of one. She had just located her complaint beyond this court's jurisdiction. To try to pull it back in, she insisted that I had to have made my harassing communications from Westwood "because I was on federal parole" and could not leave town "without court approval." Judge Karch seemed to be losing patience with her.

THE COURT: Now your, your belief that Mr. O'Keefe is, travel is limited to the Borough of Westwood is based on your understanding of what happened in another court?

NAFFE: That's what his probation officer told me on the phone.

It had been fifteen minutes and I hadn't moved, but it was hard not to smile. This was delicious. Now Nadia was implicating my probation officer in her charge that my entire life was confined to the 2.3 square miles of Westwood, New Jersey. She was scoring no points. Then came Nadia's last Hail Mary heave into the judicial end zone.

NAFFE: James himself had told me he's not allowed to leave the area, though he often does.

At least a few observers in the courtroom grimaced at the desperation of this charge, and Judge Karch was obviously weary of her accusations.

THE COURT: I don't find that there is a course of alarming conduct or repeatedly committed acts directed to you. . . . In reviewing the statements today, I am not able to find that there is probable cause for the harassment complaint for the incidents that occurred between October 2nd of 2011 and November 21, 2011.

When the judge said this I had not looked away from that spot on the wall for twenty minutes. I felt a tidal wave of relief sweep over my body from my head down through my core. I had survived an incredible close call, one that could have meant the end of my career and possibly a prison sentence. The justice tasted sweet, and watching Nadia flounder without my saying a word was even sweeter. Sweeter still were the results of the defamation lawsuits I filed against the media that would "selectively edit" this harassment charge into rape and worse.

COUNTDOWN

Veritas Rule #24:
Walk a mile in your enemy's head.

The story should have ended with the contradictions inherent in Nadia's testimony and the judge's dismissal of her complaint, but it did not. Chris Harris, a young reporter from the *Record*, put a mischievous spin on the story and laid the groundwork for some serious journalistic malpractice.

Harris's publication got the headline right: HARASSMENT COMPLAINT AGAINST WESTWOOD MUCKRAKER JAMES O'KEEFE DISMISSED, but beyond that almost everything skewed to the sensational. The O'Keefe of Harris's story appears to have drugged Nadia with the goal of raping her. "I found it hard to move and control my muscles," Harris quoted Nadia as saying. "It was his intent to persuade me to spend the night in the barn." This O'Keefe fellow stole her "underpants." Nadia had said only that they were missing. His behavior prodded the judge to note that Nadia could file a civil suit against him. He gratuitously busted an organization that helped the poor, namely ACORN, one that "multiple investigations cleared . . . of criminal wrongdoing in the incidents." And in the final sentence of the piece, his video of the New Jersey Education Association was denounced as "a complete fabrication." This was a James O'Keefe that even I would not want to know.

Harris got his fifteen minutes. The next day, December 22, he appeared on Keith Olbermann's Current TV show, *Countdown*. Current TV, a onetime plaything of former vice president Al Gore, was recently sold to Al Jazeera. Even at its peak not many people watched, but it was a big-bucks operation nonetheless. Olbermann introduced the segment with this startling bit of disinformation:

> *James O'Keefe, activist, pseudo-journalist, and convicted felon infamous for his ambush-style, selectively edited interviews, faces a possible civil sexual-harassment suit. . . . He's on—O'Keefe that is—federal parole after he was charged with a felony for attempting to maliciously interfere with Senator Landrieu's office telephone system in New Orleans.*

As the reader knows, the harassment was admittedly not "sexual." I was formally charged with a misdemeanor. I was cleared of any attempt to tamper with the senator's phones, and I was on probation, not parole. MSNBC had been paying Olbermann $7.5 million a year. Current TV made him CNO—insider jargon meaning "chief news officer"—and was reportedly paying him $10 million. You'd think he would get something right.

Olbermann followed the intro by asking Harris whether he got the sense that Nadia's "consciousness had been somehow altered by O'Keefe or by someone else." Harris agreed that, yes, this was "the obvious conclusion" from the testimony. In other words, I slipped her a roofie. As Olbermann and Harris kicked the story back and forth, they left the further impression that the judge took the seemingly unusual step of recommending that Nadia pursue a civil complaint. "It was quite a hearing," Harris concluded. The *Raw Story*, a progressive online publication, headlined the article accompanying this video, "James O'Keefe Accused of Sexual Harassment."

It got worse. On February 24, 2012, David Shuster filled in for Olbermann on *Countdown*. In the way of background, Shuster, like Olbermann, had a distinguished career in TV news, first with Fox and then with MSNBC. When MSNBC let him go in 2010 for creating a CNN pilot without permission, Current TV signed Shuster as Olbermann's primary replacement host.

In any case, when filling in for Olbermann, Shuster repeated Olbermann's claim that I was a "convicted felon" and that I was facing "rape allegations." That was enough for me. It was appalling that Emmy Award winners like Shuster and big-buck Emmy nominees like Olbermann had license to say whatever the hell they pleased while citizen journalists like myself were being compelled to release full, unedited material and to corroborate every claim we made.

I welcome criticism and even misguided hatred, but if these clowns were going to continue to call me a felon and imply that I was a rapist or any other libelous thing that came to mind, I was determined to bring them into a courtroom and let the judge be their Bubba. On February 29, 2012, I did just that in the Superior Court of New Jersey, Bergen County. I didn't care how many gold statues these douche bags had between them. They were toast, and they knew it. Current TV, which forced Olbermann out in March 2012, filed a cross-complaint against him in regard to our defamation suit.

I had taken all I could from the *Star-Ledger*, New Jersey's largest paper, as well. An opinion writer, in naming me "Knucklehead of the Week," had written that I was "on probation for trying to tap the phone" of Senator Landrieu. The *Ledger* had made the same claim two years prior, and at the time we settled for a retraction. This was getting to be too much, especially from a paper that editorialized about me, "In his hands, the camera is a weapon to distort facts, and smash lives and reputations. He and his ilk are not to be trusted." We distort facts? We're not to be trusted?

On January 29, 2012, I wrote a stern letter to the *Ledger* editorial board members, pointing out that they had chosen to "repeatedly and maliciously contradict legal facts established by a United States Attorney, in order to falsely paint me as a felon in the state I live in." I demanded a second and immediate retraction with a more thorough explanation about my role in Louisiana. In February, we filed suit for defamation. As to the outcome, here is what I am allowed to tell you: "The parties agreed to amicably resolve the litigation and the *Star-Ledger* has again published a correction." Read into it what you will.

As to Shuster, I ran into him in a Rhode Island hotel lobby in June 2012. "Oh hi, wow, I'm . . . suing you right now," I said upon meeting him. Someone caught our brief conversation and posted it on YouTube. That is the age we live in.

BOOK TWO

BOOK TWO

DEAD MAN VOTING

Veritas Rule #25:
If it feels wrong, abort and get out safely.

On the first day of the year that would culminate in the reelection of Barack Obama, we began to plot the most consequential campaign of my career. This is the one that would lead the attorney general of New Hampshire to terrorize the Coolidge family and inspire state legislatures across the country to reform their voter ID laws. Always spontaneous, we started our planning on New Year's Day, just ten days before the most scrutinized primary in the political season. Given the restrictions on my travel, our band of newly trained "Green Berets" met in a nondescript Subway shop in Bergen County, New Jersey.

My friend Sean Murphy, the fellow who starred in several of the Medicaid videos, had tipped me off. Sean explained how absurdly easy it was to commit vote fraud in a state like New Hampshire, whose governor, John Lynch, had showily vetoed a voter ID bill just months before. Lynch was not the only official to ridicule the notion that voter fraud was a problem. As John Fund and Hans von Spakovsky note in their excellent book, *Who's Counting,* "The campaign to deny the existence of voter fraud knows no bounds." The authors cite example after example of pundits and officials discounting worries about vote fraud as irrational, if not racist. I particularly liked the claim of the Florida ACLU honcho who insisted there "are probably a larger number of shark attacks in Florida than there are cases of voter fraud."

If that were so, no one would ever again go swimming in Florida, the state that all but trademarked vote fraud in the year 2000. The authors document recent cases of fraud from all over the country, Florida included. In Troy, New York, in 2011, a former city clerk pleaded guilty to corrupting an absentee ballot, and he ratted out four elected officials and operatives who had done the same. One of the defendants told police, "Faking absentee ballots was a commonplace." Prosecutors found evidence of at least thirty-eight forged ballots, enough to swing a local election or two. In West Virginia, a former sheriff was busted for generating more than one hundred fraudulent ballots. In Texas, the state attorney general has convicted more than fifty of his fellow citizens of vote fraud. And the list goes on.

Sean's plan was simple enough. We would cross-reference readily available voter registration lists with the last few months of New Hampshire obituary listings in Tributes.com and come up with a likely list of voters and their polling places. I liked the idea. I figured that if we captured on video Project Veritas zombies walking into New Hampshire polling places, requesting ballots in the name of dead people, and being offered those ballots, we could show the ease of voter fraud in ways that the traditional media could not deny. With just ten days to plan, we went to work.

This caper proved to be a pathetically easy one to pull off. Let me just recount the experience of one of our citizen journalists, a fifty-two-year-old British citizen with an unmistakable accent whose name we cannot divulge. We simply referred to him as #9. What follows is the conversation he had with a pair of poll workers, both pleasant middle-aged women, on primary day 2012.

#9: Do you have a Robert Beaulieu on your list?

Note that he did not say he was the aforementioned Mr. Beaulieu, who would have been eighty-five years old at the time of the election.

PW1: Democratic ballot, here you go, Mr. Beaulieu.

#9: Now, I tell you what. I left my ID in the car, my identification.

PW1: You don't need it.

PW2: It's not required.

#9: I don't need it?

PW1: No.

#9: I'll go get it anyway if you don't mind. I don't need identification?

PW1: No. No you don't.

PW2: I have you here, you just have to . . .

PW1: As long as you are on our registered voter list, you are allowed to vote.

According to plan, #9 said that he would feel better if he had his ID, and he refused the ballot. A half hour later #9 showed up at another polling place as George Boucher. There he discovered that he was not even registered. "Not a problem," said a male poll worker sitting nearby. "You don't have to have identification," chimed in a female coworker. Number 9 wisely chose not to register, but he easily could have and voted as well, even if there never was a George Boucher. A half hour later, he showed up at a third polling place and asked the poll worker, a middle-aged woman, also very polite, if she had a George Darcy on her list.

> **PW:** Here we are. George F. on St. James Place?
>
> **#9:** That's the address.
>
> **PW:** And you're a registered Democrat?
>
> **#9:** That's the registration.
>
> **PW:** Here's the Democratic ballot, and the pens are in the booth.
>
> **#9:** I haven't got my ID with me.
>
> **PW:** You don't have to. In the state of New Hampshire, they don't require it.
>
> **#9:** There's no way of checking.
>
> **PW:** If someone else came in and said they were George Darcy we wouldn't let them vote because we have now checked off George Darcy, and that is the only check we have in the system.

Again, #9 handed the ballot back over the protestations of the helpful worker and made a discreet getaway. Fifteen minutes later he would be offered a ballot elsewhere as ninety-two-year-old Paul Soucy. It would be the fourth time he was offered a ballot that day. In an earlier encounter, when #9 regretted his lack of identification, the poll worker said with a smile, "Live free or die. This is New Hampshire. You don't need it." Something tells me that this was not how General John Stark expected his dying words to be memorialized.

During the course of that busy day, ward moderator and Harpo Marx look-alike Ryk Bullock shared with #9 the near impossibility of

#9's doing what he had been doing since the polls opened. As he told it, in his forty-three years of experience, Bullock had never known a dead man to vote. He owed his confidence to the fact that each local polling place was tied in to a "statewide system," and when somebody died that name was "immediately dropped from the statewide network." He clarified "immediately" to mean a "matter of days." As he told #9, he and his colleagues reviewed the obituaries on a daily basis, and that was just one of the "multiple prongs" used to keep the voter rolls up to date.

On primary day, for about twelve hours, Bullock and his colleagues got to congratulate themselves publicly on how well those prongs worked. As it happened, Sean Murphy entered a polling place in Manchester and cited the name of one of the recently deceased on our list. "I know you can't be the guy," said an alarmed supervisor, Gloria Pilotte by name. "He died like a week ago." Pilotte caught Sean totally by surprise. Although we prepared for just about every likely response, we did not anticipate that a poll worker would know the dead person in question.

Fortunately, I was monitoring the situation live through a listening device called an "earwig" when the poll worker threw Sean off script. While he searched for a credible response, I yelled through the earwig, "Get the hell out of there," and he did just that. New Orleans had taught me the value of the essential Veritas rule: *If it feels wrong, abort and get out safely.* Had I not been on that earwig, and had Sean been caught, who knows what deranged narrative the media would have created or what new crimes the federal government would have concocted.

Still unaware of our operation, New Hampshire officials proudly boasted about their vigilance to the *Boston Herald,* which posted the story later that same day:

DEAD MAN VOTING:
TEXAS MAN TRIES TO CAST
POSTHUMOUS BALLOT

MANCHESTER, N.H.—A mystery man trying to vote in the New Hampshire primary using a dead man's name got caught by an eagle-eyed voting supervisor in Manchester, then disappeared before police could corral him.

"We take a lot of pride in this primary," Gloria Pilotte, the Ward 9 supervisor who stopped the voter fraud, told the *Herald*. "I'm very confident about the way we do this in New Hampshire."

The unknown man, dressed in a suit and tie, did not say why he was trying to vote as the recently deceased person and would not identify any group he was representing.

"He said 'You'll soon find out,'" Pilotte tells the *Herald*.

"I'm very confident about the way we do this in New Hampshire"? Poor Ms. Pilotte. She had no idea what was coming. The *Herald,* however, should have guessed. The only reason our agent got caught was that this older supervisor happened to know the voter who died. Given that personal recognition seemed to be the state's only screening device, its editors should have suspected that any number of zombie voters got through, and so followed up on the story. This wasn't reporting the *Herald* was doing. It was stenography.

As we knew by this time, Pilotte had more confidence in the system than her colleagues did. In another telling encounter, Adam Coolidge talked to a young female poll worker. This time he did not imply he was someone else.

AC: Do you have a Ferdinand Mitchell?

PW: What is the last name?

AC: Mitchell, Ferdinand Mitchell.

PW: Is this you, Ferdinand Anthony Mitchell?

AC: Actually, that's not me. He's deceased. I'm just checking to make sure if he's off the list.

PW: He hasn't been purged off the list.

AC: He hasn't been? Do you know if there are any other dead people on the list? We're just checking to make sure there aren't.

PW: How would I know if they are dead or not?

The poll worker sensed the absurdity of the request and laughed as she posed that last rhetorical question. Her question would go viral. More than 350,000 people would see her ask it. Within twenty-four hours, it was she, not Gloria Pilotte, who represented the true face of New Hampshire vigilance. We had no reason to doubt Pilotte's sincerity or Bullock's or that of any of the poll workers who graciously enabled our sting. We had to wonder, though, how easy it must be to commit fraud in a city or state where the poll workers were not quite so sincere.

ZOMBIE SYMPHONY

My guys sent me the raw zombie voter footage out of New Hampshire through Dropbox, and I went to work. As each file uploaded, I methodically began syncing the audio and visual. This was not much fun. Manually speeding up and slowing down footage to sync was a tedious, math-heavy exercise, but we lacked the resources major studios had to do this work automatically. In fact, we initially thought about holding all the footage for a year-end special, but after Sean Murphy met with a *Daily Caller* reporter in New Hampshire on primary night, we saw the wisdom in meeting the *Caller*'s next-day deadline.

For me, that meant an all-nighter. I put on classical music in the background and plowed through for twenty hours straight. I reviewed the footage, composed it, edited it, narrated it, and had a ten-minute video ready for the next day, January 11. I alerted Andrew Breitbart to the video and had him laughing for fifteen minutes over the phone at the comic absurdity of it all. To Andrew, watching our guys get offered ballots without even misrepresenting themselves was a "symphony to his eyes." He particularly liked the ending in which the mop-haired Ryk Bullock told #9 how very nearly impossible it was to be handed somebody else's ballot.

Given that everyone in the video was white, Andrew thought it nicely sabotaged the "voter ID is racist" narrative. He sent out one of his trademark tweets tagging his beloved *Media Matters* foes.

How's Institutional Left going to respond to @JamesOKeefeIII's exposure of how easy it is to Cheat-N-Vote®: thedc.com/xsmLmj@mmfa

I released the video through an exclusive arrangement with Tucker Carlson's *Daily Caller*. The supporting article, which was posted at 1:15 p.m., was simply titled "Dead People Receive Ballots in New Hampshire Primary." The video itself had been posted on YouTube less than an hour earlier.

Somewhere along the way someone tipped off Ryan Reilly, a young reporter for the influential insider blog *TPM* (in full, *Talking Points Memo*). At 12:54 p.m. that same day, twenty minutes before the *Daily Caller* article appeared, he sent an email to the members of an election law listserv trolling for "experts" to trash our efforts in New Hampshire. A friend forwarded me the email.

"As far as I can tell," Reilly said of our exploits, "this is the largest coordinated attempt at in-person voter impersonation fraud, and it was conducted by a group to show why voter ID laws were necessary." The language was loaded. Even before he got a single response, Reilly already knew what his narrative would be.

At 3:05 p.m., less than two hours after the *Daily Caller* posted its article, Reilly posted his article under the hopeful front-page banner "The Joke's Over." By "joke," I think he was referring to my career. The headline captured his thesis: "Election Law Experts Say James O'Keefe Allies

Could Face Charges Over Voter Fraud Stunt." The problem America faced in this critical election year, Reilly decided, was not voter fraud but illegal "stunts" pulled by the likes of Project Veritas.

Reilly found just the experts he needed to confirm his own talking points and manufactured a narrative by selectively editing their quotes. "So right off the bat, what they did violated the law," said Hamline University law professor David Schultz. How did he know we committed fraud? I don't know, because we didn't. We researched the law. Our guys never "procured" a ballot. They turned them down in every case. But why let little details stand in the way of a rousing narrative.

"Who in their right mind would risk a felony conviction for this?" Reilly quoted election law expert Rick Hasen as saying. "And who would be able to [commit fraud] in large enough numbers to (1) affect the outcome of the election and (2) remain undetected?" I would suggest Hasen ask those reform candidates who have lost local elections by as little as a single vote.

"The fact that activists can engage in a stunt is not a reason for reform," said NYU professor Samuel Issacharoff. "It means nothing." Issacharoff was reinforcing the bogus point that Reilly had made in his email, namely that we were trying "to show why voter ID laws were necessary." Reilly was implying, as would others, that we were tools of the Republican Party sent out to help pass voter ID laws or, in prog talk, "voter suppression" laws.

On the following day, Reilly wrote a follow-up article, this time challenging the funding of Project Veritas. The fact that we financed our election campaign with a fifty-thousand-dollar grant from a single donor seemed to him somehow conspiratorial. Who funds *TPM* I have no idea. Reilly also dredged up constitutional law professor Frank Askin from Rutgers, my alma mater. "It's another one of these O'Keefe bullshit actions," said Askin. "Let [our reporters] cast a vote, see what happens." In a listserv discussion Askin openly wished that our guys had voted so he could enjoy "the five year jail sentence" he foresaw for all of us.

Fortunately for me, I had a source who forwarded me the election law listserv discussion on this subject. It proved to be a fascinating intellectual and philosophical debate and much more nuanced than Reilly's reporting implied. One question that surfaced repeatedly was whether the visual truth we were exposing was—or was not—damning.

Hamline's David Schultz, citing Wittgenstein and Kant on the importance of experience, concluded, "The fact that this video depicted potentially how easy it is to commit false impersonation does not support the proposition that in fact widespread voter fraud exists."

Bradley A. Smith of Capital University Law School, ignored in all *TPM* articles, had a different take. Writing in response to Schultz, Smith made the argument that seemed obvious to the ordinary New Hampshire citizen:

> *The problem is that many in the anti-ID camp (where I basically consider myself as a policy, though not as a constitutional matter) regularly argue that not only is there no voter impersonation fraud, but that in fact it really cannot occur. . . . That latter argument now seems demolished.*

I had grown used to inciting media dustups, but to provoke a legal donnybrook—and get to observe it—was both new and deeply satisfying. The YouTube video was not only a symphony for the eyes, it was also grist for a heady philosophical discussion. I found myself speed-reading through these commentaries when not actively managing the media during these two sleepless days. The adrenaline kept me alert and engaged.

While the philosophers debated, the anti-journalists defamed. The night after the New Hampshire video debuted, Reilly appeared on Keith

Olbermann's TV show, *Countdown*. David Shuster, who was filling in for Olbermann, expanded the conspiracy to Fox News. He claimed that Fox "has been a crucial media ally for O'Keefe to promote his guerrilla exposés." I wish he were right. A Fox News documentary investigative unit requested the New Hampshire footage but did not actually use it. There were voices on Fox that had been helpful, but Beck was gone—he had turned against us, in any case—and Hannity had grown cautious. In fact, Fox would not so much as mention any of our election fraud stings until October.

As to the rest of the media, Shuster captured the gist of their thinking. "The right-wing fixation with voter fraud," he said, as though he had conjured this silliness up himself, "is largely used as a justification for passing restrictive ballot-access measures designed to suppress voter turnout among people who tend to vote for Democrats." History has shown, of course, an increase in voter turnout in states that have voter ID laws, but history has never much interested the folks at MSNBC.

Despite the claims of our antagonists, we were no one's tools. We were reporters. We were doing what reporters have historically done— exposing waste and fraud and allowing the policy makers to make what they would of it. Reilly and Shuster were practicing the fine art of anti-journalism, attacking real journalists who expose inconvenient facts. In 2012, unfortunately, there were more of them than there were of us, and there were no facts more inconvenient than the ones we were exposing.

The Reilly narrative held firm in the media, right down to the word *stunt*. The always reliable *Media Matters* headlined its article "Election Officials, Experts: O'Keefe Implicated in Another Illegal Stunt," and used my New Orleans mug shot to drive the point home. Joan Mc-Carter's *Daily Kos* article began with the words "James O'Keefe's New Hampshire stunt." Sam Favate of the *Wall Street Journal* had his law blog headlined "Might Conservative Activists Face Criminal Charges for Voter ID Stunt?" Note the absurd double standard here. The same people who insisted that there was no such thing as voter fraud were confident—or at least hopeful—that we had committed it.

The reader comments in these publications capture their audience's giddy fixation with sending me to jail. Let me cite just a few of the more printable. All of these follow the January 12 *Daily Kos* article, but you can find responses like these almost as easily at CNN:

> "How about a nice RICO Indictment for everyone involved in this conspiracy known as Project Veritas."

> "If you arrest these people and put them away for a while, you will not need voter ID check anymore."

> "[P]imple on the ass of democracy. Jail is exactly where this weasel belongs."

> "It's not a very effective scam if you actually get caught and go to jail, now is it?"

> "One can only hope Jimmy Boy O'K will step in something like a Class A felony which would carry major jail time so we can wave buh-bye to this arrogant, nicompoopish punk!"

> "This little douchebag has been doing this for YEARS. He should be in jail."

> "Go to jail. Go directly to jail. Don't stop at Go. Don't collect your paycheck from the monied interests you serve. Say hi to your cellmate, Bubba."

Who's kidding whom here? These creeps could not have cared less about our tactics. No, what bothered them were our targets. If Republicans were the ones profiting from wholesale vote harvesting and lax enforcement of the law, these same people would be following me on Twitter and friending me on Facebook, not cheering on the eternal Bubba, my imagined prison rapist. They have held me to a much higher standard of fair play than other journalists, and they have refused to admit this, even to themselves.

Maybe I missed something in my college government classes, but I thought liberals defined themselves by their sense of justice and fair play. The unfortunate fact is there are few real liberals left. "Liberals" don't cheer when the feds destroy my evidence, as they did in New Orleans, or when YouTube pulls down my Planned Parenthood videos, or when the networks censor what we exposed in New Hampshire.

Liberalism was yielding to fascism. It has happened before. We can take little consolation in the fact that our fascists are largely softcore, but that can change quicker than you can say "Nakoula Basseley Nakoula." As I write this, our friends in the media are fully silent on Nakoula's imprisonment for producing the quasi-movie *The Innocence of Muslims*. Yet when the Christian right merely protested the federal funding of Andres Serrano's equally offensive photograph *Piss Christ*, they rushed to Serrano's defense, just as they rushed to David Gregory's defense when he waved an illegal gun clip on *Meet the Press*. Worse, if you ask them about this, they won't even see the problem.

The thousand calls for my imprisonment did not go unheard. Sure enough, the day after the release of the New Hampshire video, Pat Hattersley and his supervisor showed up at my parents' house packing heat and asking questions. I was there at the bat cave that week, managing the media. When they arrived, in fact, I was sleeping on the floor, my first sleep in about forty-eight hours. My parents had no idea what was going on, but my normally reserved dad stood up for me with a resolve that made me proud. Although I slept through it, my mother and grandfather watched Dad square off against these guys in front of the house. The conversation went something like this.

"What seems to be the problem, Pat?"

"We just want to know what your son is up to," said Hattersley. "You know about his video in New Hampshire. We want to know what he did up there."

"You're going to have to ask him. He's a grown man. He does journalism. I haven't talked to him recently."

"We're just checking in," Hattersley responded. "We want to find out about what he's doing with the election."

"You know, guys," said Dad, more than a little bit exasperated, "you'd think with all the problems facing our society, the rape, the murder, the fraud on Wall Street, you'd have something better to do than come here and harass Jimmy—for what?—a Class B misdemeanor?"

When Hattersley protested, my dad overrode him. "It's a disgrace," he continued, "a complete and total failure of the American judicial system."

"You're entitled to your opinion, sir."

"No, it's not my opinion, Pat. It's a disgrace what you are doing to my son."

"That's your view."

"And it's an affront to the Constitution. Now get off my property and leave my family alone."

After that day in January 2012, Pat and his supervisor never came to my parents' house again.

THE AMERICAN WAY

Veritas Rule #27:
The truth is manifestly damning.

While the Beltway bloggers were busily ridiculing our "stunt," the citizens of New Hampshire were busy emailing their elected representatives. Just about every citizen in the state except those caught on tape was appalled, not at anything Project Veritas had done, but at what the state government had *not* done, namely protect the integrity of their ballots.

We had made the decision to ignore the national media and focus on the local, which are usually less complacent and almost always less corrupt. The local news stations in New Hampshire did not disappoint. Their coverage was impressively balanced.

Local television responded to the story because we gave them something to show. That is the beauty of video. The people who watched did not deceive themselves into thinking they had been hoodwinked by tricky editing. They understood that all TV news was "selectively edited." All journalists use excerpts to highlight the most newsworthy things said or done by their subjects. If anything, our editing was more honest than the networks'. The taxpayers of New Hampshire knew what they were seeing, and they were not happy about it at all. They quickly shared that unhappiness with their elected officials.

On Thursday, November 12, the state's Republican leaders weighed in. "This video has placed a shocking exclamation point on the need for immediate reform to New Hampshire's election laws to ensure that voter fraud does not taint the rights of our citizens to have their votes counted in an honest, responsible way," said House Speaker William O'Brien. O'Brien added that the video "horrified" the nation. He was not mincing words.

"Well, it's clear today," added House Majority Leader D. J. Bettencourt, "that the emperor has no clothes and that it's time to undo the damage of the Democrat rule and put some real teeth into the integrity of our elections by passing photo ID and residency laws to ensure that this doesn't happen again."

The New Hampshire political establishment would hear none of this. Having reassured his citizens that fraud was an illusion when he vetoed the voter ID bill just months prior, Democrat governor John Lynch saw nothing amiss but our actions. His cronies were equally myopic. They didn't want reform. They wanted revenge. "They [the Project Veritas team] should be arrested and prosecuted to the fullest extent of the law," said Manchester's *Republican* mayor Ted Gatsas. "People who pull stunts like this should be prosecuted," added Nashua city clerk Paul Bergeron, who had gotten his "stunt" talking point down. I wonder if either of these guys ever called a *60 Minutes* sting a "stunt."

The day after the video surfaced, Bergeron, who looks scarily like V. I. Lenin, appeared on Al Sharpton's MSNBC show to make the case that voter fraud is an illusion. Sharpton knows a thing or two about fraud. He first came to national attention for his stirring defense of fifteen-year-old Tawana Brawley. In November 1987 Brawley claimed that six white men, among them Dutchess County prosecutor Steven Pagones, had raped, mutilated, and smeared her with feces. In Sharpton's mind, this was just another day on the job for a white prosecutor and his pals.

The charge was absurd on the face of it, but Sharpton milked it for all the racial guilt he could extract. After months of empty theatrics, the grand jury ruled conclusively that Brawley fabricated her story. Pagones turned around and sued Sharpton for slander. True to form, Sharpton was slow to pay what the court ordered. As the Internal Revenue Service will attest, he hasn't done much better paying Uncle Sam his due. Yet, bizarrely, he is considered respectable enough to have his own show on a major cable network. Go figure.

Bergeron argued the attorney general's case for him. "Its [our team's] own activity should be looked at and prosecuted," he said, claiming that our reporters "took physical possession of the ballots." The MSNBC editors helped him with this half-truth by editing out the parts where our guys hand the ballots back. Throughout his six minutes of near fame, Bergeron spoke over a banner that read, "Right wing smear team may face legal actions from voter fraud." On the national level, this passes for television news.

Sharpton had to know better. In 1984, a New York State grand jury uncovered a widespread zombie voting conspiracy that had gone on in his native Brooklyn for at least fourteen years. One of the witnesses told the grand jury how he led a crew of eight people from one polling place to another in the course of an election day. Each member of the crew voted at least twenty times and, according to the witness, there were twenty other such crews working that same day. Write Fund and Von Spakovsky, "This extensive fraud could have been stopped if New York required voters to authenticate their identity at the polls."

The anti-journalists would hear none of this. Scott Keyes of *Think-Progress* captured the gist of their coverage in his headline "James O'Keefe's Group Appears to Commit Voter Fraud in Order to Gin Up

Hysteria Over Non-Existent Fraud Problem." Nonexistent? Note that this blogger had to use an eighteen-word headline to obfuscate what the video made painfully clear. Still, as with the law professor quoting Wittgenstein, video beats words like rock beats scissors.

Governor Lynch, meanwhile, appeared on local WMUR-TV, beating the drum for prosecution. "I hope that they should be prosecuted to the fullest extent of the law," he said of our crew, then added a kicker that made logical hash out of the whole sentence, "if in fact they're found guilty of some criminal act." No, governor, you can be found guilty only *after* you are prosecuted. Of course, these are the kind of stupid things public officials say when they are thoroughly embarrassed. At this point, the authorities were not exactly sure what we had done wrong, but they were prepared to find something they could make stick.

Not exactly sure what law we might have broken, the media began to contact the widows of the deceased to prompt them into outrage. The *Boston Herald* found its way to Rachel Groux, widow of Roger Groux. "That's awful," she told the reporter upon learning that her late husband's name had been used. "Why should they use his name? They shouldn't use anybody's name—alive or deceased." Yes, *exactly*. In trying to use the widow's comments to make us look bad, the *Herald* reinforced the point we were hoping to make.

The *Daily Kos* repeated Rachel's lament just before asking its readers to sign a petition to be sent to New Hampshire attorney general Michael Delaney and U.S. attorney John Kacavas demanding that we be investigated. So much for the First Amendment! The reader will recall that Mark Myrdeck, the investigator who worked under Delaney, floated the offended-widow theme when he tried to browbeat the Coolidge family into giving up Adam.

The *Daily Kos* would deliver more than one hundred thousand signatures to Delaney urging him to investigate "the alleged voter fraud committed by right-wing activist James O'Keefe." People for the American Way, which collaborated with the *Daily Kos* on the petition drive, insisted that voter fraud was "an extremely rare phenomenon" but that in trying to prove otherwise, I "committed fraud" myself.

What kind of "American Way," I wondered, was the attempt to silence truth-telling? We weren't advancing policy or lobbying lawmakers or giving cash to campaigns. We were videotaping reality, and this reality, as the one law professor noted, "demolished" the illusion that fraud was impossible.

To preserve that illusion, the New Hampshire authorities continued their harassment of the Coolidge family. In the weeks following the initial visit, Mary saw Merdyck drive by the house at least a half dozen times. Twice she saw him in her rearview mirror. Once she saw his car in front of hers and watched as he sped away when he spotted her behind him. She was ready to say "What in the world do you want from me?" Merdyck was around so often that Adam and I thought it might be neighborly of the Coolidges to order him a pizza. That gesture, after all, seemed much closer to the American way than hounding reporters and harassing their families.

THE RISE OF RICHARD HEAD

Veritas Rule #28:
*They may never understand your ideas,
but they will be forced to understand your results.*

Mark Myrdeck did not give up easily. On May 7, 2012, a Monday, I was scheduled to speak in New Hampshire. When I filed my travel documents with my probation officer, I told him I was going to stay in Hollis, New Hampshire, with a fellow named Mike Rogers. At 9 a.m., on the day I was scheduled to speak, Rogers, still in his bathrobe, found Myrdeck at the door with a local policeman in tow and a large briefcase in his hand. I can only guess that the state and federal authorities were communicating about my comings and goings.

Although he was at pains to suggest I was not in jeopardy, Myrdeck came with a criminal grand jury subpoena to serve me. As he did at the Coolidges' house, he placed a dossier on the counter with a photo sticking out. This one was of Skip Murphy, another local activist. "I know all about you. I read your stuff. I watched your speeches," he told Rogers, who could only surmise that they were researching any local activist in any way associated with me.

My saving grace was that Myrdeck was overeager. After he left, Rogers called to warn me. Having overslept, I had not yet left New Jersey. I called Mike Madigan. He called Myrdeck and called me right back. "I talked to this Merdeck, Merdick, Merdook guy," he told me in his unreformed Brooklynese. "They have a criminal subpoena waiting for you. You ain't going to New Hampshire." This would be one of many times Madigan saved my bacon.

I didn't go. I Skyped in my speech to a Republican fund-raiser at the Abenaqui Country Club in Rye Beach, New Hampshire. "I've been advised that if I appear physically in New Hampshire, I will be hit with a grand jury subpoena," I told them. "This is what public officials do to journalists these days." I hated to disappoint my friends, but they fully understood. This wouldn't be the last time I had to Skype into an event from New Jersey.

I suppose if your parents had named you "Richard Head," you might go through life with a chip on your shoulder, too. New Hampshire associate attorney general Dick Head certainly seemed to. Head was my Javert, the guy within the state AG's office who had the charge of bringing me to justice, or something like it, for my role in the January vote fraud sting. On this memorable day, his hounding took a truly weird turn. To advance the state's investigation, he sent a letter to a "Ms. Nadia Naffe" requesting the "electronic records" she had in her possession relating "to James O'Keefe and/or Project Veritas."

After the judge in New Jersey rejected her harassment claim, Nadia had taken her increasingly strange case public on her own highly detailed and accusatory blog. She seemed to be buying into the inferences that Olbermann and Shuster were making about rape. She accused me publicly of "false imprisonment," of recruiting my friend Tony to "intimidate" or, worse, "assault" her, of keeping her panties as "a souvenir to show off to [my] friends." The vague hint that she made at the hearing of being drugged became much more specific. "I tried to escape from the barn as quickly as I could," she wrote. "I tried to run away, but I didn't know where I was. I felt disoriented after drinking the alcohol you purchased." Blogger Nicole Belle summarized the saga: "Rape barns? Sex tapes? Intimidation by hidden older male friends? WTH? Isn't this guy on probation still? Shouldn't he be getting visits from the authorities?" Maureen O'Connor's *Gawker* blog headlined the evolving story "James O'Keefe's Panty-Stealing 'Rape Barn' Sex Scandal."

After repeating every one of Nadia's increasingly bizarre claims, O'Connor conceded, "There's a chance that Nadia is a litigious paranoiac who blows minor grievances out of proportion and misinterprets the world around her." Yes, Maureen, there is a chance of that. I was coming to believe that Nadia was in fact an agent provocateur. This was not paranoia. This was my reality. For some time, allies had been warning me about potential moles. Given the hostility we faced, I fully expected to be stung at some point. The symmetry of it would have thrilled our antagonists in the media.

In time, we were able to procure Nadia's relevant emails, and we realized that she had been in communication with half the anti-journalists in the known universe. They were slobbering over the steaming bull that they hoped Nadia would serve up. Nadia also tried to lure our common acquaintances into accusing me of thoughtcrime on matters racial. "Have you ever had any suspicions that James harbored racial attitudes towards minorities, specifically African Americans?" she asked Hannah Giles. To prod Hannah's memory, Nadia provided links to a few slanderous articles about me. Said Hannah in response, "No, I never got that feeling."

I cite all this to show that Nadia is the kind of person New Hampshire was willing to enlist in its case against me. Dick Head and his cronies were that desperate. They were so desperate that they asked Nadia for the "electronic records" that she had stolen from me. I do not make this charge lightly. A month after Nadia's brief stay at our carriage house, electronic copies of some of my confidential documents and correspondence ended up in the hands of a Washington D.C. reporter. The reporter shared the material with Madigan but would not name his source. Upon investigation, however, we discovered that the PDF files' "properties," as accessed through Adobe software, were created by one "Nadia Naffe." We promptly filed for a restraining order to prevent Nadia from disseminating any further material.

It got more bizarre still. Naffe appeared to be collaborating with Democrat campaign consultant Neal Rauhauser, an associate of convicted bomber and current paper terrorist Brett Kimberlin. In fact, Nadia had her picture taken with Rauhauser on an Amtrak train. At the time, she was traveling to a hearing in New Jersey, where the judge would issue the restraining order we had requested to secure my files.

Fortunately, bulldog Mike Madigan would tolerate none of this. "I am appalled," he wrote to Head, "that the Attorney General and chief law enforcement officer of the great and historic state of New Hampshire would be seeking data which was stolen from one or more of Mr. O'Keefe's computers without his knowledge or consent." Madigan then cited the restraining order just filed.

> *You should be aware that Ms. Naffe is the subject of a court order in New Jersey with respect to the very same stolen materials you are seeking to obtain. This court order specifically prohibits her from transferring this stolen property to anyone. Surely the Attorney General's office does not want to be complicit in a violation of Judge [Harry] Carroll's Court Order.*

If I had not lived this stuff, I might not believe it. It even stunned Madigan, who had seen just about everything. Fortunately, he had clout enough to keep Head at bay. Head backed off.

An adviser of mine would explain to me the difference between failure and success. *Failure,* he said, is sitting outside an innocent New

Hampshire family's home in an unmarked squad car for endless hours with a pointless subpoena for a non-crime. *Failure,* he continued, is soliciting the help of a person who has a restraining order against her for claiming she hacked into your Gmail. *Success,* he told me, is seeing both houses of the New Hampshire legislature pass a voter ID bill by veto-proof margins because of your efforts.

This event occurred on June 27, 2012, when the New Hampshire Senate voted 18–5 to override the governor's veto of Senate Bill 289. The bill required voters in the November 2012 election to show a photo ID or sign an affidavit. The House passed the bill 231–112, also margin enough for a veto override.

John Lynch, the governor who wanted us "prosecuted to the fullest extent of the law," had five days to sign the bill, but if he refused to, it did not matter. The bill would pass into law in any case. We're not policy people. We did not set out to accomplish this. But the passage of this hugely popular voter reform made it damn hard to prosecute the guys who made it happen. "There is nothing in this life as sweet as justice," I wrote on ProjectVeritas.com, "and nothing as motivating as injustice."

Beyond New Hampshire, at least on the surface, our success changed little. The media continued to hate us. Embarrassed state attorneys general continued to hound us. The rationalizers continued to insist that the triangle did not have three sides. But all their bluster could not compete with the truth and clarity of a video produced by a Jersey guy on probation. New Hampshire was something of a breakthrough, and they knew it. What we accomplished there had consequence.

LIVING ON A PRAYER IN MINNESOTA

Veritas Rule #29:
Rock beats scissors. Journalism beats anti-journalism.

"Matt Drudge's 15 minutes of fame may be ending on a rather nasty note," *Salon*'s Jonathan Broder assured us—*fifteen years ago*. I can identify with Drudge here. No matter what my colleagues and I did, there was some reporter somewhere ready to console America that it had heard the last of James O'Keefe.

Tommy Christopher, the White House correspondent for *Mediaite*, a prominent blog that purports to cover the media, was one such nonbeliever. On February 8, 2012, Christopher posted a story headlined "James O'Keefe's 'Fake Tim Tebow' Voter Fraud 'Investigation' Doesn't Have a Prayer." The day before, we had posted on Breitbart.com a video showing the holes in Minnesota election law. Not only did he call the video "garbage," but he also repeated the mindless media talking point that my goal was "to enact strict voter ID laws" and in the process disenfranchise "millions of voters" who tend to vote Democratic.

Yes, Tommy, our investigation did have a prayer. It woke the citizens up to the chaos that passed for Minnesota election law, and they alerted their legislators by the thousands. One of them, Representative Mary Kiffmeyer, promptly sponsored a bill to clean up the system. "If you have no system that deters and detects fraud," said Kiffmeyer, "and you don't determine the identity of voters, the electoral system cannot inspire public confidence."

What Jon Buckley and Adam Coolidge collected in Minnesota shocked even me, and I thought I was unshockable. Instead of showing up to request ballots on election day, they went from one seat of county government to another, talked to election officials in each one of those counties, and brought the videotaped conversations back for me to prepare for YouTube. We chose this strategy because Minnesota has stricter laws than other states on misrepresentation at the polling places. By going this route, we were able to expose a completely different weakness in the system. My law school education proved helpful after all.

Still trapped in New Jersey, I had an astonishing wealth of footage from which to choose, all of it provided by friendly officials who had little anxiety about the electoral house of cards they were superintending. I imagine that none of them has stolen a vote in his or her life or even thought to. Unfortunately for the citizens of Minnesota, they lived in a world where not everyone is as nice as their officials.

The weakness of the Minnesota system was embedded in a single sentence on the state's voter registration form, and it was for that reason we targeted Minnesota. The would-be voter was invited to mark the box that applied to him or her. The most lethal box reads:

I do not have a MN-issued driver's license or a MN ID card, or a Social Security Card.

No problem, the voter was still eligible. He just checked that box. The same voter did not even have to come in to register. "Is it possible for a third party to register a group of voters?" our guys asked the election officials. Yes, sure. "Can I have twenty or so registration forms?" Sure, why not. "Do I need to bring in their IDs or anything?" No, of course not. "It's just kind of an honor system?" Yes, pretty much. "We're not the police."

Jon asked if anyone was ever caught voting illegally. "Yes," admitted the clerk, "but it is, you know, after the fact. My election judges have a hard time with that. They're like, 'Change the law, change the law.'"

The judges were right. The law definitely needed changing. Jon and Adam established that the newly registered voters could vote absentee, again without anyone ever confirming they actually exist. To ease the mind of those readers who might be duped by my "idiocy," Tommy Christopher argued that the federal Help America Vote Act (HAVA) of 2002 required voters who did not register in person to provide ID the first time they voted. Unfortunately, not one of the officials our guys talked to even mentioned HAVA. I doubt if most poll workers had even heard of the law.

The greatest weakness of the system, as our video showed, was the registering and voting of people, real or imagined, en masse through the absentee process. Perversely, some of my critics ridiculed me for advocating photo IDs since it is generally agreed that the point of greatest vulnerability is absentee voting. Earth to media: I have never lobbied for photo IDs!

Christopher ignored every flash point in our video and persisted in the illusion that "successfully registering fake people is incredibly difficult, and casting fake votes is even harder." Oblivious of recent history, he insisted that manufacturing enough votes to affect the outcome of an election was "a near-impossibility, and certainly not worth the penalty." I am sure U.S. senator Norm Coleman will take heart knowing that. In 2008, he had his career short-circuited by some of these nearly impossible practices, losing his reelection bid to comedian Al Franken by 312 votes out of nearly 3 million votes cast. In fact, Coleman led after the initial count, but Franken was awarded the great majority of the 953 "wrongly rejected" absentee ballots.

Although there is no way to gauge how many fake absentee votes were cast in that election, there is reliable evidence that more than a thousand ineligible felons voted illegally. Nearly two hundred of them, in fact, were later convicted of doing just that. The felons proved a crucial voting bloc given the margin of "victory."

I suspect Christopher would respond, "How do we know they voted Democratic?" We know because felons almost always do. In 1996, as Fund and Von Spakovsky documented, Bill Clinton received an estimated 93 percent of the admittedly hard-to-track felon vote. Even when controlled for race and class, surveys show felons are much more likely to vote Democratic. I'll leave it to Christopher to imagine why.

In some cases, our guys identified their would-be absentee voters as "Tim Tebow" and "Tom Brady." The two famous quarterbacks had dueled the previous Sunday in a much-watched NFL playoff game. Christopher cited the use of these names as proof of our "idiotic smugness." He then unwittingly proved our marketing smarts by referring to our sting in the headline as the "'Fake Tim Tebow' Voter Fraud 'Investigation.'" "Tebow," in fact, was the verbal equivalent of a prop. Yes, Tommy, we branded our effort with Tebow's name, and you bought it. You gave the brand life. Much appreciated.

I am at a total loss to understand the psychology of anti-journalists like Tommy Christopher. They get up each day for work, look in the mirror, and say to themselves—what?—"Today, I am going to slime a citizen journalist, smugly predict his demise, and then, when my prediction proves laughable, hope that no one notices." Why get out of bed in the morning?

STORMING VERMONT

Veritas Rule #30:
Don't blow your cover while inside the place.

If the Academy of Motion Picture Arts and Sciences ever decides to give out an award for best actor in an election sting video—admittedly, not a likelihood—our man Jon Buckley, #3, would be odds-on favorite to win for his performance in Vermont. Well versed in the dark art of political espionage, Jon is a seriously versatile guy. He combines the seeming innocence of the Dustin Hoffman character in *The Graduate* with a Bogart-like ability to back authority figures down. Helping him too is his ethnically—and even chronologically—amorphous appearance. If he tells you he's a Russian, you believe him. If he tells you an Egyptian, you believe that, too.

At one polling station, in an accent that he likely picked up from *Borat*, Jon requested a ballot for a fellow whose first name just happened to be "Mohammed." When the poll worker pronounced "Mohammed" the way you or I would, Jon haughtily corrected her:

PW: Mohammed?

JB: Moccchhh-med. Please, Moccchhh-med.

PW: Moccchhh-med?

JB: The name is Moccchhh-med.

PW: Moccchhh-med?

JB: Moccchhh-med.

Jon then attempted to show the poll worker his ID, and she, like every other clerk that day, insisted that no ID was necessary.

JB: You don't need ID?

PW: You said you are who you are. Your name is on there.

JB: This vote, you need ID?

PW: Nope.

JB: You don't need ID? In Kazakhstan, you need ID.

I laughed all through the editing of this one. In fact, the Vermont primary proved as easy to crack as New Hampshire, maybe easier. Sean Murphy, who lives nearby in New Hampshire, secured a list of registered Vermont voters. He did it legally. Figuring that only a minority of people vote in primaries, even presidential ones, our guys requested and were handed ballots under the names of six living people and two dead ones. Every time we asked, we received.

Fluent in French, Sean Murphy requested a ballot for a fellow whose name sounded vaguely French-Canadian. "You need my passport?" he asked in heavily accented English. When the worker said no, he replied, "You don't need my ID? In Quebec we always need to show license."

This all would have been much funnier if the future of the republic were not at stake. Despite all the clues that he might not be a citizen, the poll worker blithely offered Sean a ballot. This was one of six locations at which we were offered ballots.

To give Vermont's voter law context, Jon stopped in a Burlington bar, ordered a beer, and declined to show ID. When the bartender refused him, he indignantly insisted on talking to the bar's manager, a very polite female. Not only did Jon have his talking points down pat, but he also managed to express them in a pitch-perfect progressive whine.

SM: You require a photo ID here?

BM: Yes, we do. Actually, the state of Vermont does.

SM: So you follow it because the state says so?

BM: Well, we follow it because we don't want to be shut down and lose our liquor license.

SM: So you're just following orders.

BM: Absolutely.

SM: That's an alcohol suppression law. It's a piece of legislation that disproportionately affects minorities.

BM: I am very sorry that I can't serve you without an ID.

SM: You don't care. That is racist. . . . I don't have the time. I don't have the resources and the money to say, "Look, I have to quit my job and go down to the DMV and do this."

BM: Then you don't want to drink badly enough.

If only Vermont secretary of state Jim Condos approached his job as logically and ethically as the manager of this Burlington bar! Advising me

on questions of beer and constitutional law was one of the real authorities on both subjects, J. Christian Adams. If the name sounds familiar it
is because Adams, a civil rights attorney, very publicly quit the Department of Justice for its failure to prosecute the New Black Panther Party.
This was the case where billy-club-wielding Black Panthers stood outside
a polling place in 2008 intimidating would-be voters. After an investigation, Adams and other Justice Department lawyers filed charges. The
Panthers failed to respond, and a federal court in Philadelphia entered
a "default" against them. Then, incredibly, Obama political appointees
in the Justice Department intervened and got the case dismissed. This
eye-popping offense caused less hand-wringing in America's newsrooms
than did our innocent voter stings. The White House counted on that.

After our guys came back from Vermont, Adams argued that or-
dering a beer and voting were not really parallel acts. The latter was a
constitutional right. The former was not. In Vermont, however, what
was a constitutional right, at least according to the state constitution,
was gay marriage. "I'll bet the state requires photo ID before they issue
a license," said Adams.

Gay marriage, of course! This made for a much better constitutional
analogy than drinking and a perfect visual juxtaposition as well. Our
adversaries would be hard-pressed to argue that gay unions were not
a constitutional right. We did not, however, have time to send anyone
back to Vermont to ask for a marriage license, especially since we had
agreed to release this video the next day.

So we settled on nearby Emerson, New Jersey. Talk about spontaneous—we had only twenty-five minutes to get to the Emerson City Hall
before it closed for the weekend. There were three of us, and I was the
only one with a car, and that was a two-seater. Not quite sure how to
look "gay," I grabbed a pair of thick, nonprescription black glasses and
put on a skintight shirt. Then I drove Jon and Adam Coolidge there in
separate trips.

Breathlessly, Jon and I asked the clerk to process our impending civil union—Governor Chris Christie had just vetoed a gay marriage bill. After I handed over the twenty-seven dollars for our license, the clerk casually asked, "Now I do need to see your papers." We grew appropriately outraged. "We don't actually have identification," I told her. "We can't afford it." When the clerk insisted that we could not proceed without it, I asked her how it was that we could vote without ID but not get married.

"They're both constitutional rights," Jon, my intended, chimed in. "It's a marriage repression law," I added. Throwing every likely riff in the mix, Jon turned into Rain Man and started pounding the counter, chanting, "ethnic minorities, ethnic minorities." He was supposed to be an Arab. Adam was casually recording all this on his iPhone. This was one flak catcher, bless her heart, who was unmoved by our mau-mauing. "There is nothing I can do," she told us. "This is what the state is asking you to do," I inquired. "You ask for ID?" She said, "Yes," and that was that.

We posted the Vermont video on March 13 through Breitbart's BigJournalism.com. I thought it was one of our more entertaining and informative efforts. Although we never said where the civil union scene was shot, I was expecting the purists to object on the grounds that it was shot in New Jersey and not in Vermont. That did not happen. What did happen was that my probation officer, Pat Hattersley, thought that I had gone to Vermont without telling him. In a fit he called me, ready to suspend my probation.

"James," he yelled, "what were you doing in Vermont?! You didn't have permission!"

"No, Pat, I was in Emerson, New Jersey."

"But James, your video was about the Vermont election."

"But it was also about getting a license for a civil union. Vermont doesn't have civil unions. They have gay marriage. Don't take my word for it. Just look up the law."

That seemed to put his mind at ease, but the absurdity of it all had to weigh even on Hattersley. Here he was thinking I had gone to marry some guy in Vermont and he was relieved to learn that I had actually gone to marry some guy in New Jersey. This was pure screwball comedy. What was less amusing was the thought that Pat, or more likely his supervisor, was really upset because I had ticked off still another muckety-muck from some other state, in this case, Vermont secretary of state Jim Condos.

Chunky and mustachioed, Condos looks like a guy who has sat behind a desk for far too long. Worse, he seems to have spent most of that time memorizing media talking points. Forgetting that Vermont was not exactly Bedford-Stuy—it is whiter even than New Hampshire—he responded to our efforts with the kind of feigned outrage Al Sharpton had. As he told a local reporter about our sting, "It's an attempt to suppress particular classes of voters."

The classes he cited were three: "college students, minorities, and senior citizens." I shook my head in bewilderment when I read this. Don't these guys ever think about what they are saying? For starters, Condos could hand-deliver an ID to all the black and brown people in Vermont. The state is less than 1 percent black. For another, Republicans carried the over-sixty-five vote by an astounding twenty-point margin in 2010. If we were Republican operatives as accused, why would we suppress the votes of our best constituency? And finally, being young enough to remember, I can assure you—the problem for students in any state is not the difficulty of securing a photo ID, but the ease.

A few months later, an African-American named Derrick Grayson, a self-appointed "Minister of Truth," posted a short and funny video that speaks to just how patronizing guys like Condos can be. After mimicking the "this is going to make it harder for students, the poor, and minorities" refrain, Grayson lights up. "Do you not see the insult in this, negroes. They saying you are too goddamn stupid to have voter ID." He then wonders why anyone would block efforts to require ID, "unless, of course, they want that voter fraud to take place." Bingo!

True to form, Condos assured his fellow citizens that our sting was "an attempt to show a problem where none exists." The real problem, of course, was the sting itself. "The perpetrators of this video actually did commit voter fraud," he told the local news. He then sicced Attorney General William Sorrell on Project Veritas. This, of course, made no sense. None of our guys ever took a ballot or voted. It is as if we shot footage of an open bank vault to show the ease of stealing money and then were arrested for bank robbery.

As it happens, incumbent Sorrell was challenged in an August Democratic primary by T. J. Donovan. Although Sorrell would ultimately prevail, primary day ended without a clear winner. The race was that tight, a final margin of fewer than seven hundred votes. Condos estimated that only 8 to 10 percent of registered voters went to the polls. What this means is that a crew of vote thieves could have moved from polling place to polling place early that morning with only the remotest chance of asking for a ballot in the name of someone who had already voted. Of course, that would never happen in Vermont.

MORTE D'ANDREW

Veritas Rule #31:
Keep your mind open to people who know more than you do.

I was lying in bed the morning of March 1 when I got the call. For me, and for many Americans, it was one of those jolts that imprint the time and place of your first awareness into your memory banks. It was Matt Boyle, a reporter at the *Daily Caller*, who phoned me. "James," he said, "did you hear this thing that Breitbart's dead?"

Only half awake, I was unsure whether I was dreaming. "Let me call you back," I said confusedly. I checked my messages. They were flooding over. I was not dreaming. Andrew had died. He had collapsed on a Brentwood street of apparent heart failure. He was forty-three years old. He left behind a loving wife and those four inspired little kids. He was one of a kind. There was no duplicating him.

"People are going to say whatever and try to claim whatever to try and take us out," Andrew told me a few days before he died. "They have an irrational fear of us. They want us on a leash. We're not going to be on a leash. They want us to dance. We're not going to dance with them."

Andrew confirmed the reality of this every time he appeared in the mainstream media. Time and time again he was attacked in every way and from every angle imaginable, and time and time again he refused to be leashed and refused to dance. In our country today, to inform your fellow citizens and to advocate for those positions your conscience dictates is not an easy thing. It can be a battle. Battles need warriors, and Andrew was our warrior. Like Achilles, he had a vulnerable spot. It proved to be his heart. Although he did not smoke, he tested that heart every day in a thousand ways. The man never stopped. I'm not sure he slept. If he slept, he never rested.

Andrew had long been a source of comfort and advice for me because he knew better than anyone the challenges we citizen journalists face. Better than anyone he understood the effort and energy required to fight, not just the big fights, but the small fights as well. With every article, every email, every tweet, every day, he battled to get the truth out. He struggled against the forces of conformity and compliance, and he prevailed far more often than not.

While Andrew and I were very different people in many respects, we thought much alike. When we engaged, there was a special creative flow between the two of us. "What if?" he posited mischievously. "Why not?" I would respond, our dialogue drifting into a veritable theater of the absurd. At one event, I was speaking to a friendly audience about a future video concept, "Earth Supply and Renewal," in which I planned to take a government subsidy to an outlandish extreme—digging holes and refilling them. Andrew immediately got the gist of what I planned to do, and he and I started scheming with each other right there in front of the crowd. The video, released in July, brought hell down on a local legislator who admitted on tape, "Between you and I, a lot of these Green Jobs program are bullshit." Andrew never got to see the video.

Many people in the media and in the wider world waste their time pursuing power, money, and glory. Not Andrew. He was set on this earth to expose the facts, right the wrongs, and pursue the truth wherever it might lead. I am honored that he took me along for the ride. Many of the friends who called that March morning asked, "What are you going to do now?" In my head, I heard the response Andrew was channeling: "What are *you* going to do now?"

I wish I could leave this chapter here, but to understand the war Andrew was waging, you need to see the response to his death. On that same March 1, only hours after I heard the news, *Rolling Stone* magazine posted its eulogy, "Andrew Breitbart: Death of a Douche," by Matt Taibbi. "So Andrew Breitbart is dead," wrote Taibbi. "Here's what I have to say to that, and I'm sure Breitbart himself would have respected this reaction: *Good!* Fuck him. I couldn't be happier that he's dead." The tweets were worse:

They say not to say anything ill of the dead, but to only mention the good. Andrew Breitbart is dead. Good.

Breitbart is dead? Good riddance, rot in the ground.

Congrats to Andrew Breitbart on the promotion from "fucking asshole" to "controversial figure."

I never wished Andrew Breitbart dead, but don't ask me to give a fuck about that hate mongering lying son of a bitch because he is dead.

Andrew Breitbart was a piece of shit yesterday and he's a piece of shit today. Death changes nothing.

Just took a huge shit and flushed it as a tribute to Andrew
Breitbart's life.

Wow! Just heard Andrew Breitbart died. Hele-fucking-lujiah.
NOT sorry to see that asshole gone. So Andrew, how's Hell ya
fucking cunt?

These go on and on. To be fair, Andrew emerged from the same cultural
swamp as the people he offended. He could be rough even on the dead,
but not that rough, not that vile, not nearly. A child of Hollywood, he
directed himself on life's stage and kept honing that direction. What we
need are just a few good citizens to follow his lead. God bless you, Andrew Breitbart. Thank you for all you have taught me and all that you
have taught the world.

TEBOW SCORES

Veritas Rule #32:

Brand your action, and it will have legs.

Shortly after midnight on April 3, after a nine-hour debate, the Minnesota House voted by a 72–57 margin to send a new constitutional amendment to the voters in November. Later that afternoon, the Senate approved the same measure by a 35–29 vote. If the voters approved the measure, Minnesotans would have to show a photo ID when they voted, and they would no longer be allowed to "vouch" for someone else's eligibility. The amendment, if passed, would also result in reforms to the system of provisional balloting.

In the debate leading up to the vote, Representative Steve Drazkowski began his defense of the proposed bill like this: "Many of you have received as I did emails that showed a YouTube video of a Thomas Brady and a Timothy Tebow." For me, still confined to New Jersey, this was pure ear candy. Our "Tebow" brand still had legs. If you recall, Tommy Christopher of *Mediaite* boldly predicted our Minnesota sting did not "have a prayer." Obviously, it did. Had the Yes Men ever prompted a state senate to amend its constitution?

Drazkowski elaborated on what our video revealed. He focused, as we did, on the section of the voter registration form that allowed a would-be voter to check the box "I do not have a MN-issued driver's license or a MN ID card, or a Social Security Card" and jump right into the electoral process. A majority of Minnesota legislators found that Grand Canyon–sized loophole troubling. The purpose of their reform was simple enough. "So we know for sure people are who they say they are," said Drazkowski, "and they live where they say they live."

If this seems unprovocative to you, it provoked the hell out of every legislator in either chamber without an *R* in front of his or her name. Watch the video of the debate and you will be treated to some world-class caterwauling, in this case from the distinctly Minnesota Democratic-Farmer-Labor Party (DFL). Not a single one of its members, in the state House or Senate, voted for the bill's passage.

I thought I had heard every conceivable lame rationale to keep the system porous. I had not. Raising the bar on foolishness, DFL senator Katie Sieben worried out loud that election judges might not hand over a ballot "if a person changed hairstyles." In that the Transportation Security Administration reviews 1.7 million photo IDs a day and has, as far as I know, never mistakenly rejected a passenger because of a change in hairstyle, I do not think this will be too great an issue.

As I tweeted our success proudly from my New Jersey bat cave, I was moved to coin a new Veritas rule: *They may never understand your ideas, but they will be forced to understand your results.* Previously hostile reporters were starting to take note. Among them was David Weigel of *Slate.* Earlier in his career, Weigel had resigned his position at the *Washington Post* after posting in a discussion group vicious comments about the conservatives he was supposed to be covering. This was the notorious JournoList, a private site in which allegedly objective reporters could go down low and out themselves in all their partisan splendor.

Perhaps because we are of the same generation, Weigel seemed to have had a special contempt for me. After I had been arrested in New Orleans, he posted a nearly endless string of "hahahas" and added, "O'Keefe is either going to get a radio talk show or start a prison ministry. That's what successful conservative ratfuckers do for their second acts." I can safely say he was no fan. Now, however, he was singing another tune with tweets like "@JamesOkeefeIII quietly scoring huge victories on Voter ID."

One unexpected victory came in New Hampshire. Under Section 5 of the landmark federal Voting Rights Act of 1965, New Hampshire needed the approval of Attorney General Eric Holder's Department of Justice before the legislated changes in voting procedure became law. Although many were hopeful that Holder would immunize the states against the scourge of voter ID, Holder went ahead and "precleared" New Hampshire.

According to whistle-blower J. Christian Adams, there was little straightforward about Holder's decision. The DOJ lawyers who argued for preclearance had previously argued against voter ID in other states. In a Texas voter ID case, one of the attorneys, Gerry Hebert, insisted that the threat of voter fraud was "merely a pretext, a cloak" for voter suppression. He claimed, in fact, that the Texas effort had been "tinged with race from day one." He asked that the court find that the Texas law was enacted with a discriminatory purpose, which it promptly did in a unanimous decision.

There was no real difference between the Texas law and the New Hampshire law except that Texas is farther south and thus presumed to be more racist. If Holder had failed to clear New Hampshire, it would have revealed just how perversely partisan the whole process was. Thank goodness, we mostly stung northern states like Minnesota, New Hampshire, and Vermont. Lord knows how racist we would have been had we invaded the polling places of Texas, the state whose blatant ballot stuffing back in the day made "Landslide Lyndon" Johnson a U.S. senator and ultimately president of the United States.

In the way of postscript, a cabal of unions and other like-minded groups raised nearly $3 million to challenge the Minnesota voter ID amendment that came before the public in November 2012. Their arguments ranged all over the place: the amendment disenfranchised students, old people, rural people, and, of course, the few minorities that lived in the state. The unifying theme, as one ad actually spelled out in the text, was that "Minnesota has no voter fraud." So, the ad implied, why bother with an amendment at all?

Before the advertising started, the measure had widespread support among Minnesotans, but the scare ads frightened off much of the state's do-gooder population. At the end of the day, although the amendment mustered more votes than Mitt Romney did, it lost narrowly. Still, for me at least, the campaign had educational value. I began to understand that almost nothing scares the government-media complex more than the threat of an honest election. No wonder they hate us so.

BECOMING ERIC HOLDER

Veritas Rule #33:

You will get a wave of creative adrenaline from time to time. Go with it.

Back in the bat cave, kicking around ideas for future stings, Sean Murphy had a wonderful "aha!" moment. What if we solicited the ballots of D.C.'s leading anti-ID proponents, none more vocal or visible than Attorney General Eric Holder? Holder surely deserved to be stung. On the night of March 14, 2012, NBC's *Nightly News* did a feature on pending voter reform. "There is no proof that our elections are marred by in-person voter fraud," Holder insisted. "Solutions that have been proposed go to things that don't exist, problems that don't exist."

As anchorman Brian Williams made clear, when Holder wasn't busy covering up the Fast and Furious scandal or burying the voter intimidation case against the New Black Panthers, he spent his time challenging state laws that require government-issued ID to vote. Okay, Williams did not make all that clear. As usual, he failed to mention Fast and Furious or the New Black Panthers. No, NBC stuck to the anachronistic civil rights narrative that had an heroic Eric Holder blocking voter ID legislation in Texas and South Carolina and taking aim at Mississippi—given their legacy and all, you understand.

I liked Murphy's idea. He drew his inspiration from his work on another research project related, indirectly at least, to the upcoming District of Columbia presidential primary, to be held on April 3. Initially, we thought about repeating the New Hampshire voter ID success, but while researching the deceased on the voter checklist, Murphy had come upon the names of celebrities who had publicly protested voter ID. These included Alicia Menendez of MSNBC, NAACP chief Ben Jealous, David Brock of *Media Matters,* and Bill Maher of HBO. Some of these names he could verify as the celebrity in question, some he couldn't.

Best of all, in reviewing the complete checklist of D.C. voter rolls, Murphy found Eric Holder's voter criteria. To verify that it was indeed *the* Eric Holder, he validated the name with the attorney general's birthday against the one stored in the District of Columbia Board of Elections website. Murphy started cross-checking the other celebrity names against voter rolls and realized we just might pull this off. If so, this would be the ultimate use of the Alinsky tactic *"Pick the target, freeze it, personalize it, polarize it."* I made the gutsy call without even consulting Valerie Jarrett: "Let's roll."

We were keyed up for this one. We were doing our best to expose hypocrisy and corruption at the highest level, and we knew they would do their damnedest to stop us, to humiliate us, maybe to arrest us. We spent three days in prep work on legal and marketing before sending the Project Veritas team to Washington. As it happened, the day the team arrived, the Minnesota legislature was enacting voter reform legislation. God was surely smiling on us.

When our team brought the raw video back—I still couldn't travel—I knew that if He saw what I saw, heaven would be resounding with belly laughs. Although still raw, this video was pure gold. Project Veritas's executive director at the time, Shane Cory, was so psyched by the content—and remember, content is king—he sent out a fund-raising letter that was over-the-top even by our own brash standards. Here is how it started, and it got more triumphant as it went on:

> *Without hesitation, what you are about to see is the boldest work that Project Veritas has done to date and I have absolute confidence that it will make an immediate impact. What we have done—legally exposing hypocrisy and corruption at the highest levels—isn't just going to "stir the hornet's nest," it's going to crack it WIDE OPEN.*

We put the finished video up on April 9 through Breitbart.com and the *Daily Caller*. It was compelling. In the opening scene, Jon Buckley, our top special ops guy, approached the poll worker, a middle-aged white male, and casually solicited Eric Holder's ballot. Overlooking the fact that Jon was half a foot shorter, several shades paler, a generation younger, and almost criminally less well groomed, one could easily confuse him for the attorney general.

JB: Do you have an Eric Holder?

PW: H-O-L-T-E-R or D-E-R?

JB: H-O-L-D-E-R. That's the name.

PW: I do. [He confirms address, censored on video.]

JB: Northwest. That's the address.

PW: Please sign your name there.

JB: I actually forgot my ID.

PW: You don't need it, sir. It's all right.

JB: I left it in my car.

PW: As long as you're in here, you're on our list, and that's who you say you are, you're okay.

JB: I would feel more comfortable if I just had my ID. Is it all right if I go get it?

PW: Sure, go ahead.

JB: I'll be back faster than you can say "furious."

Murphy and I had been trying to incorporate the name of the gun-running scandal into the script. We sampled "I'll be back fast and furious" and "I'll be fast and furious about getting my ID," but we settled on "I'll be back faster than you can say furious." It had the right tempo, the right rhythm. We rehearsed it, and it worked as planned. People remember the line. In fact, it elicits the most laughter and loudest cheers every time I show the video to an audience. After this sequence, the video cuts to Holder telling Brian Williams, "There is no proof that our elections are marred by in-person voter fraud." It made for great theater.

We wondered whether the poll workers asked for a signature to compare it to one on file, and so we tested that possibility at another polling station. This time Jon requested the ballot for David Brock. We are not sure it was *the* David Brock, but it was certainly *a* David Brock. To facilitate the test, Jon had his right hand wrapped in a bandage and claimed he had burned it "seal-coating a driveway." A great method actor, Jon will spend weeks in an area doing recon. He calls this the "silverback in the wilderness" phase of an op. Lesser actors will sprain their wrists. Jon burns his seal-coating a driveway. Ask yourself, which of the two explanations is more believable?

When asked to sign, Jon said, "My hand is kind of tied up at the moment."

"Literally," joked a bystander. The poll worker asked Jon "to make an X or whatever you do."

"But you won't be able to compare it to my regular signature," Jon answered, expressing heartfelt fake concern.

"We don't compare anyhow," said the worker. Case closed.

In the middle of the video, I dropped in an old black-and-white clip of Saul Alinsky telling an interviewer, "One of the most effective tactics is making you live up to your own book of rules." To demonstrate this point, Jon visited the Department of Justice, the domain of Attorney General Holder.

"This is the Department of Justice, correct?" he asked a guard standing outside the building. When the guard affirmed that it was, Jon deadpanned the quintessential irate citizen:

JB: Do you need an ID to meet someone in the Department of Justice?

GUARD: Yes, you need an ID.

JB: That strikes me as ironic because the Department of Justice strikes down voter laws imposed by state governments. You can't have voter ID laws. Yet I need an ID to get into the Department of Justice.

The guard was unmoved. Jon had no better success getting beyond the front desk at *Media Matters* without an ID. Only on one occasion was a team member not offered a ballot. Here is why. When one of our female reporters, #8 by name, asked to vote in the name of television commentator Alicia Menendez, the poll worker asked for her ID. By asking, the poll worker prevented #8 from receiving a ballot and proved on camera that photo IDs do discourage impersonation. Cinema verité. No wonder people want to censor us.

Drudge gave us top billing all day, and the video seemed to sober up the opposition. In a response shockingly free of ad hominems, *Media*

Matters was left to sputtering that our video "fails to show actual voter fraud being committed, and it doesn't prove the existence of a widespread conspiracy to throw an election." The writer followed with a loopy non sequitur: "That's because both are extremely rare." How would she know? According to this logic, conviction on a voter fraud charge would be 100 percent dependent on a YouTube video showing an attempt by the accused.

The *Media Matters* response was pretty much standard among the anti-journalists. Alex Koppelman, writing for the once-credible *New Yorker*, took it a step further, attacking our creative sense as well as our logic. "It's a cute little trick, and a lot of people on the right have gotten a nice little laugh at Eric Holder's expense today," he pouted. "But it doesn't prove anything—actually, if anything, it shows just how limited O'Keefe's talents are." He then lectured us on the hard work involved in real "investigative journalism," the kind that exposes actual criminals committing voter fraud. "Do that, and come up with something good, and then we can talk about voter fraud."

Koppelman, of course, didn't consider the time it took to cross-reference the names and the checklists, pull voter rolls in the District of Columbia, verify and validate the names, do the legal research, write the script, and follow up with the board of elections for comment. When we did ask for comment about signatures, what the District of Columbia employee told us contradicted what we caught on tape. The media will not invest their own resources to investigate voter fraud for an obvious reason: they are afraid of what they will find.

The day after our Eric Holder sting aired, the D.C. board swung into action. They did what the reader will by now have come to expect they would do, namely "condemn" our video. "I have directed our attorneys to conduct a thorough investigation and refer all evidence to law enforcement authorities for appropriate action," said board chairwoman

Deborah Nichols. "Our polling places are open to the media and observers who want to legally document our procedures for checking in voters. There is never any justification for disrupting the voting process with fraudulent activity."

The press release was so sanctimonious it could have been written by a Puritan divine. We were mere "pranksters." We had pulled a "stunt." The board of elections would grant "zero tolerance" to anyone tampering with an election. We were likely guilty of a "criminal offense." No, nothing could possibly be amiss in a city that reelected Marion Barry mayor *after* he was convicted of drug possession and served six months in a federal pen.

Despite the wild-eyed condemnations of the board of elections, Holder soon enough gave me a totally unexpected gift, a veritable get-out-of-jail-free card. He was testifying before the House Judiciary Committee regarding the oversight of the Justice Department. Questioning Holder was Representative Steve King of Iowa. Here is how the conversation played out.

> **KING:** I wanted to also ask you about your reaction when you saw the video of the young man who claimed your ballot here some months ago. And your action—reaction towards requirement for a photo ID after you saw that video?
>
> **HOLDER:** You know, I mean it's an attempt to show something I suppose. But I think what I drew from that—the video was that that guy was very careful not to say he was Eric Holder. Not to actually get a ballot. He didn't do the kinds of things that would have subjected him to criminal . . .

Whoa! Stop the presses! Would someone please email this quote to the various politicos and pundits who called us criminals? In New Hampshire alone, Manchester mayor Ted Gatsas said our guys "should be arrested and prosecuted to the fullest extent of the law." Nashua city clerk Paul Bergeron insisted, "People who pull stunts like this should be prosecuted." Even New Hampshire governor John Lynch chimed in: "I hope that they should be prosecuted to the fullest extent of the law." Their minions had been harassing me and my colleagues for months. "Lynch law" indeed. Steve King continued:

KING: Yeah and I—I'm not worried about [criminal charges]. But, he could have obtained your ballot with ease. It was offered to him. And so I just suggest this, that it—it may not be impossible, but I think it's been determined here today in the questioning of Mr. [Dan] Lungren that—that visiting a federal building, even your building, it may not be impossible, but difficult without a picture ID. And if you—if it's difficult or impossible to visit a government building without a photo ID then how can we allow someone to help choose our government without a photo ID?

HOLDER: Well you see I think the question is—if you look at for instance South Carolina. They had in place measures that protected the integrity of the ballot before they went to the photo ID. And I don't per se say that photo IDs are necessarily bad. The question is now the structure is put in place? How they are distributed. Whether or not it has a disproportionate impact on people of a certain race or ethnicity? A certain age group?

KING: Why would it?

At this point, King's time has expired. But from our perspective, he had more than done his job. Earlier, King had asked FBI director Robert Mueller about our Holder video. Said Mueller, "This is the first I've heard about this incident." It is amazing what they do not know in Washington.

NORTH CAROLINA

Veritas Rule #34:
Double-check your facts before going public.

On this pleasant Tuesday in May, the Project Veritas crew descended on North Carolina to explore some additional holes in the Swiss cheese that is America's electoral system. The hot item on the ballot that day was Amendment 1, which, if passed, would "provide that marriage between one man and one woman is the only domestic legal union that shall be valid or recognized in this State." All eyes were on North Carolina.

For starters, we wanted to explore whether noncitizens were able to vote. We had chosen two test cases. The one fellow, William Romero, was listed as a native of Colombia. The other, Zbigniew Gorzkowski, was from Poland. To come up with their names, we cross-checked jury refusal forms in Wake and Durham counties respectively against the registered-voter list. We chose these two fellows because their apparent lack of citizenship disqualified them from jury duty, but they were registered to vote just the same. Gorzkowski had actually voted in two recent elections.

As to props, imagine if the Von Trapp kids had two demented older brothers, and these brothers traipsed about unself-consciously in goatherd outfits complete with semi-authentic feathered alpine hats. Jon Buckley even dyed his hair blond for the operation, which made little sense when he presented himself before the poll worker pretending to be a Colombian and speaking in a mysterious accent of his own contrivance.

JB: William DeJesus Romero.

PW: Is Romero your last name?

JB: The name, William DeJesus Romero.

Note that Jon never claimed to be Romero. He merely recited his name.

JB: I get pasaporte.

PW: We don't need the passport, sir. All we need to do is have you verify that you are who you say you are. We don't require an ID. We just require that you state your name and address.

JB: I get pasaporte.

PW: No, we don't need it. We don't need it.

JB: I get pasaporte Colombiano.

PW: Sign your name right there and you may vote.

At this point Jon began to wave around his right arm, which was conveniently in a sling.

PW: Okay, you can't sign.

JB: I feel better with pasaporte, feel better with pasaporte.

PW: If you want to get the passport you may do that but we don't need it. You simply need to make an X in this box. Just like this.

JB: Voy a tener pasaporte Colombiano.

To be fair, the clerk was as polite as she could be. Jon did all in his power to make himself suspicious, and she simply refused to notice. I suppose suspicion is outside her job description. As planned, Jon did not accept Romero's ballot and left to get his mythical passport.

At a second polling place, in an even more mysterious accent, fellow goatherd Adam Coolidge told the clerk the name of the Polish guy, Gorzkowski, and he too was offered a ballot. When he said he lacked a passport, he was assured he did not need ID. "I don't need it?" he said incredulously. "I can still vote? I'd just feel more comfortable if I had my passport. I will go get my passport." He too left without accepting a ballot.

No longer dressed as a goatherd, Jon visited with a fellow seemingly born to the job of assistant dean of students, given that his name is "Dean," as in Dean Blackburn. After gratuitously telling Jon that he self-identified as "bisexual," Dean Dean referred us to Terri Phoenix, the director of the LGBTQ Center at the University of North Carolina, to get some advice on voting in the hotly contested Amendment 1 election. If you are wondering, yes, the "Q" stands for "Queer." I guess you are allowed to use that word in North Carolina.

Terri Phoenix—a name, one presumes, of her own creation—proved to be a charmless person of indecipherable gender. When Jon explained to Phoenix that he had voted both in Ohio, where he lived, and in North Carolina, where he went to school, Phoenix offered some sage advice: "Hopefully, no one will figure that out."

Our crew also met with Adam Limehouse, the director of the ambitiously named "Coalition to Protect All NC Families." This outfit was formed to defeat Amendment 1 and raised more than $2 million to do just that. When the subject turned to vote fraud, and the illegality thereof, Limehouse said flippantly, "You know what else is against the law? Speeding?" Translation—wink, wink—everyone does it. Of course, we were recording all of this.

That evening, as the votes came in and the LGBTQ gang realized that their $2 million investment purchased less than 40 percent of the vote, they partied, if a shade bitterly. Jon joined them at a local disco. For a former goatherd, he did a mean Cupid Shuffle, now captured forever on video. At the party, he met a cynical Durham County election judge. When asked if he would take the required oath to uphold the state constitution, the judge answered, "Either I'm not going to do it, or I'll make a show of saying I *mostly* uphold the constitution of the state of North Carolina." Again, the moral elite choose to enforce or not enforce the law based on "the greater good" as they conceive it.

A week later, on May 15, Breitbart.com posted the video summary of these events under the headline "O'Keefe Strikes Again—in North Carolina," and the anti-journalists went busily to work. They focused on the individuals with discrepancies in their public record, William Romero and Zbigniew Gorzkowski. *ThinkProgress* went back to both men that same day our video aired and asked if they were citizens. At 2 p.m. on May 15, just hours after the video was posted, Scott Keyes of *ThinkProgress* posted a piece claiming the Polish guy was a citizen. How did he know? The guy apparently said so.

"O'Keefe has a responsibility as a journalist to ensure the veracity of his facts before he makes wild charges like these," wrote Keyes. "A simple phone call or Nexis search would have sufficed, yet doing so would have undercut his spurious argument that voter fraud is a widespread problem in the United States." Keyes was writing this for people who may have heard about our video but did not see it. They would not have known we went well beyond "a simple phone call."

In fact, we combed the public record and found a hard discrepancy. We interviewed both men, one in person, one on the phone. We aired the interviews. We asked each if he was a citizen. Both awkwardly evaded our question. The viewer saw or heard all of this. Keyes did not bother to explain that the men had been denied jury duty, let alone why. Where, I wondered, was Keyes's videotape showing what Gorzkowski told him?

A day later, *ThinkProgress* tracked down the "family" of the Colombian, and the family assured Keyes that their man was a citizen, too. There was no proof beyond that for either man: no video evidence, no public records, no sworn affidavit, not even a direct quote from the men in question. Still, that was evidence enough for the *Huffington Post* to headline its story on *ThinkProgress*'s research "James O'Keefe Voter Fraud Video Further Debunked: Another U.S. Citizen Falsely Accused."

Speaking of fact-checking, Keyes also claimed in reference to our conversation with the Colombian man, who was alone when we talked to him, that "O'Keefe proceeded to ambush the family at their home." Happily, my probation officer does not read *ThinkProgress*. He would have been unhappy to learn that I had busted out of my New Jersey gulag without permission. I wish I could have.

TPM took another tack. Its headline tells the tale: "Widow Unnerved by James O'Keefe Voter Fraud Stunt." Within a day of our posting the video, *TPM* had hunted down the widow of the one dead man whose ballot we had requested and told her what our video showed. "If he were my son I would spank him," Winifred Bolton told *TPM*'s Ryan Reilly.

Here, I have to give Reilly credit where it is due. Bolton also told him, "I agree that there should be picture ID. I don't understand why you don't have to have picture ID. I don't understand how that is so hard to get," and he reported it. I think he did so just to show that Bolton was not a political ally of his, but I appreciated the gesture nonetheless.

A few months after our sting, I received a forwarded email from a fellow on the Wake (N.C.) County Board of Elections, who was then undergoing mandatory training. His identity shall remain under wraps:

> *They're talking about O'Keefe right now—exhibit about the video is on the screen at today's statewide, several hundred person training. They're using it as an example of "red flags" for officials to look out for—lederhosen and arm casts. The recording inside polling stations issue has come up repeatedly. If I thought there were enough lederhosen in the Raleigh area, I'd consider getting a bunch of folks together to wear them and vote (legitimately) on election day.*

North Carolina officials may have been worried about the wrong indicators—lederhosen and arm casts come to mind—but at least they were paying attention.

UNDOCUMENTED JOURNALISTS

Veritas Rule #35:
Be prepared to release your unedited tape.
Ask your adversaries to do the same.

"It might as well be Harry Potter's invisible Knight Bus, because no one can prove it exists," began Stephanie Saul's dismissive, three-thousand-word article on voter fraud in the September 16, 2012, *New York Times*. The "it" refers to a literal unseen bus, but Saul used the bus as metaphor for vote fraud in general.

About 2,500 words into the article, Saul dissected our efforts in North Carolina, where she was sure we were up to no good. "Not only were Mr. Romero and Mr. Gorzkowski citizens," she said definitively of the two North Carolinians we had profiled, "but the State Board of Elections concluded that Mr. O'Keefe's operatives may have broken several laws, and turned over evidence to prosecutors."

Saul presented this as breaking news, but the first response of embarrassed state officials has always been to attack us. More troubling, she offered no evidence that Romero and Gorzkowski were actually citizens. We highlighted these two individuals for a very specific reason: they had refused jury duty claiming they were not citizens but registered to vote nevertheless. For her part, Saul could not locate Romero and simply took Gorzkowski's word that the state documents we had unearthed were somehow wrong. This might be acceptable reporting for a blog like *ThinkProgress*, but for the *Times*, it is pathetic.

Equally disturbing, Saul did the kind of selective editing we are accused of doing, to make our reporting look reckless and slipshod. First comes Saul's direct quote of what the narrator, namely me, says on the video:

> *William Romero is registered to vote in North Carolina. Here is a copy of his voter registration form, where it says he was born in Colombia, South America. He is not, however, a United States citizen.*

The final sentence ends with a period and a closed quote. According to any good stylebook, including the *New York Times'* own, words left off at the end of a sentence should be acknowledged with ellipsis marks. To leave off the ellipsis is journalistic fraud if the clipped words affect the meaning of the quote. What follows is the quote as I delivered it in my narrator's role in the North Carolina video:

> *William Romero is registered to vote in North Carolina. Here is a copy of his voter registration form, where it says he was born in Colombia, South America. He is not, however, a United States citizen* **according to jury refusal records obtained by Project Veritas through a public records request in Wake County, North Carolina.**

In boldface is the last half of the critical sentence, which text Saul consciously omitted. By cutting off the sentence in the middle, she fully changed the impact of what I was saying. I was not voicing my opinion as to Romero's citizenship. I was citing the county records. If she were really being fair, Saul would have also included the sentence from the narration that follows the quote above: "His name and address fell under the category that says 'true' for non-citizenship."

Let me here add detail to what we discovered. Unlike the *New York Times,* we sent a reporter and a cameraman to Romero's house and talked to a man we presume to be Romero. We found the fellow outside his house wearing an "I (heart) Univision" T-shirt.

"Hello, is William Romero home?" our reporter asked politely.

"How can I help you?" the fellow replied. When the reporter explained that he was there to talk about Romero's jury refusal form, the fellow turned defensive and demanded that we turn our cameras off.

As I explained in the video, we made a public records request in Wake County for jury refusal records and discovered that a William Romero at that same address was listed under the category of "true" for noncitizenship. It would seem that either he lied on the jury refusal form or lied on his voter registration form.

When our reporter asked the fellow at the Romero house, "Is [Romero] a United States citizen, sir?" the fellow asked belligerently, "Who are you with?" He again demanded that we turn the camera off. "You ever put that on TV anywhere," he threatened, "and I'm gonna sue your ass." We did put it on TV, and our ass has yet to be sued.

Saul was nearly as reckless in her analysis of the Zbigniew Gorzkowski case. A Project Veritas reporter had telephoned Gorzkowski. He did not deceive Gorzkowski in any way about our intentions. We aired the recorded interview without tricks. It went as follows:

PV: We noticed you were called for jury duty in the last two years and were disqualified on the grounds that you were a noncitizen. We would like to check and see if that is still the case.

ZG: No it's not the case.

PV: It's not the case? You are a citizen now of the United States?

ZG: I don't know. Who are you calling from?

Gorzkowski's thick accent and imperfect command of the language made it sometimes difficult for our interviewer to follow.

PV: I'm sorry?

ZG: I don't know.

PV: Sir . . .

ZG: Yes.

PV: You are a citizen?

ZG: I don't know who you are and what the interest is for you.

PV: We are an independent agency that monitors public records.

When Gorzkowski told us to go check the county records to answer our question, we informed him that we already had, and that was why we were calling. He found it "weird" and "dangerous" that the county would make such records public. The concept of transparency eluded him. We never did get an answer out of him as to whether he was a citizen or why the discrepancy existed.

Saul did not provide an answer about the discrepancy, either. She did not even raise the question. Having done her reporting under the premise that election fraud was a myth, she apparently saw no reason to challenge that premise. As she saw it, that myth had become enshrined in what she mockingly dismissed as "the election fraud gospel." In fact, however, the orthodoxy was all hers. Only a zealot could dismiss our work so unquestioningly at this stage of the election. Curious about her motivation, I wrote to Saul and asked, "Is there a particular reason why you chose to selectively edit out the following events over the last eight months?" I then listed some of the information she chose to overlook.

- Our video in New Hampshire was cited in passing a voter ID law.

- Our video in Minnesota was cited during the passage of a constitutional amendment for voter ID.

- Our video showing the attorney general's ballot being offered to a stranger was cited in a House Judiciary Committee hearing.

- Our video showing the attorney general's ballot being offered to a stranger was discussed with the director of the FBI.

- Our videos in Washington, D.C., prompted an investigation by the district board of elections.

- Attorney General Holder, while under oath, effectively cleared us of breaking the law.

- Attorney General Holder precleared the voter ID law in New Hampshire after representatives mentioned Project Veritas during the passage of that law.

- The state of New Hampshire attempted to issue a criminal grand jury subpoena against me despite Attorney General Holder's statements.

- Our Vermont investigation showing ballots offered in the name of the dead prompted an investigation by the secretary of state in Vermont.

"I'd be happy to do an interview on our upcoming stories documenting fraud and abuse," I concluded, "but it is unfathomable to me how a reporter could edit out all of the above and still claim to be fair." By this time, I was imagining a new slogan for Project Veritas: "Undocumented journalists—doing the work that American journalists refuse to do."

THE FLUKE PROTOCOLS

Veritas Rule #36:
Mau-mau the flak catchers.

One unusual inspiration for Project Veritas was Sandra Fluke—yes, *that* Sandra Fluke, the overaged Georgetown University Law Center student famous for being insulted. She intrigued me from the beginning, but her speech at the Democratic National Convention provided us some real ammunition. In it, she drew a picture of a dystopian America so thoroughly anti-woman that, if accurate, it would have had Todd Akin voting Democratic. Upon watching this, we knew what were the passion points for the young and restless.

In January 2012, the Democrats launched their contraceptive offensive for which Fluke would become the poster girl. The point man on the offensive was the always reliable George Stephanopoulos. On this occasion, the former Clinton operative was playing ABC's debate moderator. Out of nowhere, he asked candidate Mitt Romney whether he believed the Supreme Court should overturn a 1965 ruling that a constitutional right to privacy bars states from banning contraception.

Romney did a double take. He had surely attended thousands of Republican events, public and private, without ever hearing the issue of contraception raised, let alone debated. Now, on national TV, Stephanopoulos expected him to address an issue about as relevant today as stagecoach regulation. For his part, Romney dismissed the question as a "silly thing" and refused to engage. Not easily embarrassed, George wrestled with this bone for another three painful minutes.

A month later, Fluke whined about the cost of birth control at a press conference disguised as a congressional hearing. She would have passed quickly into obscurity had not Rush Limbaugh ridiculed her on the air. Afterward, Georgetown locals pointed out that she could have bought a month's supply of birth control pills at the neighborhood Target for nine dollars, but that did not undo her talking points. At the convention in August, she was still reminding her audience, "Access to birth control is controlled by people who never use it."

To understand Fluke's thinking is to understand the psychology of too many young people who enlisted in President Obama's grassroots reelection organization, Organizing for America (OFA). In their eyes, an employer who refuses to pay for their birth control pills, even if for religious reasons, somehow "controls" their access to birth control. Okay, so the nation is $16 trillion in debt. So 23 million people are out of work. So our borders are overrun. So the Middle East is in disarray. What motivated these young people to get politically active was the lure of free birth control bills. Forgiveness of their student loans would have been nice, too.

It was important that our Project Veritas reporters understood that motivation as they prepared to infiltrate OFA. We knew that the primary mission of OFA was to harvest votes, however they could, but we had seen enough in our vote fraud investigation to suspect that some activists would not care whether the votes harvested were legal. We wanted to out those activists.

As we explained to our reporters, what the Flukes of the world were doing was mau-mauing to get what they wanted. They used emotion freely and applied it to the various race, sex, and class pressure points. Their goal was to force their targets into a corner where they had a choice between yielding or being denounced as anti-woman, racist, rape advocates, or worse.

We intended to use their strategy against them. Our reporters would express an interest, say, in voting in multiple states. If an organizer hesitated, we would make an emotional appeal to the various race, sex, and class causes du jour. "Don't you care about women?" "You're not anti-woman, are you?" As Sandra Fluke reminded us, we knew what "this America" would look like if we did not prevail in November, and it would not be pretty. Fear of the scary future that Fluke described gave our reporters their motive to steal votes. Accordingly, we developed talking points (TP) to use in any situation with OFA.

FLUKE: It would be . . . an America in which access to birth control is controlled by people who will never use it.

TP: *If we do nothing, that America will be the one our children inherit.*

FLUKE: It would be an America . . . in which politicians redefine rape so survivors are victimized all over again.

TP: *I'm not allowing that to happen. That's why I'm voting twice.*

FLUKE: Many women are shut out and silenced.

TP: *That's why I'm voting in multiple states, to amplify the female voice.*

FLUKE: I'm here because I spoke out, and this November, each of us must do the same.

TP: *I'm speaking out by voting more than once. Do you have my back or will you turn your back?*

We also encouraged our reporters to use props like, say, a birth control pill container. A female reporter could show that it was empty and talk about the fact she was too broke to raise another child. A male reporter could show the picture of his girlfriend's kid he was already taking care of and generally create an atmosphere of desperation and urgency. If the OFA employee refused to help our reporters vote twice, they would argue he was sexist and trying to control their birth control. They could also talk about the white male politicians who could not possibly understand what it *feels like* to be in this position. We urged them to mau-mau, to use emotion, appeal to shared values. What follows is an instructional memo we distributed among them:

FOR INTERNAL USE ONLY

The first rule is "Content is King." The last rule is "Don't get caught."

If you fail at getting content, the solutions are easy to find; dig deeper, switch your angle, etc.

Investigations can fail in various ways: a) the subject ignores your damning statements; b) the subject notices them but doesn't really find them relevant; c) the subject misunderstands you; d) you get found out.

So what about "d"? What if you get "found out"? Some PV reporters may think the only option at this point is to "get the hell out of there," but it is possible to capitalize on this situation if the reporter has a wonderfully creative, devious mind.

In fact, if you do get caught, you may have no choice but to have a wonderfully creative, devious mind, since you violated one of the most important rules.

If they find out your real name during your video investigations, your only option isn't just to run in the opposite direction. You can 1) say that you are publicly conservative in some ways, but "choice" is an area that you can't compromise on, so you are committed to helping out

O in this election; 2) say that you were infiltrating the right; 3) create a double bluff; 4) mau-mau them.

Turn a negative into a positive. When conducting your operations always leave an escape route built into your conversation.

We did not misunderstand the hot buttons or underestimate their potential. In October, a Project Veritas reporter embedded within the Organizing for America campaign developed a relationship with Houston OFA director Stephanie Caballero. Using the Fluke protocols as rationale, our reporter told Caballero that she intended to vote twice: once in Texas, and once in Florida via absentee ballot. Caballero did nothing to discourage the illegal act. Quite the opposite; in fact, she laughed throughout the explanation. "Oh my God! This is so funny," said Caballero on video. "It's cool though!"

Within hours of the video's release, Stephanie Caballero was fired from her position in the Houston OFA office. Democratic National Committee spokesperson Melanie Roussell made the following statement: "There is obviously a history here of making selective use of taped material, and we will certainly not vouch for the completeness of what was released. However, what we saw was enough for us to take the action that we did." The Houston OFA office was shut down following the termination of Caballero. This was only one tape from one OFA office. Imagine if we had a hundred reporters with video cameras.

TAMPA BAY BLUES

Veritas Rule #37:
Ask forgiveness, not permission.

If multiple threats of criminal subpoenas from embarrassed state attorneys general and secretaries of state were not enough, now the Secret Service had involved themselves in managing my life.

The James Madison Institute (JMI), a Florida-based nonprofit, had invited me to speak on the role of the citizen journalist, at a luncheon held in conjunction with the Republican National Convention in August 2012. I never got there. On August 22, 2012, six days before the event, my attorney's office sent a request to my probation officer, Pat Hattersley, explaining the logistics of my trip. "Please let me know if you have any objections to the requested travel or if you require any additional information," we asked innocently.

As KGBish as it may sound, the federal government had to alert people in various jurisdictions every time I would travel to a location outside New Jersey. Even though I was a reporter, and had a constitutional right to do my journalism, the probation office would have to contact the organizer of any event at which I was scheduled to speak. This made organizers uneasy. People tend to shy away from controversy.

The reply from the government this time was quick and harsh. "Offender was to complete 100 hours of [community service] the first year of supervision," Hattersley responded. "We are now on year 3 of probation. No future travel will be considered until the community service is completed."

"Thanks Pat for your quick work on the request," probation officer-in-charge Kevin Mullens weighed in, "and I absolutely concur that the request is denied." He claimed that I was not in full compliance with the conditions of my supervision and that I should have submitted my travel request at least two weeks in advance. Readers should recall that all of this energy was being generated to keep in check a first-time offender on a dubious misdemeanor charge nearly three years after the offense.

Shocked, I responded promptly to my attorney, "I informed the probation officer that I would be performing community service all this weekend fri-mon. He went ahead and emailed US Attorneys that I hadn't completed it. Why is he emailing all these people?" The rules had mysteriously changed just a few days before this critical political convention.

Two days before the event I received an email from Pat Hattersley. "I did speak with Deborah," he said of Deborah Cox-Roush, an event organizer at the 2012 Republican convention, "and she is no longer issuing the ticket." Somehow, the commotion around my travel requests had pulled the Secret Service into the decision making and they put the fear of God into Cox-Roush. For "safety" reasons, the authorities revoked my ticket for the event. Three years ago, I walked into a U.S. senator's office and said I "was waiting for somebody" when I wasn't. Who knows what I might do in Tampa?

My probation officer told me, "I have not made any calls to the

Secret Service. I was going to call them, but [Cox-Roush] told me she was not issuing the ticket, so I did not bother." In the way of eliciting sympathy, I suspect, he added, "I am also on the hot seat for this, for allowing travel for the last one and a half years."

Hot seat. That's what the probation office was concerned about. I was causing the feds discomfort. My very freedom to move had become too hot to handle. No one wanted to take responsibility for the situation a federal judge put them in when he raised our stillborn stunt in New Orleans to the level of terrorism. Unusual or not, I was at the mercy of the court. I thought of talking to my congressman about getting the rules changed governing travel, but I wasn't even sure there were rules.

"Who or what prompted the Secret Service to contact Deborah Cox-Roush?" I asked Pat. "Did your supervisor contact them? These people, including JMI, have gotten burned now and they have donors and contacts that help my efforts. My board chairman is asking me why the Secret Service is involved."

Pat responded, "I don't know, you may have to ask the Secret Service that question. I do know they do backgrounds on everyone who is on the invite list, so they may have seen your name and arrest record and inquired with Deborah."

Ultimately I could not go to Florida. It was nearly impossible to discuss publicly because the media would have spun it as "Even the Republicans Reject O'Keefe at Convention," which is not what happened.

With no better recourse, I Skyped into the JMI event, talking about "The Role of the Citizen Journalist," showing the voter fraud videos through MacBook Pro, which often proves frustrating to do remotely. Within minutes, Tarini Parti at *Politico* published a piece telling the world I was not allowed to go to Tampa. I did at least get a chance to remind *Politico*'s audience that the federal government had destroyed my evidence. "It's grossly disproportionate at best or unconstitutional at worst," I was quoted as saying, "to restrict the travel of a journalist for three years following a class-B misdemeanor."

A few minutes later Drudge immediately put in all caps, "GOV'T BARS JAMES O'KEEFE FROM TRAVELING TO TAMPA." I sat back in my chair in my New Jersey bat cave, away from all the action, and contemplated the reality that to be a muckraker in these perilous times means taking on the full weight and force of the federal government. Although I have never met or even spoken to the man, I knew instinctively that wherever Matt Drudge is, he gets it.

HIDDEN CAMERAS FOR ME BUT NOT FOR THEE

Veritas Rule #38:
Remember, some journalists are more equal than others.

James Carter IV, the unemployed thirty-four-year-old grandson of former president Jimmy Carter, did not much like Mitt Romney. "It gets under my skin," he told NBC News, "mostly the weakness on the foreign policy stuff. I just think it's ridiculous. I don't like criticism of my family." He also harbored a grudge against Romney's company, Bain Capital, and capitalism in general. "I'm a partisan Democrat," he said. "My motivation is to help Democrats get elected. If there is anything I can find in any race, I try to do that."

Carter had heard about a video that had been recorded at a fifty-thousand-dollar-a-plate fund-raiser at the Florida home of Marc Leder, a private-equity financier and chief executive of Sun Capital Partners. Through Twitter, he located the anonymous possessor of the video and encouraged him or her to share it with the publication *Mother Jones*. *Mother Jones* promptly posted a provocative segment of the video in which Romney seemed to write off 47 percent of the American public.

"James: This is extraordinary. Congratulations!" former president Carter emailed his grandson. As to the media, they responded as enthusiastically and uncritically as they did when Osama bin Laden was killed. Hidden video camera? Anonymous source? Dubious chain of custody? Who cared?

Twitchy Media got the story straight. "Naturally, the media directed their pearl-clutching accusations of ethics violations and criminality at O'Keefe and Andrew Breitbart rather than the corrupt organization they exposed," said *Twitchy* of our ACORN videos. Now, however, the media were all but celebrating "Romney's campaign-ending missteps." *Twitchy* shared some tweets that caught the gist of the hypocrisy:

> Remember how outraged the press was over O'Keefe's "selectively edited," "unethical" "gotcha" videos? I guess they've evolved.

> Hey @JamesOKeefeIII check out the media harassing the undercover romney recorder . . . wait a minute.

> if @JamesOKeefeIII had made this tape, the media would slam him and the DOJ would look to prosecute. MoJo gets a pass.

> Funny how the left hated hidden video when it came from Brietbart and O'keefe, right?

When interviewed by *Yahoo News*, I described the Romney tape as "an effective tactic that has a place in a democracy." Yahoo put that quote in the headline. What did not make the headline was my follow-up comment: "I think that there's definitely been a double standard amongst professional journalists here because they've been pretty much raking Project Veritas over the coals for about three years." Buried deep in the article were my comments about the failure of anyone in the media to scruple about laws that may have been violated or whether the video had been dubbed or doctored.

The Romney camp had its own suspicions. Romney himself claimed this video was edited and asked that the person who had the video "put out the full material." David Corn of *Mother Jones* responded in a tweet, "Romney says we posted 'snippets' & not full answers in the secret videos. Uh . . . no. See for yourself." He then provided the link for the "full tape." The media were quick to insist that Romney was wrong. "*Mother Jones* Releases Full, Unedited Romney Video," read a typical headline, this one from NPR, which did not exactly applaud us when we released the full tape of our NPR sting.

"Romney is not the only one who has called for the release of the full 49-minute video," *Mother Jones* proudly declared on its website. "And we're more than happy to oblige. The complete video demonstrates that Romney was not snippetized and that he was captured raw and uncut. Here it is, in two parts."

While the major media were busy congratulating *Mother Jones*, William Jacobson of *Legal Insurrection* took up Corn's challenge to "see for yourself" and was promptly rewarded for his efforts. He discovered that the "full tape" cut off right after Romney's controversial 47 percent remark:

> **ROMNEY:** We do all these polls—I find it amazing. We poll all these people to see where you stand in the polls but 45 percent of the people vote for the Republicans and 48 or 49 . . .

Although shot from the same angle, the tape picks up anew at this point:

> **ROMNEY:** . . . about twice as much as China, not ten times as much like is reported. And we have responsibility for the whole world; they're only focused on one little area of the world, the South China Sea.

Romney himself did not know what was missing. The tape was recorded several months before it was released. If he was clarifying his remarks, that clarification has been lost to history. When Jacobson emailed David Corn of *Mother Jones* asking for an explanation, here is what he got back from Corn: "According to the source, the recording device inadvertently turned off. The source noticed this quickly and turned it back on. The source estimates that one to two minutes, maybe less, of recording was missed."

The device "inadvertently" turned off at the crucial moment? I can only imagine the response if I had said anything half that stupid. How does a device turn off inadvertently? Corn would not know. He likely had no idea whose hands the recording passed through before it got to him. The media had little interest in finding out.

The story gets more outrageous. By selectively leaking segments of the video, *Mother Jones* was able to produce headlines like this one from the *Huffington Post*: "Romney Video Remarks on Palestine Peace Process Stir Outcry." His remarks stirred outcry because they were cut off again mid-thought. The clip that the public was first fed went as follows:

ROMNEY: The Palestinians have no interest whatsoever in establishing peace.

Although the comment was presented as a complete thought, it was part of a longer, more speculative observation.

ROMNEY: I'm torn by two perspectives in this regard. One is the one which I've had for some time, which is that the Palestinians have no interest whatsoever in establishing peace, and that the pathway to peace is almost unthinkable to accomplish.

Romney then goes on to explain the second, more hopeful perspective. This would come out later, but not until after the headlines were written and the first impression made.

To be sure, my anti-journalist friends would not let me enjoy this humble moment of satisfaction. "James O'Keefe: Not Vindicated," read the headlines of a *Salon* article, one of several just like it. The article author, Alex Seitz-Wald, wrote of our efforts, "He and his operatives have donned costumes and assumed invented back stories to pretend to be pimps, telephone workers and even Attorney General Eric Holder." Seitz-Wald had no such problems with the Romney video: "The only deception that may have occurred (we don't know) is at the door when the person entered the fundraiser."

Oh, the irony! *"The only deception"*? I didn't even use deception entering the federal building in New Orleans, and the same people cheering on young Mr. Carter were urging my cellmate Bubba to make short work of me. As for those missing minutes at a crucial juncture in the tape and the duplicitous editing of the Palestine remarks, no big deal. Journalists need to edit things down for time, don't you know.

THE BUTTERFLY EFFECT

Veritas Rule #39:
Big things have small beginnings.

In chaos theory, they call it the "butterfly effect." A butterfly flaps its wings in Ohio and, weeks later, as a result, a hurricane washes away the Florida coast. More tangibly, a careless camper drops a cigarette, and within days half a million Californians are forced to flee their homes. In Ridley Scott's film *Prometheus,* an alien engineer drinks a bubbling liquid, disintegrates, and the DNA in his remains elides with a cascading stream, setting off a biogenetic reaction that, if I interpret things correctly, allows for the creation of all life on this planet, quite possibly earth. "Big things have small beginnings," says a humanoid later on, after he gives the new human race a drop of the same black liquid—spawning a new alien species.

In today's media universe, the flap of the butterfly's wings goes by the name of "tweet." On the afternoon of October 24, 2012, I watched for a worthy tweet, hoping for one. That morning, you see, I had put a new Project Veritas video on YouTube. I had little choice but to fall back on YouTube. All the networks passed on the video and the story behind it, Fox News included. Two weeks before the election, with so much at stake, I assumed I was just too "controversial."

Still, I understood something they did not: media science. I knew what set the butterfly's wings a-fluttering. It was content. *Content is king.* I had trust in the content of my reporter's work, and I hoped that our video would shake up the battleground state in question, alarm the country, and put the world on notice. But this news had to start small, on YouTube, my one dependable resource, and from there disseminate like the alien's DNA through Facebook and Twitter, grass roots at its media purest.

Humble start or not, the video went public. People were watching it, digesting it, vetting it. Adversaries were fact-checking it, honing their invectives, preparing their dismissals. The pace accelerated. *WND* picked up the story, headlined it, and captured its gist in the opening graph:

> *The son of Rep. Jim Moran, D-VA—who serves as the field director for his father's campaign—has been caught on video advising an undercover reporter how to fraudulently cast ballots in the name of registered voters by forging utility bills and relying on the assistance of Democrat lawyers.*

Weeks of research and production came down to this moment. I was hoping the material would cascade down the media stream to the networks, but if I was wrong, and I could have been, I would have set myself up once again. I knew that drill all too well—and the chill.

I sat at my desk in front of my monitors, deep inside my warehouse bunker in an industrial section of a working-class town in New York State. There were no windows, no names on the door. Three locked doors separated me from the outside world. Only a tiny GE screen, linked to a security camera, told me whether it was day or night, what the weather was like, and who it was that might stop by to say hello or slash my tires. In this line of work, I make enemies. The menace *is* always there. Still, I would much rather work here, hunkered down, than preen pointlessly in a D.C. cubicle like my foes.

As I sat, I monitored the grassroots Twitter feeds and waited for any type of government reaction, however small—a squeak or a tip, an echo or a hint. Anything. The reaction is the important thing. This I have learned through experience. So I monitored people who mentioned my original tweet.

The mainstream media monitored the tweet as well, but in a totally different spirit. Unlike me, they did not want a reaction. They could ignore our video and the story it told as long as there was no large-scale public response to it. They would have to cover that. They would rather not have to. They had a president to reelect.

Then suddenly, I sensed the butterfly flapping his wings in an obscure corner of our shared universe. "Come on, come on," I yelled at my monitor. "Happen." I held my breath. Time stopped. In the mention section of my tweet deck, I saw a message that sent a thrill up *my* leg:

"@jamesokeefeiii @DelRayPatch:

Patrick Moran has resigned as field director of his father's campaign"

Space and time faded away. Everything was silent. I asked myself, "Wait, be cautious. Is this true? Can it be?" My gut said yes. I let out a shriek to alert my staff in the other room. I was too focused to explain why I was shrieking, but this felt like *it*, and I was seeing it here first.

I clicked on the Twitter handle, that is, the source of the information, to determine its validity—"Local Arlington patch reporter." Hmmm. I had never heard of this guy or his publication. I looked at his Twitter bio: "Drew Hansen is editor of Del Ray Patch, a community news site for the Del Ray neighborhood of Alexandria, Va. You can reach him at drewh@patch.com."

My mind raced. I wanted to be the guy who informed the world, but I did not know how legit the tweet was. That uncertainty forced me to focus. "Okay," I thought to myself, "apparently this *Patch* is a local journalism operation, very local. Our butterfly, the reporter breaking the news on Twitter, may not have understood the larger consequences of his flapping." For the moment at least, the news item perched on this obscure *Patch* account as mindlessly as an obit or a high school football score. As I saw it, the very innocence of this source argued for its validity.

I could not wait. I had to get the news out to everyone, right then, as fast as I could. The news cycle waits for no man, no woman, no whatever. It was 3 p.m. already, and I wanted this starburst in everyone's face by close of business. My hands shook as they stumbled across the keyboard. I could feel the weight of the congressman's future on my fingers as I typed each character. The computer lagged because I had so many damn windows open. My colleagues yelled at me to close some windows. I hollered back, "Buy me more RAM!"

Okay, I asked myself, "Where do we stand?" I did not know how reliable the source was, so I had to cite him. This way, I protected myself—at least a little bit—if there was blowback. I typed out the tweet, double-checked, and triple-checked because, like toothpaste, once it was out, there was no putting it back in. Ask Anthony Weiner.

Local reporter says Patrick Moran has RESIGNED— RT@DelRayPatch: Patrick Moran has resigned as field director of his father's campaign.

I slammed the enter button. Now things *really* happened. Within seconds there were a hundred retweets. That is right, *hundreds, seconds*. I checked to see if reporters were among the tweeters. There were, several.

I applaud them for plugging their senses into one monitor or another, day in day out. Someone has to, I suppose. I could not do it.

Today, reporters like scoops that arrive on their iPhone or their Samsung Galaxy SIII. Saves on footwear. Now they began making phone calls to determine if the information was true. It appeared to be. The match had been lit, the flames were spreading, the Californians were packing their bags in front of the advancing fire. Within minutes the *TPM* blog broke. It was the blog's acerbic voter fraud beat reporter, Ryan Reilly. He was first on the story, as he often was. As a hostile witness, when he verified the story's authenticity it was game on. I tweeted, "It's OFFICIAL," and linked to him.

Then came a comment from the campaign. Now *Politico* was covering the story. Now the Associated Press. Holy sheeeeiiiiiit! The story was on the WIRE. It was going national. This was all happening within minutes. My fingers shook all the more as I went to one of my other tabs, Google's Gmail. I reminded myself to use Google's native Chrome software. Firefox could not keep up with all these windows open. I felt like I was gliding through the Matrix now. Time may have stopped, but I was moving at light speed. The humanoid's DNA had jump-started the evolutionary process.

I fired off an email to a few major news executives and producers with a subject line, "AP REPORTS Congressman Moran son resigns." One major executive, who earlier rejected the story, responded, "Got it. Covering tomorrow." I did not even have the time to do an end zone dance. I focused on those contacts that simply had to see this, and it was getting close to COB. Everything was now about priorities. I fired off a dozen personal emails to media people and power brokers I had met in my travels. They got the news ahead of the media stream. They would take pride in that.

I was thoroughly and totally *in the zone.*

The BBC now, the *New York Times,* the *Washington Post.* Thousands of tweets, hundreds of retweets. Radio hosts were on hold. I morphed into a quasi-human information-processing machine. I had self-inflicted ADHD. I scanned all the new data, synthesized, and responded. Eating? Drinking? Peeing even—they could wait.

Every millisecond on Facebook someone shared the news. The constant buzz of Facebook alerts created an electronic hum like a casino's. The TweetDeck app popped and crackled in ways I had not heard before. My iPhone blew up with texts and notifications. I tried to turn off the sound alert, but I fumbled. I did not want to take my eyes off the computer screen. My responses to emails became pithy to the point of indecipherable.

As I monitored this madness, I was on the radio with national radio guy Rusty Humphries. He heard the buzzing and dinging in the background and asked what it was that he was hearing. "Rusty," I told him, "that's the sound of news breaking," and a beautiful sound it was.

VERITAS

Veritas Rule #1:
Content is king.

There we were in the Veritas Bunker a week before the 2012 election. We hadn't slept all night. Our hearts were racing, our adrenaline rushing or whatever adrenaline did. We were sleeping on floors, couches, and futons, eating whatever anyone went out and scrounged.

And then another tweet popped up at 7:30 a.m. from a classic "hater." He was angry with CNN for talking about me. "What is this?" I thought. "Does this mean CNN is actually talking about the Moran video? Can't be."

I shouted at a colleague relaxing on the couch, "Turn on CNN!" Oops! I woke him up. He didn't want to miss this anyhow. The chairwoman of the Democratic National Committee, Debbie Wasserman Schultz, was on with CNN's Soledad O'Brien. Unbelievable. Soledad was grilling her over the video, and Schultz apparently was caught off guard. My mind was racing a mile a minute. "Are they doing this to protect President Obama?" I asked myself. Who cared! I had to get that CNN video out to the public immediately. But we did not have it screen-captured. I tweeted around to find someone who had. Yes, *Mediaite* had picked it up and made it available for everyone. Thanks, *Mediaite*, pricks though you may be!

After hours of emails and media monitoring in the morning—no more food, minimal bathroom—my girlfriend called begging me to take twenty minutes off. I could not afford to miss breaking news, I told her. And I was right. Just then I noticed something else quite peculiar in the Twitter mention feed.

Arlington News @ARLnowDOTcom
BREAKING NEWS—ACPD has opened a criminal investigation into the video of Patrick Moran that was released yesterday http://bit.ly/PtNsz2 . That's HUGE (if true).

It happened again! Same thing. I tweeted. Other reporters retweeted. They broke their own articles. You could only imagine the panic mode the campaign was in. Now things were beginning to get really interesting, mind-bendingly interesting.

Journalists and anti-journalists alike were infected with the virus and beginning to see a trend. Even my enemies were finding it hard to criticize our work. "James O'Keefe does something right," read *Salon*'s headline. "Even a broken clock is right twice a day," read the grudging headline on Rachel Maddow's blog. "Believe It or Not, People Are Praising James O'Keefe's Latest Scheme," headlined the *Atlantic Wire*. "This is a fact," wrote David Weigel in *Slate*, "and it will piss off liberals, but: James O'Keefe has had more of an impact on the 2012 election than any journalist."

Whoah! That was a first. In fact, that was unbelievable. It was now wall-to-wall on local TV. The reports on the D.C. stations of ABC, Fox, and NBC were comprehensive. Their reporters were even interviewing Moran's opponent, Pat Murray. Now it was on BBC. The *Guardian*.

British media had picked it up. Drudge had a link in red with another link underneath. NPR posted a flaccid, heel-dragging four-line AP story. So did the *New York Times*. I had to smile. They *hated* the fact they had to report on this story, but the story's power was forcing them to. *Content is king.*

I walked out into the main room of the bunker. It was suddenly 6:30 p.m. I had lost track of time totally. On the bunker TV was Bret Baier's *Special Report* on Fox News. Fox's Eric Shawn was doing a three-minute feature on the results. For months I had been asked, "Why hasn't your stuff been on Fox News?" I answered, "Hell if I know." But now suddenly, there it was! Hell if I knew why.

My staffers' eyes actually began to tear up. We were not rejoicing because of incoming donations or media attention. Hell, if we wanted money and attention, we'd have been attacking Republican congressmen and causes. If we had, Oprah would be on my speed-dial by now. Spielberg would be in my Google circle.

No, we got emotional because we had infiltrated the mainstream media. We did it, step by step. We did it as a team, all year long. And in this moment, we began to realize that our thesis about the media was absolutely correct. At the end of the day, it was all about content. It was about original stories and their butterfly effect. With the right content, we could surmount any media or government obstacle. Win or lose on November 6, we felt like anything was possible.

To this point, the anti-journalists had thrown everything at us. I was a sexual harasser, hoaxer, a rapist, a felon. Even the damn Secret Service had my number. Our reporters were deceivers, lawbreakers, widow agitators. We had been chained together, dispatched to cages, threatened by subpoenas, investigated by election boards. I still needed permission to take a whiz, but we kept coming. We knew that for all the power of the government and their media allies, they did not have power enough to stop something as simple as a tweet broadcasting original content.

They had used all the arrows in their quiver, and we were still standing. Not only were we standing, we had *broken through*.

Still, we had a long way to go before we could claim anything like victory. The forces aligned against us were powerful. We witnessed that power two months after Patrick Moran's resignation when he was arrested for fighting with his girlfriend outside a bar. According to the police report, he slammed "her head into a metal trash can cage." Police officers on the scene described her as "bleeding heavily from her nose." They also observed "that her nose and right eye were extremely swollen." But this was Washington and Moran was wired. As punishment, young Patrick was sentenced to one year of probation to my three.

While the congressman's son was slinking away from what easily could have been a prison sentence, the Arlington County, Virginia, police were coming after me. They wanted the raw tape of our reporter Jon Buckley's conversation with Moran. The twenty-six unedited minutes we posted online did not satisfy them, allegedly because it had subtitles. The police, of course, claimed to be investigating potentially criminal wrongdoing by Moran. Madigan and I sensed they were trying to exculpate him by claiming we had somehow doctored the tape or shortened it. "I've been falsely accused of committing crimes in the past by 'cooperating' with guys like you before," I told a detective who called me.

After the phone conversation, one that I recorded for posterity, I told Madigan to offer the police a raw tape of the Moran exchange with Buckley complete and unedited. Madigan did so, and we never heard from the detective again. A few weeks later I saw a headline pop up on *Atlantic Wire*, "Cops Blame James O'Keefe for Sinking Investigation into His Voter Fraud Sting."

I thought about releasing the audio of my phone conversation with the detective, but opted against it. Better to live to fight another day. That was the long view. The short view was a statement to the *Washinton Post* saying, "The video and subsequent actions of both Patrick

Moran and Congressman Moran speak for themselves. What we saw on the video was so obviously damning and inappropriate that Pat immediately resigned, and his father's office released a statement saying that what he had done was wrong. I don't need to make any comment beyond that." Brevity worked. A few days later the Virginia Senate passed SB1256, a state bill that would require voters to produce photo ID. Virginia senator Richard Black went so far as to read the transcript of the Moran video during a committee hearing. Breakthrough.

You know the outcome, at least most of it. While we were busy trying to save the republic, the mainstream media were busy reelecting Barack Obama president. Victorious or not, they saw what was happening as clearly as we did. While we surged, they surrendered ground every news cycle. Their days were numbered. The butterfly had flapped its wings, and its effect, when multiplied, was blowing the *New York Times* away. Sowing the Seeds of Destruction read a *New York Post* headline about our work proudly displayed in our bunker. Yes, okay, destruction perhaps, but creative destruction. By rooting out media deceit, we were preparing the ground for truth to flourish. No one said it would be easy, and it wasn't.

Veritas!

★　☞　★

Back in that bunker, back at the end of the day the Moran twitter chaos exploded, I got up from my chair, my muscles aching. I felt like the guy in the movie *Limitless* who woke up after taking a powerful stimulant. I grabbed a huge trash bag and threw everything from the previous three days of my life into it—clothes, laptop, business cards, everything I'd need for my trip in a few hours to California. Then I went to the mailbox and found my "permission slip." Nearly three years after New Orleans, I still needed approval from my probation officer to travel out of state. Does that suck or what?

It was now 8 p.m. As I walked to my car in a dark alley along the elevated railroad tracks, I listened to a couple of cops argue with a citizen about a ticket. It was like stepping back into a different dimension. They couldn't have cared less about what had just transpired in our bunker. Being a stranger in this town was comforting. People here were much more earthy and real—something about that New York accent—than the prideful clowns of the Beltway.

Now silence. The streets were pocked with puddles and potholes. Unforgiving Westchester transit buses zoomed by. The evening was warm, and game-changer Sandy, the superstorm, was still a few days away. I lowered the top on my two-seater and took off. As I sped down the highway, I held on to my garbage bag to stop it from flapping and proudly threw the probation slip out the window. Lost in thought, I approached the Tappan Zee Bridge. I could see the stars overhead and the shadowy Palisades across the Hudson. I remembered the times my dad and I sailed under this bridge. Those were the eternals. No one could take them away from me.

The Havana Brown song "We Run the Night" came on the radio. Soon enough, I thought to myself, "We're going to rule the day and change the world."

ENDNOTES

PROLOGUE

Three years later: Sari Horwitz, "New Orleans U.S. attorney resigns amid scandal over anonymous online postings," *Washington Post,* December 6, 2012.

HOLLOW MEN

On the night: Names and other incidental details have been changed to protect the identity of those involved.

"A society with no other scale": Alexander Solzhenitsyn, "A World Split Apart," delivered at Harvard Class Day, June 8, 1978.

THE BOOK OF RULES

"the exceptional scholar": "Stamp immortalizes Paul Robeson," *the Daily Targum,* February 29, 2004.

"Orthodoxy means not thinking": George Orwell, *1984* (New York: Signet Classic, 1950), p. 53.

"The major premise for tactics": Saul Alinsky, *Rules for Radicals* (New York: Vintage Books, 1989), p. 129.

"Make the enemy": Ibid., p. 128.

"Mau-mauing was the ticket": Tom Wolfe, *Radical Chic & Mau-Mauing the Flak Catchers* (New York: Picador, 1970), p. 90.

MR. O'KEEFE GOES TO WASHINGTON: PART I

"Whenever possible": Alinsky, p. 127.

An outspoken abortion foe: The O'Reilly Factor, May 17, 2007.

BUSHWHACKING

"to prevent the sexual": Margaret Sanger, *The Pivot of Civilization* (New York: Brentano's Publishers, 1922), p. 108.

"a known anti-choice extremist": Hilary White, "Planned Parenthood Attacks the Whistle-blower after Student Group Reveals Racism," *Lifesitenews.com*, March 17, 2008.

In the 2008 election: "Barack Obama: Top Contributors," *OpenSecrets.org.*

One young woman: Hannah Giles, "The Truth Is Too Scandalous for YouTube," *Townhall.com*, September 23, 2008.

CHINCHILLA JOURNALISM

At the end of the day: Robert Travis Scott, "ACORN embezzlement was $5 million, La. attorney general says," the *Greater New Orleans Times-Picayune*, October 7, 2009.

On the eve of the 2008 election: Matthew Vadum, *Subversion, Inc.: How Obama's ACORN Red Shirts Are Still Terrorizing and Ripping Off American Taxpayers* (Washington, D.C.: WND Books, December 2011).

Protesting too much: Clark Hoyt, "The Tip that Didn't Bear Out," *New York Times*, May 16, 2009.

When we explained: "Acorn Prostitution Investigation," *YouTube*, September 10, 2009.

Jon Stewart would later: "The Audacity of Hos," *The Daily Show with Jon Stewart*, September 15, 2009.

In November 2007: Sam Graham-Felsen, "ACORN Political Action Committee Endorses Obama," *my.barackobama.com*, February 21, 2008.

MR. O'KEEFE GOES TO WASHINGTON: PART II

Monitoring the news: "Report: Is ACORN Intentionally Structured as a Criminal Enterprise?" *oversight.house.gov*, July 23, 2009.

MEETING BREITBART

Let me jump ahead: goodidealist, "The Acorn Pimp: The bully behind the costume (I found his blog)," the *Daily Kos*, September 14, 2009.

According to the New York Times*:* Jacques Steinberg, "An All-Out Attack on 'Conservative Misinformation,'" *New York Times*, October 31, 2008.

As ABC News reported: Michael James, "Census Severs Relationship With ACORN," September 11, 2009.

In Washington: "ACORN DC Prostitution Investigation Part I," *YouTube*, September 11, 2009.

Before they saw: Lou Dobbs Tonight, CNN, September 11, 2009.

He believed in: James O'Keefe, "ON WHY I DON'T RETURN PHONE CALLS FROM AN INTREPID CNN PRODUCER," *breitbart.com/Big-Government*, September 11, 2009.

On his departure: Brian Stelter, "Jonathan Klein to Leave CNN," *New York Times*, September 24, 2010.

ON TOP OF THE WORLD

estimated that as many: Matthew Vadum, "ACORN leader avoids prison for voter fraud conspiracy," *Daily Caller,* January 12, 2001.

The video showed: "NYC ACORN Prostitution Investigation," *YouTube,* September 14, 2009.

On September 29: Bill Whittle, "Afterburner," *PJTV,* September 29, 2009.

Andrew had cautioned me: "Fox & Friends," *Fox News,* September 14, 2009.

"That is how": John Wellington Ennis, "The Lynching of Acorn," *Public Record,* September 29, 2009.

THE EMPIRE STRIKES BACK

"You could mold this": "ACORN Prostitution Investigation LA Pt 1," *YouTube,* September 16, 2009.

In a Washington Examiner *article:* Byron York, "The stunning, total defeat of ACORN," *Washington Examiner,* September 17, 2009.

The first of the articles: Darryl Fears, "ACORN to Review Employees' Conduct After Hidden Camera Videos," *Washington Post,* September 17, 2009.

On September 18: Carol Leonning, "Duo in ACORN Videos Say Effort Was Independent," *Washington Post,* September 18, 2009.

Trusting the Washington Post: Sharon Theimer and Pete Yost, "Now in hot water, did ACORN grow too big for its own good?" *Associated Press,* September 19, 2009.

Fearing litigation: "Newspaper Issues Correction After Implying ACORN Video Filmmaker Motivated by Race," *Fox News,* September 22, 2009

The paper ran: Scott Shane, "Conservatives Draw Blood from Acorn," *New York Times,* September 15, 2009.

When Shane weighed: Scott Shane, "A Political Gadfly Lampoons the Left via YouTube," *New York Times,* September 18, 2009.

For starters: Clark Hoyt, "The Acorn Sting Revisited," *New York Times,* March 20, 2010.

PIMP PROTOCOL

Cited deep in: Charlie Savage, "Justice Department Says Acorn Can Be Paid for Pre-Ban Contracts," *New York Times,* November 27, 2009.

Apparently, Vera originally: "San Diego ACORN Employee Fired After Offering to Aid in the Smuggling of Child Sex Slaves," *YouTube,* September 18, 2009.

THE YES MEN

One video of theirs: "Halliburton's Survivaball," *YouTube,* October 1, 2010.

Yet Moore has been: David Hardy and Jason Clarke, *Michael Moore Is a Big Fat Stupid White Man* (New York: ReganBooks, 2004), pp. 67–80.

An article in the: Sahil Kapur, "The new politics of guerrilla activism," *The Guardian,* June 15, 2011.

LOUISIANA WATERGATE

As we would soon see: Meet the Press, NBC, December 23, 2012.

"Tragedy occurs": Whittaker Chambers. *QuotesWave.com.* Accessed March 22, 2013. *http://www.quoteswave.com/text-quotes/185052.*

"It is the role": Julian Assange, interviewed in "Afghanistan war logs: Story behind biggest leak in intelligence history," *Guardian Media,* July 25, 2010.

The message was: Campbell Robertson and Liz Robertson, "4 Arrested in Phone Tampering at Landrieu Office," *New York Times,* January 26, 2010.

Greg Marx: Greg Marx, "A Bad Cartoon," or "A Big Nothing"? *Columbia Journalism Review,* January 27, 2010.

The paper began: David Hammer, "ACORN 'gotcha' man arrested in attempt to tamper with Mary Landrieu's office phones," *The Times-Picayune,* January 26, 2010. (Since revised.)

Leonning may still have been: Carol Leonning and Garance Frank-Ruta, "Acorn Foe Charged in Alleged Plot to Wiretap Landrieu," *Washington Post,* January 27, 2010. Online version has since been revised to "ACORN foe charged in alleged phone tampering plot."

Now, Leonning was reporting: Carol Leonning, "Suspect in Senate office sting tweeted about upcoming action," *Washington Post,* January 28, 2010.

"If this is true": Mark Silva, "Conservatives distance themselves from arrested activist," *Los Angeles Times,* January 28, 2010.

Hannah Giles: Hannah Giles, "Once Again, James O'Keefe Strips Away the MSM's Mask of Neutrality, Revealing the Bias Below," *breitbart.com/Big-Journalism,* February 2, 2010.

Breitbart, as always: Andrew Breitbart, "MSM Leaps to Conclusions—While Big Government Waits for Facts," *breitbart.com/Big-Journalism,* January 26, 2010.

In December 2012, Letten: Campbell Robertson, "Crusading New Orleans Prosecutor to Quit, Facing Staff Misconduct," *New York Times,* December 6, 2012.

ABC GOES FOR THE JUGULAR

The first of our census: "Undercover Census Fraud Investigation—New Jersey," *YouTube,* May 31, 2010.

After introducing us: George Stephanopoulos, *Good Morning America,* ABC, June 1, 2010.

As Andrew pointed out: Andrew Breitbart, "ABC's George Stephanopoulos: A Profile in Media Courage," *breitbart.com/Big-Journalism,* June 1, 2010.

One by Shaughn: "Undercover Census Fraud Investigation—Louisiana," *YouTube,* June 2, 2010.

Not surprisingly: "Activist Filmmaker Targets Census Bureau, Cites Payroll Fraud," *Fox News,* June 1, 2010.

Morse rattled off: In public comments on his blog, Morse attacked "the shoddy editing techniques used by James O'Keefe in his 'undercover sting' videos." He also distanced himself from the conservative label despite writing for Breitbart's BigGovernment.com.

BEAUTIFUL SWIMMERS

It can come anytime: William Warner, *Beautiful swimmers: watermen, crabs, and the Chesapeake Bay* (New York: Penguin, 1977), p. 33.

A little background: "Right on the Edge," CNN, aired October 2, 2010.

I was shooting: Christian Hartsock, "Landrieu Dance," CNN, April 18, 2011.

As I would later tell: Howard Kurtz, "Reliable Sources," CNN, September 29, 2010.

Then came the CNN: "Newsroom," CNN, September 29, 2010. In its online version, Scott Zamost, "Fake pimp from ACORN videos tries to 'punk' CNN correspondent," *CNN.com*, September 29, 2010.

The press release: "Brown Releases Report Detailing a Litany of Problems with ACORN, But No Criminality," State of California Department of Justice, April 1, 2010.

In a terse statement: Andy Newman, "Advice to Fake Pimp Was No Crime, Prosecutor Says," *New York Times*, March 1, 2010.

Even Andrew: Andrew Breitbart, "O'Keefe Owes His Supporters an Explanation," *breitbart.com/Big-Hollywood*, October 1, 2010.

TEACHERS GONE WILD

"When Schoolchildren start": although routinely attributed to Albert Shanker, this quote has no firm provenance.

The story hit on Monday: Matthew Boyle, "New O'Keefe video shows teachers bragging about bulletproof tenure rules," *Daily Caller*, October 25, 2010.

In an article: Steve Baker, "Video released by conservative activist claims to show undercover footage at NJEA conference," *NJ.com*, October 26, 2010.

On October 26: Matthew Boyle, "O'Keefe video appears to show New Jersey union official describing voter fraud," *Daily Caller*, October 26, 2010.

It was me he wanted: "Jeff Cole Interviews James O'Keefe," *myfoxphilly.com*, October 26, 2010.

Cole cornered Goode: Don Steinberg, "Media: The Attack Dog," *phillymag.com*, December 2008.

Earlier that same day: "Hidden video by conservative activist James O'Keefe renews NJEA, Gov. Christie dispute," *NJ.com*, October 27, 2010.

Gov. CHRISTIE: *Star-Ledger* Editorial Board, "Gov. Christie shouldn't cozy up to muckraker of 'Teachers Union Gone Wild,'" *NJ.com*, October 29, 2010.

Breitbart was first: "'Go Watch This Video. It's Enlightening. It's Enraging.' Gov. Christie Raves Over 'Teachers Gone Wild.'" *breitbart.com/Big-Government*, October 26, 2010.

According to the Star-Ledger: "Jeanette Rundquist, N.J. teacher, is suspended, denied pay raise after being filmed on hidden video at NJEA conference," *NJ.com*, November 10, 2010.

"I felt like I was raped": Bob Braun, "Heroic N.J. teacher was sacrificed for political cause in hidden video," *NJ.com,* November 14, 2010.

One of its representatives: See "NJEA Warns Members to Be on the Lookout for Project Veritas," *projectveritas.org,* October 29, 2010.

GUERILLAS IN THEIR MIDST

The website proved: Jack Stuef, "PAMELA GELLER WAS TRICKED BY JAMES O'KEEFE'S SHARIA WEBSITE," *Wonkette,* March 9, 2011.

What the world saw: "NPR Muslim Brotherhood Investigation Part I," *YouTube,* March 8, 2011.

THE EMPIRE STRIKES BACK *AGAIN*

To its credit: Dana Davis Rehm, NPR's senior vice president of marketing, communications and external relations released this statement, *npr.org.* March 8, 2011.

This inevitably leads: James Poniewozik, "Hatchet Job: The Video Hit Piece that Made Both NPR and Its Critics Look Bad," *time.com,* March 17, 2011.

These comments usually: mediadecoder.blogs.nytimes.com, March 8, 2011.

In a piece titled: Bill Keller, "Traditional News Outlets—Living Among the Guerillas," *New York Times,* March 27, 2011.

On March 18: Bob Garfield, "On the Media," March 18, 2011. *onthemedia.org/2011/mar/18/james-okeefe/transcript/.*

ROAD GANG

Subjection in minor affairs: Alexis de Tocqueville, *Democracy in America* (Volumes 1 and 2) (Stilwell, KS: Digireads.com, 2007), p. 495.

As the Courthouse News: Maria Dinzeo, "Acorn Foes Face Trial for Undercover Film Work," *Courthouse News Service,* May 26, 2011.

"James O'Keefe not": GottaLaff, "James O'Keefe not protected by First Amendment, has to stand trial in CA," *Political Carnival,* May 26, 2011.

MILKING MEDICAID

So Together: "Ohio Medicaid Russian Drug Smuggling Investigation," *YouTube,* July 18, 2011.

In Richmond, Virginia: "Virginia Medicaid Drug Smuggling Investigation," *YouTube,* July 21, 2011.

In two separate offices: "Portland Maine Medicaid Official Counsels 'how to get around' Assets," *YouTube,* August 18, 2011.

The New York Times: Clifford Levy and Michael Luo, "New York Medicaid Fraud May Reach into Billions," *New York Times,* July 18, 2005.

Jeremy Holden: "James O'Keefe's Medicaid Sting Is Still a Fraud," *mediamatters.org,* August 11, 2011.

The Daily Kos: Joan McCarter, "O'Keefe's Medicaid Sting Attacks Public Workers for Following the Law," *The Daily Kos,* July 20, 2011.

"We need to be": Rebekah Metzler, 'Sting' video stirs fraud debate, *The Portland Press Herald,* August 12, 2011.

TO CATCH A JOURNALIST

The journalist's name: Sam Stein, "James O'Keefe's Newest Target Appears to Be a Small, Progressive Economic Think Tank," *The Huffington Post,* October 17, 2011.

Our decoy: "To Catch a Journalist: Rutgers Education Professor in Pay-for-Play," *YouTube,* October 24, 2011.

Two of them shared: "Occupy Wall Street Solicits Wall Street Banker," *YouTube,* October 11, 2011.

The word reached: Jim Treacher, "TheDC Morning: What Is OccuList?" *The Daily Caller,* October 18, 2011.

There I talked to: To Catch a Journalist: *New Jersey Star-Ledger, YouTube,* November 10, 2011.

This one focused: "To Catch a Journalist: *New York Times,* Jay Rosen, Clay Shirky," *YouTube,* October 27, 2011.

According to Wemple: Erik Wemple, "O'Keefe wrong about Shirky," *Washington Post,* October 27, 2011.

The Atlantic Wire: Adam Clark Estes, "James O'Keefe Burns His Own Straw Man in a New Video," *atlanticwire.com,* October 27, 2011.

So in our next installment: "To Catch a Journalist: Jay Rosen says Clay Shirky has had 'Consulting Gigs,'" *YouTube,* November 1, 2011.

Speaking of newsrooms: Rob Kall, "HBO's Newsroom Kicks Ass, Scares the Hell Out of Right Wingers and Probably the MSM," *opednews.com,* June 25, 2012.

On his blog: Jay Rosen, "A note to my conservative friends," *pressthink.org,* October 30, 2011.

WITNESS FOR THE PROSECUTION

Nadia's testimony was strange: "State of New Jersey vs. James O'Keefe: Transcript of Probable Cause Hearing," December 21, 2011.

COUNTDOWN

Harris's publication: Chris Harris, "Harassment complaint against Westwood muckraker James O'Keefe dismissed," *NorthJersey.com,* December 21, 2011.

The next day: Keith Olbermann, *Countdown,* Current TV, December 22, 2011.

It got worse: David Shuster, *Countdown,* Current TV, February 24, 2012.

An opinion writer: Star-Ledger Editorial Board, "N.J. activist James O'Keefe is knucklehead of the week," *NJ.com,* January 22, 2012.

DEAD MAN VOTING

As John Fund: John Fund and Hans von Spakovsky, *Who's Counting?: How Fraudsters and Bureaucrats Put Your Vote at Risk* (New York: Encounter Books, Nook version, 2012), p. 31.

I particularly liked: Ibid., p. 31.

"Faking absentee ballots": Ibid, p. 31.

In West Virginia: Ibid., p. 32.

In Texas: Ibid., p. 33.

What follows is: "Dead People Receive Ballots in NH Primary," *YouTube,* January 11, 2012.

Still unaware: Joe Battenfield, "Dead man voting: Texas man tries to cast posthumous ballot," *Boston Herald,* January 11, 2012.

ZOMBIE SYMPHONY

The supporting article: "Dead People Receive Ballots in New Hampshire Primary," *Daily Caller,* January 11, 2012.

The headline captured: Ryan Reilly, "Election Law Experts Say James O'Keefe Allies Could Face Charges Over Voter Fraud Stunt," *TPM,* January 11, 2012.

On the following day: Ryan Reilly, "James O'Keefe Says $50K Donation Funded Voter Fraud Stunt," *TPM,* January 12, 2012.

The night after: David Shuster, *Countdown,* Current TV, January 12, 2012.

The always reliable: "Election Officials, Experts: O'Keefe Implicated in Another Illegal Stunt," *mediamatters.org,* January 12, 2012.

Joan McCarter's: Joan McCarter, "New Hampshire Officials Says James O'Keefe Should Be Indicted for Voter Scam," *Daily Kos,* January 12, 2012.

Sam Favate: Sam Favate, "Might Conservative Activists Face Criminal Charges for Voter ID Stunt?" *wsj.com,* January 12, 2012.

THE AMERICAN WAY

"This video has": Staff, "Polls video slammed as a 'fraud,'" *UnionLeader.com,* January 13, 2012.

"Well, it's clear today": Jake O'Donnell, "NH Dems Respond to Bettencourt," *Salem-Patch,* January 13, 2012.

They wanted revenge: Sarah Jones, "Possible Criminal Charges for James O'Keefe Debunk GOP Voter Fraud Paranoia," *PoliticusUSA,* January 12, 2012.

"People who pull": Ibid.

The day after: Al Sharpton, *Politics Nation,* MSNBC, January 12, 2102.

Sharpton knows a thing: Alan Feuer, "Sharpton's Debt in Brawley Defamation Is Paid by Supporters," *New York Times,* June 15, 2001.

In 1984, a New York State: Fund and Von Spakovsky, p. 44.

Scott Keyes of: Scott Keyes, "James O'Keefe's Group Appears to Commit Voter Fraud in Order to Gin Up Hysteria Over Non-Existent Fraud Problem," *ThinkProgress,* January 11, 2012.

Governor Lynch: "Group Says It Got Primary Ballots with Dead People's Names," *WMUR 9,* January 12, 2012.

"That's awful": Erin Smith, "N.H. widow shocked by ploy at polls," *Boston Herald,* March 21, 2012.

The Daily Kos: "Sign a Petition to Indict James O'Keefe for Voter Fraud," *thecentristword.wordpress.com.*

THE RISE OF RICHARD HEAD

She accused me publicly: Maureen O'Connor's "James O'Keefe's Panty-Stealing 'Rape Barn' Sex Scandal," *Gawker.com,* March 22, 2012.

Blogger Nicole Belle: Nicole Belle, "James O'Keefe's Former Accomplice Spills Some More on Antics," *Crooks and Liars,* March 22, 2012.

Naffe appeared to be: "Is the New Hampshire A.G. Investigating James O'Keefe Working with Brett Kimberlin Associate Neal Rauhauser?" *Patterico.com,* June 15, 2012.

This event occurred: Jess Bidgood, "N.H. Approves Voter ID Law," *thecaucus.blogs.nytimes.com,* June 27, 2012.

LIVING ON A PRAYER IN MINNESOTA

Matt Drudge's 15 minutes: Jonathan Broder, "Matt Drudge's 15 minutes of fame may be ending on a rather nasty note," *Salon,* August 15, 1997.

On February 8, 2012: Tommy Christopher, "James O'Keefe's 'Fake Tim Tebow' Voter Fraud 'Investigation' Doesn't Have a Prayer," *Mediaite,* February 8, 2012.

One of them: Peter Nelson and Harry Niska, "Debating Voter ID: A Means to Increase Confidence in Election," *Bench & Bar of Minnesota,* August 14, 2012.

What Jon Buckley: "Registering Tim Tebow and Tom Brady to Vote in Minnesota," *YouTube,* February 7, 2012.

I am sure U.S. senator: Byron York, "When 1,099 felons vote in race won by 312 ballots," *Washington Examiner,* August 6, 2012.

In 1996: Fund and Von Spakovsky, p. 17.

STORMING VERMONT

At one polling station: "Caught on Tape: Dead People and Clones Offered Ballots in Vermont Primary," *YouTube,* March 13, 2012.

As he told a local: Kyle Midura, "Vermont elections open to fraud?" *wcax.com,* March 13, 2012.

A few months later: Derrick Grayson, "Photo ID Keeps Negro from Voting," *YouTube,* August 15, 2012.

Although Sorrell would ultimately prevail: "Sorrell Wins Democratic Primary for AG; Donovan Concedes," *vpr.net,* August 29, 2012.

MORTE D'ANDREW

On that same March 1: Matt Taibbi, "Andrew Breitbart: Death of a Douche," *Rolling Stone,* March 1, 2012.

TEBOW SCORES

Shortly after midnight: Evan Paskach on, "SENATE PASSES VOTER ID CONSTI-TUTIONAL AMENDMENT, NOW HEADED TO VOTERS," *Minnesota State News,* April 4, 2012.

Raising the bar: Jim Ragsdale, "Voter ID amendment is now up to Minnesota's voters," *Star Tribune,* April 4, 2012.

After I had been: daveweigel.com, January 26, 2010.

According to whistle-blower: Christian Adams, "Eric Holder Approves Voter ID . . . in New Hampshire, *pjmedia.com/tattler,* September 5, 2012.

In the way of postscript: Michael Brodkorb, "The Photo ID Constitutional Amendment Debate: Does Voter Fraud Happen in Minnesota?" *politics.mn,* September 17, 2012.

BECOMING ERIC HOLDER

On the night: Nightly News with Brian Williams, *NBC,* March 14, 2012.

We put the finished video: "US Attorney General Eric Holder's Ballot to Vote Offered to Total Stranger," *YouTube,* April 9, 2012.

In a response: Chelsea Rudman, "O'Keefe's Video on 'Eric Holder's Ballot': Still Not Voter Fraud," *mediamatters.org,* April 9, 2012.

"It's a cute little trick": Alex Koppelman, "James O'Keefe Still Hasn't Found His Voter Fraud," *newyorker.com,* April 9, 2012.

They did what: D.C. Board of Elections, "Board Condemns Video Showing Fraudulent Activity on Election Day," Media Release, April 10, 2012.

Questioning Holder: UNITED STATES DEPARTMENT OF JUSTICE, HEARING BEFORE THE COMMITTEE ON THE JUDICIARY HOUSE OF REPRE-SENTATIVES, *charitableplanning.com,* June 7, 2012.

NORTH CAROLINA

As to props: "NC Non-Citizens Voting, Dead Offered Ballots, UNC Officials Embrace Voter Fraud," *YouTube,* May 15, 2012.

At 2 p.m. on May 15: Scott Keyes, "'Non-Citizen' Voter in James O'Keefe's Voter Fraud Video Is Actually a Citizen," *ThinkProgress,* May 15, 2012.

Still, that was evidence: Nick Wing, "James O'Keefe Voter Fraud Video Further Debunked: Another U.S. Citizen Falsely Accused," *Huffington Post,* May 17, 2012.

Its headline tells: Ryan Reilly, "Widow Unnerved by James O'Keefe Voter Fraud Stunt," *TPM,* May 16, 2012.

UNDOCUMENTED JOURNALISTS

"It might as well be": Stephanie Saul, "Looking, Very Closely, for Voter Fraud," *New York Times,* September 16, 2012.

THE FLUKE PROTOCOLS

The point man: ABC New Hampshire Republican Debate, *thecritical-post.com/blog/* January 7, 2012.

At the convention in August: "Sandra Fluke DNC speech," *Politico,* September 5, 2012.

Using the Fluke protocols: "EXCLUSIVE: DNC Staffer Assists Double Voting in Support," *YouTube,* October 10, 2012.

Within hours: Ryan Reilly, "DNC Fires Employee Featured In James O'Keefe Video," *TPM,* October 11, 2012.

TAMPA BAY BLUES

Within minutes: Tarini Parti, "James O'Keefe not allowed to fly to Tampa," *Politico,* August 29, 2012.

HIDDEN CAMERAS FOR ME BUT NOT FOR THEE

"It gets under my skin": "Mother Jones Romney Video Release 'Poetic Justice,' Says Jimmy Carter's Grandson," *inquisitr.com,* September 19, 2012.

Twitchy Media got: "Boom! James O'Keefe highlights media hypocrisy over hidden camera videos of Romney," *twitchy.com,* September 18, 2012.

When interviewed by: Chris Moody, "James O'Keefe on secret Romney video: 'an effective tactic that has a place in a democracy,'" *Yahoo! News,* September 18, 2012.

"Mother Jones Releases": Eyder Peralta, "'Mother Jones' Releases Full, Unedited Romney Video," *npr.org,* September 18, 2012.

"Romney is not the only one": David Corn, "WATCH: Full Secret Video of Private Romney Fundraiser," *MotherJones,* September 18, 2012.

He discovered that: William Jacobson, "Critical audio gap in 'complete' Romney tape released by Mother Jones," *Legal Insurrection,* September 18, 2012.

"James O'Keefe: Not Vindicated": Alex Seitz-Wald, "James O'Keefe: Not Vindicated," *Salon.com,* September 19, 2012.

THE BUTTERFLY EFFECT

WND picked up: Art Moore, "Video snags Dem boss plotting vote fraud," *WND.com,* September 24, 2012.

Within minutes the TPM blog: Ryan Reilly, "Rep. Jim Moran's Son Resigns Over James O'Keefe Video," *TPM,* October 24, 2012.

The chairwoman of the: "Starting Point with Soledad O'Brien," *CNN,* October 25, 2012.

"James O'Keefe does": Alex Seitz-Wald, "James O'Keefe does something right," *Salon.com,* October 24, 2012.

"Believe It or Not": Adam Clark Estes, "Believe It or Not, People Are Praising James O'Keefe's Latest Scheme," *atlanticwire.com,* October 24, 2012.

"This is a fact": David Weigel, "The Power of James O'Keefe," *Slate,* October 25, 2012.

"Cops Blame James O'Keefe": Elspeth Reeve, "Cops Blame James O'Keefe for Sinking Investigation into His Voter Fraud Sting," *atlanticwire.com,* January 13, 2103.

The short view: Allison Klein, "Patrick Moran won't be charged in connection with possible voter fraud," *Washington Post,* January 31, 2013.

A few days later: "Virginia Bills Tighten Voter ID Requirements," *Daily Kos,* February 15, 2013.

SOWING THE SEEDS: Ginger Adam Otis and Tim Perone, "Sowing the Seeds of Destruction," *New York Post,* September 20, 2009.

ACKNOWLEDGMENTS

On more than a few occasions, the support and encouragement of my family kept me going when almost nothing else could. Let me thank my mom, my dad, and my artistic sister, Amanda, who came up with the cover concept. Our family runs deep and strong, so let me also acknowledge my grandparents, Robert McHaffie, James O'Keefe Sr., and especially Shirley O'Keefe, who lent me her now iconic chinchilla stole.

Without the help of my stalwart guerillas, I might still be stuck in the pipe-dream stage. Kudos to the Rutgers crew, several of whom still work alongside me—Maureen Wagner, Daniel Francisco, David and Samantha Maxham, Brian Meinders, Audrey Andrews, Aaron Marcus, Tony Gioia, Ryan Peene, Bethany S. Mandel, and Kevin Nezda. Thanks to Ben Wetmore, John Burns, and Laura Elizabeth Bush, who planted the first seeds (like dressing similar to Secret Service agents and meeting with the LeMoyne college dean). Thanks to Christian Hartsock and Gabby Hoffman for sticking by my side and Ryan Sorba for the early adventures (especially with Gloria Steinem). Many, many thanks to the original female warriors, the intrepid Lila Rose and Hannah Giles. A deep nod of gratitude to the New Orleans guys—Stan Dai, Joe Basel, and Bob Flanagan. They paid their dues. Did they ever.

For a whole string of great projects from HUD to Medicaid to election fraud, highest honors go to our fearless corps of Green Berets unnamed and those named—especially Jon Buckley, Sean Murphy, and Spencer Meads, and also Kemberlee Kaye, Chris Heneghen, Erin Haust, Travis Irvine, Brady Wells, Traci Connors, Cynthia Jeub, Kaiser Johnson, Ryan Girdusky, and Josette Chmiel. Thanks also to "Simon Templar" and Shaughn Adeleye for their inspired work on the NPR sting. Thanks to the two intrepid warriors from Oregon; Dan Sandini and Mike Strickland. I could write another book on the unfinished investigations alone.

Let me thank Congressman Steve Stockman, who in 2006 bought me the computer that made some of the original videos possible; Congressman Franks and Congressman King, who spoke our election fraud videos in Congress; Leonard Leo, who introduced me to Mike Madigan; Shane Cory and Kate Doner, who helped build Project Veritas into a sustainable c3; Ed Hulse, Benjamin Light, Benjamin Barr, John Pitts, and Brooke Daley, who helped with due diligence; David DesRosiers for helping communicate our vision to others; Charles Johnson for his brilliance in understanding the minds of my adversaries; Mallory Factor for his introducing me to so many; Francisco Gonzalez, Colin Sharkey, and Greg Walker for their service as board members; Richard Viguerie for connecting us to the grassroots; Jennifer Ridgley for her kindness and for always being there for me during the book writing process; Eric O'Keefe and Jason Stverak for their roles in the citizen journalism movement; my California comrades Gary Cavicchio and Corey Garriott, who kept me sane in law school; my best friend, Anthony Dini, who reminded me to have fun, and whose music appeared in many videos; the Dunbar family for housing me in Los Angeles when I met Andrew Breitbart; and, of course, the inimitable Andrew Breitbart himself.

On the media front I have had no greater supporter than the inspiring Michelle Malkin as well as the rest of the blogosphere. Thanks specifically to Patrick Frey for his exclusive reports on my cases in New Jersey and Louisiana. Essential too have been Joseph Farah of WND, Tucker Carlson of the *Daily Caller*, Dana Loesch, Mike Savage, Curtis Sliwa, Frank Morano, Sam Nunberg, and Roger Stone. Great help out of the gate were Rush Limbaugh, Sean Hannity, Glenn Beck, and many others. Thanks to Alex Jones for promoting our latest 2nd Amendment video series of 2013. Thanks to Laura Ingraham, Day Gardner, Bill O'Reilly, Matt Drudge, and Jill Stanek for covering the initial Planned Parenthood tapes. Thanks to John Fund, J. Christian Adams, Deroy Murdock, and Eric Shawn for their coverage of our voter fraud exposés. Talented reporters Dave Weigel, Ryan Reilly, Ken Vogel, and Erik Wemple have sparred with me, but still manage to show their humanity in the process.

I'd also like to thank the people who helped with the book itself: Alex Hoyt, who suggested a book in the first place; Anthony Ziccardi for seeing its potential; Jack Cashill for helping shape the story; and Mitchell Ivers at Simon & Schuster for nurturing it to completion. Also at Simon & Schuster: Louise Burke, publisher; Al Madocs, production editor; Natasha Simons, editorial assistant; Lisa Litwack, art director; Michele Martin, associate publisher; Mary McCue, publicist; and Stephen Manfredi of Manfredi Strategy Group.

And to my probation officer, Patrick Hattersley, you have been a decent guy just trying to do your job. It's too bad you work in a system that doesn't encourage decency.